York St John
Library and Information Services
Normal Loan

Please see self service receipt for return date.
If recalled the loan is reduced to 10 days

RETURNED	2 5 MAR 2011	
27 JAN 2009	RETURNED 2 5 FEB 2011	
3 1 MAR 2009 RETURNED	RETURNED 1 2 SEP 2011	
RETURNED 30 NOV 2009	RETURNED 2 5 NOV 2011	
RETURNED 0 2 FEB 2010	RETURNED 2 5 NOV 2011	
RETURNED 2 4 MAY 2010		
RETURNED 1 9 FEB 2011		
Fines are payable for late return		

RELIGION AND THE INDIVIDUAL

This volume brings together a significant set of reflections on the meaning of religion for the individual as well as society. In doing so it makes a timely and valuable contribution to our understanding both of individualizing tendencies within religion, and of appropriate theoretical and methodological responses to that shift.

Professor Linda Woodhead, Director AHRC/ESRC
Religion and Society Programme, Lancaster University, UK

What does religion mean to the individual?

How are people religious and what do their beliefs, practices and identities mean to them?

The individual's place within studies of religion has tended to be overlooked recently in favour of macro analyses. *Religion and the Individual* draws together authors from around the world to explore belief, practice and identity. Using original case studies and other work firmly placed in the empirical, contributors discuss what religious belief means to the individual. They examine how people embody what religion means to them through practice, considering the different meanings that people attach to religion and the social expressions of their personal understandings and the ways in which religion shapes how people see themselves in relation to others. This work is cross-cultural, with contributions from Asia, Europe and North America.

THEOLOGY AND RELIGION IN INTERDISCIPLINARY PERSPECTIVE
SERIES IN ASSOCIATION WITH THE
BSA SOCIOLOGY OF RELIGION STUDY GROUP

BSA Sociology of Religion Study Group Series editor:
Pink Dandelion and the publications committee

Theology and Religion in Interdisciplinary Perspective Series editors:
Douglas Davies and Richard Fenn

The British Sociological Association Sociology of Religion Study Group began in 1975 and provides the primary forum in Britain for scholarship in the sociology of religion. The nature of religion remains of key academic interest and this series draws on the latest worldwide scholarship in compelling and coherent collections on critical themes. Secularisation and the future of religion; gender; the negotiation and presentation of religious identities, beliefs and values; and the interplay between group and individual in religious settings are some of the areas addressed. Ultimately, these books reflect not just on religious life but on how wider society is affected by the enduring religious framing of human relationships, morality and the nature of society itself.

This series is part of the broader *Theology and Religion in Interdisciplinary Perspective Series* edited by Douglas Davies and Richard Fenn.

Other titles published in the BSA Sociology of Religion Study Group Series

A Sociology of Spirituality
Edited by Kieran Flanagan and Peter C. Jupp
ISBN 978-0-7546-5458-2 (HBK)

Materializing Religion
Expression, Performance and Ritual
Edited by Elisabeth Arweck and William Keenan
ISBN 978-0-7546-5094-2 (HBK)

Reading Religion in Text and Context
Reflections of Faith and Practice in Religious Materials
Edited by Elisabeth Arweck and Peter Collins
ISBN 978-0-7546-5482-7 (HBK)

Religion, Identity and Change
Perspectives on Global Transformations
Edited by Simon Coleman and Peter Collins
ISBN 978-0-7546-0450-1 (HBK)

Religion and the Individual
Belief, Practice, Identity

Edited by

ABBY DAY
University of Sussex, UK

ASHGATE

Published by
Ashgate Publishing Limited
Gower House
Croft Road
Aldershot
Hampshire GU11 3HR
England

Ashgate Publishing Company
Suite 420
101 Cherry Street
Burlington, VT 05401-4405
USA

Ashgate website: http://www.ashgate.com

British Library Cataloguing in Publication Data
Religion and the individual : belief, practice, identity. – (Theology and religion in
   interdisciplinary perspectives)
   1. Religion and sociology – Congresses 2. Faith – Congresses 3. Rites and ceremonies
   – Congresses
   I. Day, Abby II. British Sociological Association.
   Sociology of Religion Study Group
   306.6

Library of Congress Cataloging-in-Publication Data
Day, Abby, 1956–
   Religion and the individual : belief, practice, identity / Abby Day.
       p. cm.—(Theology and religion in interdisciplinary perspective series) (BSA
sociology of religion study group)
       ISBN 978-0-7546-6122-1 (hardcover : alk. paper) 1. Experience (Religion)—
Congresses. 2. Spirituality—Congresses. I. Title.

   BL53.D39 2007
   204—dc22

                                                                              2007036262

ISBN 978-0-7546-6122-1

Printed and bound in Great Britain by MPG Books Ltd, Bodmin, Cornwall.

Contents

List of Figures and Tables

Figures

Tables

List of Contributors

David M. Bell (Emory University)

Ali Çarkoğlu (Sabanci University)

Peter Collins (Durham University)

Sylvia Collins-Mayo (Kingston University)

Jayeel Serrano Cornelio (National University of Singapore)

Douglas Davies (Durham University)

Andrew Dawson (Lancaster University)

Abby Day (University of Sussex)

Alvin C. Dueck (Fuller Theological Seminary)

Janet Eccles (Lancaster University)

Michael Keenan (Nottingham Trent University)

Deborah E. Kessel (Fuller Theological Seminary)

Yaojun Li (University of Manchester)

Xiaowen Lu (Shanghai Social Science Academy)

Richard O'Leary (Queen's University, Belfast)

Joshua P. Morgan (Azusa Pacific University)

Kevin S. Reimer (Azusa Pacific University)

Russell Sandberg (Cardiff University)

Rob Warner (University of Wales)

Introduction

Abby Day

As with other books in the series, this collection was inspired by an international gathering of scholars discussing an important theme within the sociology of religion. The focus of the conference of the Sociology of Religion Study Group of the British Sociological Association (BSA) held at the University of Manchester in 2006 was 'Religion and the Individual', a theme chosen to provoke dialogue between psychologists and sociologists of religion. Eleven of the papers in this volume were commissioned from scholars who presented at that conference; a further two were commissioned from presenters at the 2007 BSA conference who contributed to a specially designed stream, *Religious Identity in Contemporary Contexts.*

Contributors to this volume shaped their work to reflect a common theme: how do individuals engage with religion to create and express meaning? Although it is a commonplace within the sociology of religion that the individual's religious beliefs, practices and identities are influenced by social contexts, the question for individuals is often 'what does this mean to me'? The work published here discusses that question from a variety of disciplinary perspectives: sociology, psychology, anthropology, and theology. Much of the work is empirical, drawn from international contexts, but some is expressly theoretical. Methods vary according to the questions being explored: we have large-scale quantitative studies and micro qualitative work. What matters here is not epistemological preference, but rather how in fact people are religious and what their beliefs, practices and identities mean to them.

Accordingly, the collection has been organised into three parts. The first explores 'belief' in terms of what belief means to the individual. Douglas Davies begins by exploring why the individual became sidelined in sociology and, rather more importantly, why we lack an analytical category within which sociological and psychological factors can complement each other to allow the individual to reappear within sociological studies. Janet Eccles conducted doctoral research in north-west England, revealing what she described as the 'hiddenness' of relational forms of the sacred, and what those mean to two kinds of women: those who are active church-goers, and those who have left the church.

Exploring belief amongst those do not attend church is also taken up in the next chapter by Sylvia Collins-Mayo as she looks at the nature and meaning of prayer in young people's daily lives in the UK, particularly amongst those who have little or no contact with institutional religion. Xiaowen Lu, Richard O'Leary and Yaojun Li look in depth at the meaning of religious belief in China. Although China is the most populous state in the world, there has been limited inquiry into the relationship between socio-economic development in contemporary China and the individual value orientations of Chinese people.

Part II of the book explores different ways in which people are religious in practice, considering the different meanings that people attach to religion, and the social expressions of their personal understandings. From Singapore, researcher Jayeel Serrano Cornelio considers what may account for the success of what is termed 'new-paradigm Christianity'. Another form of religious practice and its related meaning is explored by Kevin S. Reimer, Alvin C. Dueck, Joshua P. Morgan and Deborah E. Kessel. Here, we move explicitly from an exclusive Christian context as explored thus far in the volume and consider life experiences, attitudes and practices of exemplar Muslim and Christian peacemakers who effect positive change under difficult and often dangerous circumstances. The theme of autonomous practices within a wider religious context is picked up by Rob Warner in the UK with his study of Spring Harvest, the largest charismatic-evangelical conference in Britain. From practices of commitment, peace-making and individual choice-making, we conclude this section on a more prosaic note: what do religious people mean by 'giving' and how do they practise their religion through what they do with their material wealth? Ali Çarkoğlu used survey data to probe how Muslims in Turkey practised philanthropy.

Finally, what religion means to people often shapes and reflects how they see themselves. This does not happen in isolation, but necessarily in relation to others. In Part III of the book we explore identities and the tensions between external and internal meanings and constraints. David Bell dresses the stage theoretically by arguing that the meaning of religious identity has been clouded and ill-defined. He provides a theoretical foundation for measuring religious identity and proposes further research into types of religious institutions that promote different aspects of religious identity.

From his perspective as an anthropologist, Peter Collins seeks initially to interrogate two apparently opposite modes of being in religious contexts – individuality and sociality. He introduces what he describes as a complicating factor, the plane of 'secular discourse', to show how the terms 'religious' and 'secular' represent a second dichotomy which may contribute fundamentally to a misunderstanding of religious contexts. Russell Sandberg discusses how lawyers and sociologists have often wrestled with the question of defining religion, and yet there has been little sociological commentary on the various definitions and conceptions of religion found in law. He works to address this omission within a Durkheimian theoretical framework. A struggle to define a sense of identity is described by Michael Keenan as he looks at how Anglican male gay clergy manage the coexistence of gay, Christian and clerical identities. The way that the men connect life sectors, such as sexual and professional identities, provides a meaning framework for individuals. Concluding our volume, Andrew Dawson explores the new religion of Santo Daime in Brazil and discusses the fabrication of religious identity by urban middle-class *daimistas* through their appropriation of millenarian motifs traditionally associated with Brazil's rural poor.

I am grateful to all the authors for their work and for the privilege and pleasure it has been working with them. We hope you find this volume engaging, provocative and useful in your learning, teaching and research.

Acknowledgements

On behalf of all of us, thanks go to Ashgate Publishing and in particular to its supportive, professional and seemingly tireless commissioning editor, Sarah Lloyd. We are also grateful to David Voas at the University of Manchester who organised the 2006 *Religion and the Individual* conference and selected the theme. Finally, special thanks to the Sociology of Religion Study Group: its support for the discipline through conferences, postgraduate events, study days, and publications has helped many of us to develop our work in the field.

PART I
Belief

Chapter One

Cultural Intensification: A Theory for Religion

Douglas Davies

Nor love thy life. Nor hate: but what thou liv'st
Live well, how long or short permit to Heav'n.

Here, as throughout its length, John Milton's *Paradise Lost* presents a volume in a phrase (Book XI:550). Such poetically descriptive brevity permits a wisdom not easily achieved in prose. Its power lies in a literary intensification of thought and feeling: cognitive and affective dimensions of life unite in a heightened impact upon the hearer. Drama, too, takes recognizable problems normally requiring decades to play themselves out in life and presents them in an hour. Religious ritual, for its part, also integrates texts and drama, and often enhances this pervasive process. Yet, despite its omnipresence, there is no general analytical category available to embrace these social contexts in a manner that allows sociological and psychological factors to complement each other in such a way that the individual may reappear within sociological studies.

One potential candidate for this theoretical vacancy lies in the notion of 'cultural intensification'. Accordingly, the purpose of this chapter is to define the term and consider reasons for its acceptance as such. While Milton's lines reveal a literary case of 'cultural intensification' other examples could as easily be drawn from iconographic, ideological or musical domains as from historical, contemporary or mythical individuals and their social effects. To approach such contexts in terms of 'cultural intensification' is, potentially, to gain a new and expanded socio-psychological perspective upon familiar things.

'Cultural intensification' can be taken both as a category embracing a wide variety of behaviours and as a process identifiable within them in which the values of a group are brought to a behavioural focus and emotionally appropriated. It assumes an integration of sociological and psychological ideas in the interpretation of social life whilst providing a reference category for diverse and well-known social scientific analytical concepts not least those of embodiment and rites of passage, as well as less familiar notions such as rites of intensification from which this category has been developed by extension. The rest of this chapter explores these issues on the assumption that the individual is the focal point of embodiment.

Uniting Divisions

Historically speaking, the sociological study of religion has often assumed the procedural necessity of distinguishing between methods utilizing what it defines as social facts on the one hand and psychological ones on the other. Here Durkheim's formal influence in seeking sociological explanation only in terms of what he saw as social facts and not from psychological causes has been overly effective irrespective of whether he followed the distinction himself in accounting for totemic ritual, and despite his affirmation that 'the study of psychological facts' is valuable for the sociologist (1938, 111). In the process the individual was lost amidst the social group. Other contemporaries, including anthropologists Rivers (1916, see Slobodin 1997) and Bateson (1936), did seek to integrate these domains as did numerous later anthropologists (for example, J. Davies 1982) though sociological work on religion could easily ignore these dimensions and also leave the individual in theoretical exile. David Lyons' (2006) recent reflections on the body, for example, has a focus more upon the 1990s including Bryan Turner (1996) and Mellor and Shilling (1997), with an absence of anything anthropological (for example, Blacking 1977). This divide between anthropology and sociology is widespread and as regrettable as that between sociology and psychology, though there is no guarantee that either will bring the individual as such into greater prominence

Today, however, little is to be gained by isolating the social facts constituted by values, beliefs and the social organization of life from the psychological facts constituted by emotions and varieties of feeling states as is increasingly acknowledged within religious studies at large (Rue 2005), even though the formal study of emotions is, itself, in its early stages (Frijda 1986). It is with that recognition in mind that this chapter explores the notion of 'cultural intensification' as a means of fostering the integration of cognitive and affective streams of life.

Cultural Intensification: Theoretical Issues

Theoretically, cultural intensification has obvious intellectual roots beginning with the fundamental sociological, psychological and theological challenge of understanding the relationship between individual and society. Within those disciplines the interface of socially or divinely established rules for social life and the personal and collective emotional engagement with them assumes primacy of place. More specifically, within the social sciences of sociology and, to a lesser extent, anthropology 'meaning-making' has generally been credited with a philosophical background, especially in phenomenological philosophy, an issue I have analyzed in association with the question of how 'meaning' might relate to the notion of 'salvation' in religious traditions (D.J. Davies 1984). Psychology, by contrast, has been more experimental in pursuing the meaning achieved in and through the processes of human cognition as well as their limits (Pinker 1997). What is often ignored is just how individuals achieve meaning within the broad bands offered by their society and by their personal temperament. Here the study of biographical narrative is invaluable, but demands a sense of plasticity between 'the social group' and personal construal of life.

The more specific origin of 'cultural intensification' in this chapter, however, is anthropological, developed from Chapple and Coon's (1947) anthropological notion of 'rites of intensification', ritual moments in which a group gathered to re-engage with their basic values, an approach clearly echoing Durkheimian notions of society generating the very categories of thought and fostering the emotional experiences bringing them to practical life. Chapple and Coon do, however, offer a specific term that easily identifies the issue of a person's affective engagement with the values of their society and it is unfortunate that it never gained the popularity of Van Gennep's notion of rites of passage. While the latter have not only become popular but are often abused through inappropriate application the former have been largely ignored. In seeking to correct this omission it might be valuable, for example, to identify rites of passage as one subset of rites of intensification, for Chapple and Coon's concept denoted ritual behaviour in which participants do not engage in transition but in a repeatedly renewed familiarity with and commitment to their group's values. In this sense, for example, Christian participation in the Eucharist or daily prayer, or the Muslim's daily prayers all serve as rites of intensification even though some loose interpretation might be tempted to see them as rites of passage into and out of 'holy' states. The sheer familiarity with concepts is a temptation for inappropriate application, certainly as far as rites of passage are concerned. A wider familiarization with rites of intensification could, alone, be valuable in fostering more appropriate application of ideas and allow for individual appropriation of values and not simply for shifting status positions.

The move from Chapple and Coon's rites of intensification to the idea of cultural intensification is relatively simple, involving a shift from the specific to the general. Cultural intensification simply describes the wider process of which rites of intensification are narrower manifestations. It describes a wide collection of rites, events and phenomena in and through which the values and beliefs of a society are related to the emotional and sensory dynamics of individuals as members of a society. Cultural intensification is a concept able to direct analyses of a multiplicity of social events whilst also giving them both a sense of direction and of family resemblance. The remainder of this chapter sets out a variety of such events and discusses a selection of more theoretical concepts in current use to illustrate the value of this relatively abstract and unifying notion of cultural intensification.

Culture

Despite the potentially crippling critical possibilities that a commitment to notions of 'culture' may involve this chapter maintains its use in the firm opinion that 'culture' is, itself, a compound notion in need of benefit from an integrating of cognitive and affective elements within any particular society or group. Accordingly I take 'culture' to be the outcome of the processes by which values and beliefs pattern social and individual identity and are, in turn, influenced by them. On that basis 'cultural intensification' is adopted as a shorthand expression summarizing many ideas at once, including 'sociological' and 'psychological' ideas, to furnish a perspective that otherwise might not be so easily available. What cannot be ignored, however, is the fact that creative individuals can radically influence the cultural life of a society, indeed of the world, as studies of prophets and political leaders would demonstrate.

Cognitive and Affective Dimensions

There are, of course, many ways of approaching this configuration of concept and affect, here I mention only Durkheim, Turner, Bloch and Geertz. Durkheim (1915) argued for an essentially sociological treatment of ritual as a process in which members of a group bring their basic ideas to mind and engage with them in and through the acts performed, the objects used and the place of performance. Yet his work is rooted in the experiential mood shifts of ritual participants. Geertz (1973) by contrast, admits moods into the motivations of devotees in the symbolic ritual of religious institutions as his much debated cultural definition of religion made clear. In a very similar fashion Victor Turner (1996) also directly linked thought and feeling in his notion of ritual symbols as constituted by ideological and sensory poles and by the process of condensation of many ideas onto a single focus that echoes Freud's psychological notion of condensation. That kind of integration of the rational and emotional, the cognitive and affective domains of life, in ritual performance exemplifies Chapple and Coon's rite of intensification and can, as already indicated, be taken as a subset of 'cultural intensification'. Finally, Maurice Bloch's (1992) theory of rebounding conquest can also be interpreted as an expression of cultural intensification, especially in the way he developed both van Gennep and Victor Turner's emphasis upon liminality in transition rites to stress that individuals do not simply change status through initiation but may also be emotionally or existentially changed to some degree.

Values, Beliefs and Identity

At this point it is worth trying to clarify the meaning of the 'values' that are manifest in ritual and identify them as ideas invested with a degree of emotional intensity. Most often such values are the ideas by which a society directs its communal life with the members of society not being neutrally related to them. The very process of socialization involves the inculcation of values that become second nature to the individuals concerned whose sense of identity is partly composed of these values, but there is always the possibility of idiosyncrasy emerging whether perceived as deviant or revelatory.

It is also useful to distinguish between ideas and values, taking ideas to be foundational concepts grounded in basic social categories that are constitutive of a society's way of life. An idea is usually a word or phrase that summarizes a way of understanding part of the world around us and, indeed, of understanding ourselves. Ideas are often names of or for things, helping us relate to our environment, they are foundational to the process of meaning-making that is a characteristic activity of human beings. The expression 'to have an idea' takes this process a little further, describing the way in which a person makes new connections between things, and this reveals the creative capacity to adapt to the world. And there may be no emotional charge associated with such an idea. Ideas may, however, come to assume the status of a value in which emotion is vested and identity aligned. Such is the contemporary situation with the idea of evolution when it comes either to frame an atheist identity or an anti-evolutionist stance whose identity is emotionally lodged in creationism. In the latter case 'creation' becomes transformed from an idea into a value.

So, not all ideas are values. Many ideas are abstract labels for things both in the tangible world as in the realms of imagination, but values emerge from ideas as those ideas becoming increasingly significant for identity, for the organization of life and its many forms of relationships. The idea of a 'father' for example can remain simply at the level of an idea and can be compared in different societies in which the 'father' is viewed in a wide variety of ways. But when individuals speak of the place of the 'father' in their own smaller world then 'father', or perhaps we might say 'fatherhood', comes to be a value: it is an idea in which particular forms of emotion are invested.

What then of the notion of 'belief', how does that resemble and differ from 'idea' or 'value'? Here I will not examine even a fraction of the extensive academic discussion that has gone into analyses of belief (for example, Needham 1972) but will simply regard beliefs as the way in which people describe the values they perceive as central to their own sense of identity and to the meaningfulness of the social group to which they belong. So we may say that key or prime values function as beliefs. The focus lies on the subjective and social function of the belief within identity formation and the meaningfulness of the world rather than on any objective content of the belief.

By approaching beliefs by this route of values as ideas vested with emotional significance, there is no need to argue for beliefs as pertaining essentially to what is often called religion. Religious beliefs can simply take their place alongside other forms of belief for these are simply ideas relating to what a particular society may define as religion, politics, the natural environment or whatever. I will not assume that a belief concerning what a person regards as invisible and supernatural beings or powers is any different from a belief that there are laws governing how history unfolds or how individuals align themselves through marriage, work or play. Finally, it is worth mentioning 'attitude' as a means of pondering the nature and degree of the emotional charge brought to bear upon an idea. Quite often we find that attitudes bear a very strong family resemblance to values in that they involve a degree of emotional attachment or detachment. In many contexts an attitude would be thought to express a lower degree of investment of emotional energy than would a 'belief'. When ideas are invested with an emotional energy to form a value we often find it occurs through some kind of group activity, and when values are described as beliefs that activity often takes the form of ritual behaviour.

Embodiment

To pay so much attention to the emotional charge vested in ideas to yield values, and to identify the core values of a group in terms of belief that involves ritual behaviour, means that it is inevitable that we arrive at a discussion of what has come to be called embodiment (for example, Csordas 1994). By embodiment I refer to the process by which beliefs come to be part of the very way in which a person comes to be constituted and behave, acknowledging the integration of 'nature and nurture' factors within the individual. In more traditional terms one often speaks of ideas as something one thinks about, in the present context one would wish to speak more in terms of values as something practised. If those values hold primacy of place such that they may be viewed as beliefs then one could easily speak of 'behaving belief'. To behave, practise or perform a belief is a perfectly natural way of 'thinking' about human life.

The entire process of human socialization as babies and children, along with the many subsequent learning experiences as people become parts of new groups or institutions, involves the acquisition of new behaviour patterns. As a body we imitate others amongst whom we live, and we learn new forms of activity that are, themselves, grounded in particular beliefs. The body itself is a complex system in which biochemical processes are of fundamental importance in providing a feeling-state for the individual. Some of the feelings that our bodies give us are provided with names by our societies whilst others remain unnamed and are known only to the individuals concerned. The use of the word 'emotion' is valuable in describing some of these feeling-states and different societies tend to favour particular lists of their own as numerous anthropological studies spotlighting emotion have shown (Corrigan 2004; Milton and Svasek 2005). But our biochemical systems are, themselves, open to influence by our thoughts, by new experiences and by old memories (d'Aquili et al. 1979). To recall a particular life event may, for example, bring a feeling of pleasure or of pained embarrassment even if we are alone when the memory occurs, such is biography embodied. The interface between personal experience and social life is, for example, clearly evident in contexts of justice, injustice and law. This intricate intimacy I have emphasized elsewhere through the notion of 'moral-somatic' relationships that describes how the moral domain of social values pervades the very somatic base of individual life (D.J. Davies 2001).

Language, Narrative and Place

Groups are grounded in their own moral-somatic syndromes and exist to foster sentiments, feelings and memories binding believers and cherished ideas. Ritual and ceremonial behaviour, fired by narrative language and calculated silence serves the purpose of cultural intensification as in the obvious cases of legal and religious institutions. Laws and legal judgments as well as doctrines and liturgical formulae offer clear examples of how a society's values are expressed, embodied and implemented. When the fact that a convicted criminal shows no remorse is noted by a judge it is because the moral-somatic domain appears to be untouched. It is the social recognition of the dynamics of moral-somatic factors that has, for example, seen the wisdom of allowing victims to speak in court and express their own distress. In many religious contexts the place of confession, of testimony and of worship has long engaged in the moral-somatic interface of ideology and embodied emotion. And such experiences tend to be enhanced through the built environment in which they are pronounced. The court of law or the church helps frame the linguistic forms of a vow or a prayer in a dramatic way, often bringing a sense of history and a society's past to bear upon the present and, in that very moment, contributing to the intensifying of the prime values involved

The role of particular places or buildings is also of fundamental importance in this stimulation of feeling-states as part of the wider process of cultural intensification. Cultures possessing ancient monuments and long-standing architectural features use these as environments of memory. The history of a people or group becomes embedded in them, often through the material culture of sculpture, art or memorials to individuals and past events that, together, help compose the story of that people. This narrative comes to be foundational for cultural intensification by providing a focus for the way people feel in the present about things that have happened in the past and which help interpret contemporary life and give some sense of how to engage with the future. Here memory and hope cohere (Harvey 2000). A great deal of cultural appraisal and the expression of a society's sense of itself emerges both in architecture and place. Indeed, today's dominant political issues are preoccupied precisely with the cultural intensification aligned with buildings and places deemed sacred by Jews, Moslems and Christians. Another reason why more attention is now paid to the nature of building and place than has been for centuries concerns the environment, as people see their own nature enhanced or nullified when even a single building, let alone its civic, urban, or rural environment, may be viewed as related to climatic aspects of the world's ecological destiny. Here, too, a process of cultural intensification may apply when basic values and the emotions aligned with them are brought to focus on building design. No building stands alone, none 'an island' unto itself. Lindsay Jones's (1993) insightful analysis of architecture and place embodies this in the notion of a 'ritual architectural event' in which the hopes and expectations of people interplay with the allurement inherent in a structure and its potential promise. The existence of a building such as London's Westminster Abbey exemplifies the notion of an allurement of place associated with the historical events that have taken place within it. The fact of the Abbey's geographical setting amidst other places of similar historical asociations further enhances its capacity of allurement. When a formal ritual such as a royal wedding, funeral or coronation takes place in such an architectural environment the scene is set for cultural intensification. Indeed, coronation rites offer a prime example of this process as theological ideas and deep historical resonances focus in vows taken and ceremonial acts performed upon the Monarch's body, as much of Mary Douglas's early embodiment studies demonstrate (1966; 1970). Cultural intensification of social values is, here, inseparable from their embodiment in an individual as Head of State. Here the acclamation for the monarch's life, *vivat regina*, is quite telling, uniting as it does, biological life and social office. One final example will reinforce this point: viz., the death of one of the world's greatest operatic tenors, Enrico Caruso (1873–1921), who sang at New York's Metropolitan Opera no fewer than 607 times. His sudden death in his beloved Naples was marked by the entire city with 'the sorrow of hundreds of thousands of the dead man's fellow citizens ... shared by millions all over the world', and with King Victor Emmanuel, granting the use of his royal basilica of San Francisco di Paola for the ceremony (Ybarra 1954, 222). Caruso's funerary rites present a distinctive case of cultural intensification in which national identity is complemented by the international love of music both embodied in a large-hearted individual in the vanguard of that twentieth-century celebrity culture.

Survival and Cultural Intensification

Underlying great people, the sacred places marking ethnic, national or religious identity, or natural locales of ecological health, the issue of survival predominates. It is evident in long-standing and widespread graves that should not simply be viewed as memorials of the past but also as symbols of endurance, of the ongoing survival of a society, often in the link between ancestor and descendant that is perpetuated in the rites for ancestors that are performed by the living (Prendergast 2005). Survival, perhaps the foundational drive is as evident amongst human beings as amongst other animal species and cultural intensification is a way of describing the social manifestation of biological life.

Hope and Creativity

This biological-social bond is further extended when we appreciate the elaborate schemes of creative thought that reflect upon survival and upon the nature and meaning of the life. Here the kind of optimism that underlies the drive to survive can be interpreted as a form of courage for life (Durkheim 1915, 382), of hope and desire for life (Malinowski 1974, 51–53) that, under appropriate circumstances, fosters the imagination in many forms of creativity (Stotland 1969; Desroche 1979) even twenty-first-century business management combined with human flourishing (Friedman 2005). People come to live as much in these imaginative worlds as they do in an actual physical environment. Indeed, imaginative worlds an be influenced by the very buildings in which we ponder and engage with these myths, doctrines and theories about 'reality'. Cultural intensification becomes a means of describing the ways in which the emotion of hope and the capacity for creativity combine. Moreover, the drive for meaning moves from an understanding of the environment as a source of food, drink and social support to theories about the origin and significance of life itself. The meaning-making process that psychology details in a child's development through exploration of its environment parallels the pursuit of knowing about the world that is pursued by innumerable disciplines from the natural and social sciences to the human sciences including history, philosophy, theology, music and art, as well as in sporting activity. Contemporary mass interest in computerized life-games as well as the semi-fictional chat-room possibilities of electronic life further demonstrate activities describable in terms of cultural intensification.

Intensification Behaviour

It is precisely in these activities of meaning-making that hope and creativity become apparent and show how human beings engage practically with their ideas. If left to itself meaning can seem an abstract and very neutral form of knowledge; once it becomes part of a history of a nation, institution, political party or, indeed, of a sports club or of the myth and theology of a group, then it becomes acted upon and acted out. In and through that activity the particular 'meaning' takes on new life, it becomes intensified in the lives of those related to it. While it would be very easy to introduce the idea of ritual at this point in our discussion it might draw attention to a limited area of human activity whereas my intention is to embrace very many forms of behaviour as forms of cultural intensification.

If 'meaning' left to itself may appear abstract and unrelated to life so too with 'truth', not so much in the sense of what people believe to be true but with the ways in which they engage with their truth. In other words our interest lies in what might be called the practice of truth. This is, for example, one valuable means of approaching the argument about scientific and theological explanations of the nature of life. For 'truth' becomes embodied in the lives of those engaged in its pursuit and illuminates the relative importance of where and how people live. A life spent in laboratory or other scientific action needs relating to time at home, at play or at worship. The hopes behind family life and ethics of work situations are practised just as philosophers practise their knowledge of meaning in and through seminars, lectures and tutorials. In other words there are ways of life that serve to intensify particular attitudes and outlooks: ideas seldom remain in abstract isolation. People are seldom – and cannot be expected to be – neutral about ideas in which they invest their lives. In the case of scientific and theological ideas of the meaning of life, for example, it is easy to see that scientists who practise in a laboratory and worship in church are rather different in life-orientation from those experiencing only one such context. 'Truth' is embodied, is as much a verb as a noun, as the general sociological notion of *habitus* has long acknowledged: and practice provides occasion for intensification of the values involved.

Situational Intensification

To speak of cultural intensification raises the question of different degrees of cultural intensity, which could initially be approached on a low to high spectrum. Situations in which there is a low or even negative level of intensity of value-behaviour might include discussion of, for example, classic notions such as Durkheim's *anomie*, issues of suicide, the social protest of marginalized groups or even Weber's 'disenchantment' when explored more philosophically (Tester 2001). Toulis' use of the idea of 'crisis of presence' to account for the meaninglessness preluding conversion could also be included in such a spread of related concepts.

Then there is an 'ordinariness' of intensity found in many societies as the daily life of routine finds a level of expression in degrees of informality and relative formality but without a shift into specially singled out events, never better accounted for than in Terkel's description of ordinary American lives (1974). Family members or work colleagues conduct their lives on a daily basis that varies in formality and informality depending upon the nature of the society concerned, but it is likely that on certain specific occasions this mode shifts into a different form as when, for example, American schools engage with their national flag and enact their regular pledge of allegiance, an act that would be entirely strange in the United Kingdom. With an existentialist theological purpose in mind Paul Tillich, for example, spoke of the way in which 'religion opens up the depth of man's spiritual life which is usually covered by the dust of our daily life', and did so when he wished to identify what he became famed for: viz. the 'ultimate meaning' underlying life, an ultimacy he called 'the glory of religion' (1959, 9). In the philosophical-sociological domain of phenomenological sociology the 'dust of daily life' settles within the 'everyday life world' where routines seldom evoke ritualized action involving prime values. The phenomenological notion of 'tension of consciousness' is, itself, valuable in marking the varying levels of emotional dynamism brought to human perception and social interaction. The tension of consciousness involved in casually watching passing traffic from a café is different from the purposeful scanning employed when crossing the road and very different from the electrifying message-processing triggered when driving into a motorway hazard.

So, too, with issues of social convention or moral values that are often accepted but unconsidered but become sharply foregrounded under the right circumstances. Moscovici (1993, 245), in his important study that combined a critique of sociology with an advocacy of its need to engage with psychology, echoes these distinctions of level of attention in his telling distinction between 'anonymous' and 'nominated' actions. He did so as part of his comparison and contrast between the work of Durkheim, Weber and Simmel, in which he identifies the first two as dealing with 'nominated facts' and the last with 'a host of relationships and common forms of behaviour' (Moscovici 1993, 247). This led him to what he self-critically described as perhaps the 'extreme' conclusion that *society is not a sociological notion* but a 'common sense idea' (1993, 250; original emphasis). However, one of the most significant aspects of Moscovici's analysis as far as this chapter is concerned relates to his interpretation and development of Simmel's theoretical approach to money. As a medium of exchange that helps forge society – itself the outcome of the human desire to be with others – money serves as a symbolic focus for numerous aspects of human desire. As an 'instrument of social magic', as Kieran Flanagan calls it, it need not only signify 'an estranging power' (1996, 176) for, in terms of cultural intensification, as of Moscovici's 'anonymous' and 'nominated' actions, money occupies a prime symbolic position. Within developed societies, money underlies most aspects of life and, precisely because it is the background medium of and for everyday life, it is also available as a means of intensifying any particular value of that world. Gifts of money or presents expressing monetary value regularly mark the status change of rites of passage just as financial absence often stigmatizes those of low or even marginal social status. Within the cultural domains of religion, too, money's symbolic power is enormous in its capacity to express an individual's or a group's devotion to its deity or to fellow devotees, as I have demonstrated elsewhere for the biblical case of money within the Acts of the Apostles (D.J. Davies 2004). For Judas, whose betrayal money bought a field in which he perished, for the deceitful Ananias and Sapphira who also died, and for the Simon who gave us the notion of Simony and barely escaped with his life, money turned negative. For the faithful Paul, however, who paid his own way to the end, the Acts depicts money as the medium of sincerity towards the prime value of the Holy Spirit. In a dramatic transformation, blasphemy come to inhere in financial sharp practice and ritual purity shifts from Hebrew body-fluids and food rules to the manner of handling money. The very existence of money allowed the new religious movement of Christianity to move from traditional Jewish community forms of operation to those of a voluntary organization of eclectic membership. The values of a group that was, itself, in process of formation, were intensified in and through the symbolic capacity of money.

Conclusion

In this biblical case and the foregoing discussion enough has been said to suggest that emotion and the values it pervades may find in 'cultural intensification' an appropriate interpretative category, a higher-order notion able to embrace and illuminate other ideas bearing a family likeness. It is for this reason of generality that the chapter's subtitle prefers thinking of cultural intensification as a theoretical construct with potential as a theory *for* use when discussing religion as one amongst other aspects of life rather than a theory *of* religion as a distinctive category. A great deal more needs saying on all of these sketched issues but, for now, it may be wiser to heed Milton (XII: 585) in our conclusion as in the introduction. Accordingly,

> Let us descend now therefore from this top
> Of speculation.

Bibliography

D'Aquili, E.G., Laughlin, C.D. and McManus, J. 1979. *The Spectrum of Ritual: a Biogenetic Structural Analysis*, New York: Columbia University Press.

Bateson, Gregory. 1936. *Naven*, Berkley: California University Press.

Blacking, John (ed.). 1977. *The Anthropology of the Body*, New York: Academic Press.

Bloch, Maurice. 1992. *Prey into Hunter*, Cambridge: Cambridge University Press.

Chapple, E.D. and Coon, C.S. 1947. *Principles of Anthropology*, London: Cape.

Corrigan, John (ed.). 2004. *Religion and Emotion*, Oxford: Oxford University Press.

Csordas, Thomas J. 1994. *Embodiment and Experience: The Existential Ground of Culture and Self*, Cambridge: Cambridge University Press.

Davies, Douglas J. 1984. *Meaning and Salvation in Religious Studies*, Leiden: Brill.

——. 2001. 'Health, Morality and Sacrifice: The Sociology of Disaster', in Richard K. Fenn (ed.), *The Sociology of Religion*, Oxford: Blackwell. 404–417.

——. 2004. 'Purity, Spirit and Reciprocity in the Acts of the Apostles', in L.J. Lawrence and M.I. Aguilar (eds), *Anthropology and Biblical Studies*, Leiden: Deo Publishing. 259–280.

Davies, Jon. (ed.). 1982. *Religious Organization and Religious Experience*, London: Academic Press.

Desroche, Henri. 1979. *The Sociology of Hope*, London: Routledge and Kegan Paul.

Douglas, Mary. 1966. *Purity and Danger*, London: Penguin.

——. 1970. *Natural Symbols*, London: Penguin.

Durkheim, Emile. 1915. *The Elementary Forms of the Religious Life*, London: George Allen and Unwin.

——. [1895] 1938. *Rules of Sociological Method*, trans. S.A. Solovay and J.H. Mueller, New York: The Free Press.

Flanagan, Kieran, 1996. *The Enchantment of Sociology: A Study of Theology and Culture,* London: MacMillan.

Friedman, Thomas L. 2005. *The World is Flat: The Globalized World in the Twenty-first Century*, London: Penguin.

Frijda, N.H. 1986. *The Emotions*, Cambridge: Cambridge University Press.

Geertz, C. 1973. 'Religion as a Cultural System', in Banton, M. (ed.), *Anthropological Approaches to the Study of Religion*, London: Tavistock. 1–46.

Harvey, David. 2000. *Spaces of Hope,* Edinburgh: Edinburgh University Press.

Jones, Lindsay, 1993. 'The hermeneutics of sacred architecture: a reassessment of the similitude between Tula, Hidalgo and Chichen Itza Part 1', *History of Religions*, **32**: 315–342.

Lyons, David. 2006. 'New Media, Niche Markets, and the Body: Excarnate and Hypercarnate Challenges for Theory and Theology', in J.A. Beckford and J. Walliss (eds), *Theorising Religion: Classical and Contemporary Debates*, Aldershot: Ashgate. 197–210.

Malinowski, B. ([1948] 1974). *Magic, Science and Religion*, London: Souvenir Press.

Mellor, P. and Shilling, C. 1997. *Re-forming the Body: Religion, Community and Modernity*, Sage: London.

Milton, John. (2000). *Paradise Lost*, ed. John Leonard, London: Penguin.

Milton, Kay and Svasek, Maruska (eds). 2005. *Mixed Emotions: Anthropological Studies of Feeling*, Oxford: Berg.

Moscovici, Serge. 1993. *The Invention of Society*, Cambridge: Polity Press.

Needham, R. 1972. *Belief, Language and Experience*, Oxford: Blackwell.

Pinker, Steven. 1997. *How the Mind Works*, London: Penguin.

Prendergast, David. 2005. *From Elder to Ancestor*, Folkstone: Global Oriental.

Rue, Loyal. 2005. *Religion is Not About God*, London: Rutgers University Press.

Slobodin, Richard. 1997. *W.H.R. Rivers, Pioneer Anthropologist, Psychiatrist of The Ghost Road*, Gloucestershire: Sutton Publishing,

Stotland, E. 1969. *The Psychology of Hope*, San Francisco: Jossey-Bass.

Terkels, Studs. [1974] 1984. *Working,* Harmondsworth: Penguin Books.

Tester, Keith. 2001. 'Disenchantment and Virtue', in Kieran Flanagan and Peter C. Jupp (eds), *Virtue Ethics and Sociology*, London: Palgrave. 35–50.

Tillich, Paul. 1959. *Theology of Culture*, New York: Oxford University Press.

Turner, B.S. 1996. *The Body and Society*, Sage: London.

Ybarra, T.R. 1954. *Caruso*, London: The Cresset Press.

Chapter Two

Speaking Personally:
Women Making Meaning through
Subjectivised Belief[1]

Janet Eccles

Introduction

In this chapter I report on the results of a series of interviews with a small group of women in north-west England. These were carried out to determine what influence, if any, their attendance at church, either past or still continuing, has on their present beliefs and practices, together with what influences might also have been exerted by cultural changes since the 1960s.

Research by Heelas and Woodhead (2005) into those individuals and communities pursuing the sacred, in whatever form, in a market town of northern England, suggests they fall into two distinct constituencies. The majority of those who attend church and chapel have a non-subjectivised belief in a theistic, transcendent, male, Christian god, whose word is inviolate and has been handed down for centuries by hallowed tradition, a god, who, Callum Brown (2001) maintains, legitimates the notion of the pious (domestic, submissive and self-sacrificing) female. Those who pursue the sacred through what might be called the working together of mind-body-spirit and inner-life spirituality, the holistic realm, have much more subjectivised beliefs in that they aim to improve the quality of their individual and unique lives, whether they are male or female. Only 4 per cent of the Christian church attenders they interviewed had become involved in the holistic realm. Hence they see a bifurcation of beliefs between the two groups. Those who seek the sacred belong, by and large, to either that which privileges non-subjectivised belief – submission to a male God and saviour – or that which privileges the empowering of one's own subjective life.

Other evidence (Roof 1998; Wuthnow 1998; Lambert 1999; Roof 1999; Hervieu-Léger 2000; Roof 2003) suggests, however, there is much more fluidity of belief, that many individuals are engaged in a process, a quest, which may involve moving in and out of different sacred milieux, according to perceived need at the time. Ammerman (2003, 224) believes that, 'Describing religious identities is not a matter of asking a checklist of categorical questions, but a matter of analyzing a dynamic process', because we are all made up of multiple identities which means

1   I am grateful to Professors Linda Woodhead and Paul Heelas and to Dr Abby Day for their helpful comments and suggestions during the writing of this chapter.

that no situation or identity is ever utterly devoid of multiple narratives, both public and private, sacred and secular. Thus, it is more likely that 'believers' will be placed along a continuum, indicated by the notion of 'dynamic process', from those, at one extreme, who submit to the non-subjectivised unquestioned authority of a male God all the way through to those, at the other, listening to their inner subjective selves and getting in touch with their deepest feelings.

To try and discover to what extent there is either bifurcation or fluidity of belief, I embarked on a micro-level gendered ethnographic study in southern Lakeland, where I live. Given that women are in the majority in congregations in England (Gelder and Escott 2001), and that Heelas and Woodhead found women made up the majority of the holistic realm participants, and in view of my own interest in a gendered approach to the sociology of religion, I restricted myself to studying women. The data gathering, which extended over a period of two years from 2004 to 2006, involved me conducting a series of open-ended informal interviews, lasting on average two hours, with more than 70 women, aged 40 and over. Roughly 40 per cent of these respondents attended a place of worship, another 40 per cent of them have disaffiliated, with the remaining 20 per cent being irregular attenders. The lower age limit of 40 was imposed because women younger than 40 are much less likely to have been, or remain, churchgoers. The sample cannot be representative of women in England as a whole as time and resources did not permit me to choose that kind of sample. It certainly raises questions, however, as to how much some women in church simply accept traditional orthodoxy, including the male god, salvation only through this male god and saviour, the gendered hierarchy and the prioritising of the female domestic role, and how much they have been influenced by the increasing salience of the holistic milieu and the more plural contexts in which most of life in the West is now fashioned. It also raises the question as to how much any women, attending church or not, have actually been able to shift off their domestic commitments, despite having lived through the sexual revolution of the 1960s.

There is certainly evidence that all have been affected, one way or another, by the changes brought about in that period, regardless of their beliefs. Some women continue to worship in a congregation acknowledging a Christian male god and, hence, continue to operate in an environment privileging the male. Nonetheless, there is testimony that even here faith stances are changing, sometimes influenced by the more subjectivised holistic realm and the increased knowledge and awareness of other faith traditions. Some women use Christianity's spiritual goods but subject them to considerable reinterpretation. Others have abandoned any kind of faith stance.

The evidence from the women I shall quote, therefore, representative of others in this study, suggests that there is no straight bifurcation in beliefs between the traditional attender and those in the holistic realm. Beliefs represented here span a continuum, from the traditional member of a conservative/evangelical congregation to the holistic practitioner utilising a number of 'spiritual' goods and services. Where bifurcation occurs it may be rather more between the 'seekers' of the sacred in whatever form and the more rationalist 'non-seekers'. Whatever these women may be, however, the emphasis, for most of them, will be on their own direct experience, which 'authorises' their beliefs, and the personal affirmation and empowerment they receive through the particular social relations in which they are implicated. Whether churchgoers or not, women go on attending to domestic commitments albeit with a changed attitude to these commitments.

Staying 'At Home'

The continuum of belief, which moves continuously from the completely non-subjectivised to the subjectivised, then, runs from the belief in orthodox Christianity with its male, transcendent, controlling God and his son, Jesus, as the saviour of the world, to the 'sense' that there is some kind of life force or presence, which may be male or female or genderless, sometimes immanent sometimes transcendent, but which connects us to all that is, with many variations and nuances in between. All these women are believers in something, therefore, beyond that which is directly observable by our senses. Bifurcation occurs between them and the remaining group who simply do not attend to the matter of belief and dismiss any idea of the supernatural, if asked, believing only in that which seems to be scientifically provable and rational.

The non-subjectivised believers, therefore, are the traditional, self-sacrificial women, whose faith and praxis have remained closest to the Christian 'home' – culturally and religiously, if not always geographically – in which they were first nurtured. These women see God as male and Jesus as their saviour, devote large amounts of their time, when not doing paid work or attending to home and (often extended) family, to arranging the altar flowers, cleaning the church, running the Mothers' Union, teaching in Sunday school, organising fund-raising events, taking part in services as lay preachers/readers, serving as sideswomen, elders, secretaries, treasurers and organists, as well as assisting with communion and helping their neighbours in need. Many describe their work as 'a privilege' and when they are in some difficulties, domestic or professional, simply refer to these as 'testing times'.

But the numbers of women falling within this category represented no more than 10 per cent, at the most, and none is under 50. These communities have their place for some women. As Ozorak comments in her study of 61 churchwomen, and as I found in mine, this kind of community provides opportunities for women to work together and to form close friendships with other women. They are places in which as Ozorak says, 'power emanates from the support of the community' and so is increased by being shared (1996, 7).

Nonetheless, the findings from my study suggest that women with traditional beliefs and lifestyle are diminishing and that even women in apparently traditional congregations do not always hold entirely to all that is understood as orthodoxy. The churchgoing women I spoke to for a previous (2003) study were simultaneously consumers of the goods and services of the holistic realm. A number practise yoga with a spiritual input, for example, or may go circle dancing or are members of an Iona or spiritual healing group. Churches Together in Britain and Ireland has a specific arm, Churches Together for Healing which was formed following the Anglican report *A Time to Heal* (2000). This group, of which I was a regional member for four years, is certainly happy to include various forms of holistic therapy into its programmes. Another organisation, The Churches' Fellowship for Psychical and Spiritual Studies, founded over 50 years ago, and which publishes an organ, *The Christian Parapsychologist*, certainly combines a number of aspects of more holistic belief with traditional faith and practice.

As Ammerman (2003) argues, we are all made up of multiple selves, participating in multiple narratives. Many of the women also have/had paid employment outside the home and are members of family groups as well as charitable or recreational organisations, in addition to being attached to their worshipping community These, too, have their own particular discourses and narratives in which the women are embedded.

Moving Away from 'Home'

An example of someone situated somewhat further along the continuum of belief might be Ruth, a member of a traditional congregation following much of Anglican orthodoxy most of her life, but importing newer aspects of contemporary culture into her belief system, and who worships in a downtown church in a post-industrial community on the west coast of Cumbria. She was obliged to be the main breadwinner in her first marriage, a fact she resented deeply, much preferring to be the traditional housewife. She is now remarried and quite happy that her Church still denies women the highest office, believing this is but a matter of time. She has no problem with an exclusively male priesthood, although her current vicar happens to be a woman. She felt that, 'In all honesty I prefer a male priest. I haven't got anything against women priests at all, but it wouldn't bother me if women were not involved in the clergy.' When asked to describe what roles churches offer women she dwelt largely on that of 'vicar's wife' and, although pressed during our interview, she seemed unable to conceptualise a role for women other than this one. This dissolution 'into the stronger side of partnership' (Alexander and Taylor 2006, 57) was reflected in her decision not to attend church while married to her first husband, because he did not approve, and her declaration that she will now do what she wants to do, ironically by going to church, as 'selfish'.

Ruth does wield some power, however, in her worshipping community since she is a member of the Parochial Church Council (PCC), its main decision-making body, and, as such, has considerable input into its life and activity. But she is not sure that God is male and feels that the church building is the 'last place' to find God. Ruth saw God 'out everywhere, all encompassing, so you never know where you're going to meet him'. And when pressed further about the gender of God: 'Who knows? We call nature woman and I think God's a bit of everything, nature and spiritual and when I get a spiritual feeling it's usually when I'm somewhere very natural … by a waterfall, out on the hills ... not usually in the shopping mall.'

Ruth also believes that 'there are many paths to God' while her confidence in belief in the afterlife seems to be predicated more on a firm belief in ghosts, rather than on any kind of traditional eschatology. Day (2006) has observed a belief in ghosts among those she refers to as atheists in her case study from Yorkshire. She calls this an aspect of the 'secular supernatural'. I also found a number of my interviewees whose belief in the (Christian) afterlife, sometimes expressed as a belief in resurrection, was predicated on their certainty that their dead relatives were watching over them, sensed as a not quite visible 'presence' or 'as angels'. A number pray to God or speak to a deceased parent virtually at the same time, not always distinguishing between the two.

So Ruth, traditional in her perception of suitable roles for women in church and a belief in patriarchal forms of church governance, has nonetheless recast other traditional ideas and beliefs: a pluralist stance on other religions, the turn to the more subjective, personal experience of a more panentheist male or female god and the secular-but-sometimes-sacred supernatural, thus mingling the traditional with a more expressive, individualistic kind of faith, shaped by those newer cultural influences, increasingly prevalent since the 1960s.

For women like Ruth, there is no connection between the patriarchal relations, as evinced in church governance, and the restricted roles for women with her own relatively lowly paid job (which means she needs to take in a lodger to make ends meet). For women, like Ruth, belonging to a church seems to represent groundedness in the face of much flux in the rest of life, a place to be cared for, while often caring for others at the same time. It is a place of 'connection', both physically and psychologically, and one which fosters the transfer of social capital from one person to another.

Changing One's Address (to the Sacred)

For some women, however, it is not possible for them to remain connected to the same religious institution in which these patriarchal relations hold sway. These particular women are mainly tertiary educated and have been exposed to a more cosmopolitan, pluralist environment, thus to a greater multiplicity of narratives, both public and private, sacred and secular. For these women, at the other end of the continuum, this is the moment at which they 'move out' altogether, as one might say, living an independent life, geographically removed from home, but also independent of the beliefs and the patriarchal relations which have authorised those beliefs, learned in the original home.

But, remaining at this end of the continuum for the moment, one can see that, while moving away geographically, one may remain culturally close to home, even if not always religiously. There may be a need to move to another worshipping community, one which allows for greater freedom to conceptualise the sacred in a new, possibly non-theistic, mode, one which no longer privileges the male god and saviour and hence the subordination of the female, casting her into the purely domestic role – one which allows, in sum, for much less orthodoxy. Still, there is the need to remain attached to community of some kind, an awareness that life is better for being with others who seek the sacred, however differently each may conceptualise it.

Rebecca will serve as an example of this need to move rather further away from 'home', having been immersed in other narratives, yet still wishing to 'import' into her new situation something of the original narrative which shaped her formative years. Rebecca's father is a minister in the Presbyterian Church and both parents are committed not only to their faith but also to political activism on behalf of the disadvantaged. The sense of commitment, both to a worshipping community and to the activism which they enjoined on their daughter, has remained firmly in place, but Rebecca has lived and worked abroad for a number of years on an international ecumenical project

Staying with the rigid doctrines of her past, staying within the 'parish system' as Ruth has managed to do, did not accord with how Rebecca now conceptualised what the worshipping community should be. She has subsequently become committed to the Quakers but remains, like her parents, a member of the politically active Iona group.

So far, at this end of the continuum, we have considered women firmly within a community where the male, Christian god is dominant. Even Rebecca envisages God in a fairly traditional Christian way at times, although not always. But what of the more feminised forms of religion and/or spirituality, characteristic of the holistic realm? To what extent have they made an impact on women in the pews, when numerous books on women's religions and goddess spirituality have made their appearance on the scene in more recent years? (See, for example, Christ and Plaskow 1978; Starhawk 1979; Stone 1979; Christ and Plaskow 1989; Starhawk 1990; Sered 1994; Christ 1997; Griffin 2000.) I did not come across many women during my research who were particularly interested in goddess spirituality, even among women in the holistic realm – where I came across just one Druid and a member of a drumming group who perform rituals similar to those described by Christ, Starhawk and others. But I note also that Heelas and Woodhead (2005) similarly, did not find many participants in groups which might be devoted to a goddess. Eleven were involved in 'Pagan activities', seven in a 'Women's Spirituality Group' and two in a group called 'Wild Women', compared with 128 practising yoga.

Anna, who is a keen practitioner of goddess spirituality, is part of a group attached to her local Unitarian Church, not a member of a Pagan activities group. Consequently, Anna does participate in much more orthodox theistic worship as well as goddess rituals. Carol Christ remarks that there are large numbers of women all over the Western world brought up 'in the biblical religions' who are rediscovering the language, symbols and rituals of the Goddess (1997, xiii). However, Christ implies that one is unlikely to be a follower of the Goddess and a believer in a theistic Christian (or Jewish or presumably, therefore, also Unitarian) god at the same time. 'The Goddesses are presented in the Bible as "abomination" and it is hard for scholars to shake the mind-set that has encouraged all of us to think of Goddesses in relation to terms such *idolatry, fertility fetish, nature religions, orgiastic cult, bloodthirsty,* and *ritual prostitution*' (1997, 78 – original emphasis). Despite this, Anna's group has grown and is both 'respectable' and 'respected' in a way that it was not even in the early 1990s.

Although there are few Goddess worshippers in my study, as such, Anna is one of a number of women whom I interviewed who are coming to experience a growing distaste for 'male' religion – particularly its negation of women's sufferings and the female body. Women, thus disenchanted, have, by and large, either given up on belief of any kind or turned to the holistic realm, the latter being the main finding of

Heelas and Woodhead's thesis (2005). Anna's group is possibly somewhat unusual, therefore, in practising Goddess spirituality, while being attached to a church promulgating theistic belief. Anna still joins in with singing the Lord's prayer in her church and remains a firmly committed member. She explains her ambivalence in this regard by saying,

[A]s a kid, early teens, I picked up these Bible reading things, read a bit every day. Did O level Scripture, so I think all that has remained with me but the pagan thing has developed and makes more sense. I can't say makes entire sense, but is coming together.

Here is Ammerman's 'dynamic process' at work, in which 'no situation or identity is utterly devoid of multiple narratives'. We 'import' (and export) 'resources and schemas ("rules" or categories of understanding) from one narrative to another' (2003, 212). Referring to the work of Minow (1997), she goes on to explain that all identities are 'intersectional', that we are always many things at once. Anna, Rebecca, Ruth, even the traditionalist women, in that many of them have paid work outside the home and are involved in other groups and activities, together with the women yet to be mentioned, are situated in multiple relational and institutional contexts, because that is how contemporary society is configured.

Visiting Occasionally

The women discussed so far are all regular attenders at a place of worship but Roof (1999; 2003) speaks of a 'quest', people moving in and out of sacred space, as need arises. Among such are Davie's (1994) 'believers but not belongers', those who have left off committed churchgoing but who may visit occasionally and retain belief in 'God' of some kind. My own research suggests this god varies from the transcendent, all-powerful creator, who 'fixes' things in answer to prayer in a way which is beyond our ken, to a vague kind of 'somebody or something there but we won't worry too much about it and just get on with life', to a sense that we are not simply the sum of our parts nor is the world in which we live. Ammerman claims that 'no interaction is utterly secular or utterly sacred' (2003, 222). I did meet some women who would wish to disagree that there could be anything remotely sacred in their life, but there were very few. Why women retain belief, even though they do not wish to be committed to regular attendance, can be explained in various ways, but Isobel will serve as an example. There are two compelling reasons for her to access the sacred on an ad hoc basis.

Apart from attendance at a Moravian secondary school or taking her children to mass when her Catholic husband was away on business, Isobel has had virtually no involvement with a Christian church, being too busy, domestically, professionally and in her local community. She has worked all her life in a large industrial northern city, which has seen a very high influx of families of other races and faiths. There have been tensions and some violent clashes. Isobel, in consequence, retired to a quiet village in the Lake District.

She has also experienced in recent years both the deaths of her parents and the suicide of a young friend. While all Isobel's activities have kept her occupied, they do not help her to come to terms with the two major changes in her life; going to the ancient priory church in her village, from time to time, for the very traditional, high Anglican service and visiting her old school for its end of term services do, however, help her. Sitting in the ancient priory and visiting her old school not only 'include' her in Hervieu-Léger's (2000) chain of memory – in this case, of a great ethnic Christian tradition of which she sees herself a part – but the priory's discourse of resurrection and the life to come provides comfort and meaning. Isobel was quite happy to lay aside her Christian 'resources' of the past when all seemed to be going well, but when she came up against radical change, she 're-imported' those resources, those categories of understanding, back into her personal narrative.

While Isobel is happy to 're-import' a former category of understanding to help her make sense both of her imagined loss of her ethnic-cum-Christian identity and the death of those she loves, other interviewees are unwilling, in the midst of major life events, to rely on one single tradition or 'resource' – and resource is a very apt term to describe the provenance of those goods and services on which these women rely – for their personal 'theodicy'. I use this term, although we are stretching its meaning far beyond any mere *theos* here. These women are participants in the holistic realm, indeed, they have no wish to see themselves as overtly Christian at all, but a number of those I interviewed were using Christian symbolic 'goods', alongside practising reiki, attending various spirituality groups, healing groups and self-help groups, and accessing internet sites on alternative spiritualities and healing.

It could be argued these women were the mirror image of the Christian attenders, quoted above, who sometimes visited these groups or websites but found their main source of significance, to use Charles Taylor's (2002) term, within the worshipping community. These women sometimes made use of Christian resources, often interpreted differently, alongside many others. They prefer, as one of my interviewees said, more the 'yin-yang sort of idea, not the wafty masculine God the father, son and holy spirit thing'. They are as likely to use female images and ways of relating, speaking of 'Mother Earth', and the 'interconnectedness of all things', for example, although, as noted above, very few specifically name 'the Goddess' as such.

Albanese suggests healing in the holistic realm is a 'work of reconciliation'. Its holistic ethos means that this form of healing 'emphasises a forgiveness that dissolves physical disease, emotional hurt and the collective distress of society and nature' (1992, 78). But, if one were to consult the materials put out by Churches Together for Healing, they, too, speak of the 'work of reconciliation' and the same kind of '"dissolving" forgiveness', to which Albanese refers. The difference would be that the Christian women would be urged by their clergy to pray to a transcendent male authority, or in the case of Catholics perhaps to the Virgin Mary, for help in such acts of reconciliation. Whether they only access transcendent authority, however, I think could be questionable. Interactions with others within their worshipping communities – largely female, I suggest – would also play a part. This has certainly been my observation over many years of church attendance. The holistic women, however, are resolutely self-helpers, but helping others too, let it be importantly noted.

While women like Ruth, Rebecca and Anna remain fully committed to a worshipping community and see the importance of belonging, and Isobel sees the importance of believing but also of 'belonging', in a more ad hoc sort of way, Mary would be an example of a woman situated a further step along the continuum. She does attend a church but considerably less willingly. Like many of the women in this study, Mary has had more than her share of difficult life events, the worst being the suicide of her daughter, followed by a life-threatening breakdown in health of her second husband. This has caused Mary to search far beyond the Church (Catholic or Protestant) for meaning: in India, among a number of eastern gurus, in meditative practices, in the native American spiritualities, in such holistic purveyors of the spiritual as the Conscious Creation website, in visiting spiritualist mediums who assure her she is here 'for your own soul's growth, not your neighbour's', always looking for the meaning of so much unhappiness and her part in it. She distances herself completely from the Church, which she sees as 'in control … For Christians the suppression of women has been total. If only the Church knew the potential of women. It's been taught out of them.'

But, despite Mary's vehement declaration of where her faith stance now is, she sees supporting her Roman Catholic convert husband, by attending mass fairly regularly, as well as singing in his church's choir, as part of her commitment to another in marriage, while seeking her own meaning elsewhere. Mary concludes that we are all 'selves-in-relation', we're all connected to everything that is, part of the continual cycle of birth, life and death. This convinces Mary far more than the sense that all her unhappiness is simply a (male postulated) theodicy of 'God's will' or a trial of her faith or one of the traditionalist believers' 'testing times'.

Her belief in connectedness and how this relates to issues of finitude and death resonates well with Christ's 'web of life' (1997, 113–134) and, as Christ would suggest, translates into a passionate commitment, for Mary, for various animal welfare charities, as well as promotion of green issues and battling with medical practitioners for some degree of active participation and control in the management of one's own health. Knott and Franks (2007), in their study of a medical practice, have also identified this subject as a site for women's rather than men's contestation and resistance.

Living Independently

The remaining small group of interviewees, while churchgoers at some time in their past, felt no need of invocations or prayers or rituals or healing groups or connection to distinct communities of seekers after the sacred. These women, similarly implicated in intersectional narratives, just like all the other women interviewed, do not talk to dead relatives or to any form of deity. In fact they rarely give the sacred (or the dead) another thought. When I asked them about such matters as belief in an afterlife, for example, it was clear they viewed this as irrational, preferring to invest in belief in the life processes themselves. As one interviewee told me,

> When you look at any other living being, animals … the emphasis is on survival and their future is in their offspring, so their purpose is to secure a future in life and for their genes to be carried forward. I sometimes see our purpose in life is more with our children, to give them the best grounding, to set them up, but then not all people have children. But

all these people dying and existing somewhere else. Where is it happening? I don't know.
And for what purpose? What are they doing?

These women generally feel they live their life by certain principles and morals,
trying to be kind and helpful. They admit that they don't know if they are always
successful but feel that, if there is somebody making a judgement at the end of the
day, they're not going to be 'that narrow-minded whether you went to church or not,
it's more important how you've lived your life'. We note that Abby Day, in her case
study from Yorkshire, has documented 'belief' in family and friends as the alternative
form of 'belief' she observed in those of no religious persuasion. 'Most people I
interviewed believe in their affective, reciprocal human relationships as the main site
for sourcing and expressing emotions, morality and transcendence' (Day 2006, 5).
Day terms this a secular 'believing in belonging'. She could detect no notion of 'the
sacred' in their discourse and neither could I in that of my interviewees. But this was
a fairly small proportion of my interviews as a whole.

Conclusions

As can be seen, it is hard to argue for the bifurcation of belief theory in this study,
except between the believers in something sacred and the believers in belonging.
Some women combine, to a greater or lesser degree, traditional elements of belief
with a much more expressivistic, subjectivised and individualistic kind of faith,
arising out of their own direct experience. Some women have cast off Christian
tradition altogether, either in favour of other forms of the sacred or of combining some
reconceived elements of Christianity with other forms of the sacred derived from
other cultures and traditions, as commentators such as Roof, Lambert and Hervieu-
Léger maintain. Others see no need of the sacred at all: they have effectively laid
aside those 'categories of understanding' and have no need, at least not presently, of
those 'resources'. But all these women are engaged in multiple narratives, situated
in multiple relational and institutional contexts. How these women make meaning,
how anybody makes meaning, one might argue, arises as a consequence of the
intersectionality of one's multiple identities. Given that women are members of a
family, may work both inside and outside the home, may be engaged in recreational
pursuits and may attend a church, as a committed or a casual attender, the multiplicity
of their narratives has increased quite significantly in recent times. There is fierce
competition. Sometimes the church may win a – greater or lesser – share in that
competition, sometimes it cannot.

As to Christianity reinforcing the role of dutiful wife, we note that regular
churchgoers may embody this role to some extent, but they may well exercise
agency and be empowered by such roles as the one Ruth holds on the PCC and/or
through the shared support of the community of women within the church. What we
do observe is that all these women have commitments of one sort or another, whether
attending church or not. There is little sign these have been abandoned as Hochschild
(2003) testifies (see also Christ, 1997, and Hartsock 2000, on the 'double shift'),
while Day similarly comments that 'Responsibilities for offspring are maternal …

I did not find anyone in my study who questioned the norm of family care being women's work' (2006, 75–76).

But I would argue that because these women all have (or have had) paid work, there is much less a sense of dependence, hence no need for dutiful submissiveness. Moreover, Day (2006) points to the suggestion that women's inability to spend time on themselves is probably not to be viewed as self-denial but rather as self-fulfilment. She quotes the work of Strathern who argues that we must, as researchers, be aware of the process of denigration which exists in our culture and renders women's domestic labour of such little value that the women themselves are not seen as full persons (1984, 13–31). There was a sense, to me, in these interviews, of each woman playing her own part in a partnership, even though its equality may be more apparent than real. Similarly they perceive their family, friends and colleagues within their various sacred/secular communities/groups as offering an empowering sense of connection *as equals*.

Although it would be hard to argue that any of these women had achieved anything like gender equality, whatever we may mean by that, it would be equally hard to argue for their dissolution 'into the stronger side of partnership' (Alexander and Taylor 2006, 57). Regardless of their social location, these women have cleared themselves a space to create their own identity(ies). This is an act facilitated by their increased financial independence, almost certainly, but also, importantly, facilitated and empowered, by the community and social relations in which they find their 'home'.

Moreover, these women, as we have seen, cannot be simply categorised into theistic versus holistic believers, as Heelas and Woodhead argue. As a result of the intersectionality of their multiple selves, an intersectionality to which we are all subject, they import, in varying degrees, and for many different reasons, other narratives into their belief systems from the social positioning and culture in which they are embedded; hence it is not surprising that we see a continuum of belief not a bifurcation. Bifurcation only occurs where there is a refusal to import any kind of religious or spiritual discourse into the narrative one currently relates.

We might ask, therefore, whether these women become more subjectivised in their belief as the influence of the church decreases in their life, or whether it is the other way round. Given the salience of the holistic in our culture at large (see Heelas and Woodhead 2005, for elaboration of this thesis) and the evidence here, I would hazard a guess it is the latter, but this is an area which might well merit further research.

Bibliography

A Time to Heal. 2000. London: House of Bishops of the General Synod of the Church of England.

Albanese, Catherine L. 1992. 'The Magical Staff: Quantum Healing in the New Age.' In J.R. Lewis and J.G. Melton, eds, *Perspectives on the New Age*, Albany: State University of New York Press. 66–84.

Alexander, Sally and Barbara Taylor. 2006. 'In Defence of "Patriarchy".' In Sue Morgan, ed., *The Feminist History Reader*, London and New York: Routledge. 56–58.

Ammerman, Nancy T. 2003. 'Religious Identities and Religious Institutions.' In Michelle Dillon, ed., *Handbook of the Sociology of Religion*, Cambridge: Cambridge University Press. 207–224.

Brown, Callum G. 2001. *The Death of Christian Britain: Understanding Secularization 1800–2000*. London and New York: Routledge.

Christ, Carol P. 1997. *Rebirth of the Goddess: Finding Meaning in Feminist Spirituality*. New York: Routledge.

—— and Judith Plaskow, eds. 1978. *Womanspirit Rising: A Feminist Reader in Religion*. New York: Harper and Row.

——, eds. 1989. *Weaving the Visions*. New York: Harper Collins.

Davie, Grace. 1994. *Believing without Belonging: Religion in Britain since 1945*. Oxford: Blackwell.

Day, Abby F. 2006. 'Believing in Belonging in Contemporary Britain: a case study from Yorkshire.' Ph.D. dissertation, Lancaster University.

Eccles, Janet B. 2003. 'New Leanings and Meanings: Investigating Changes in Belief of Twelve Church Members and the Implications for the Future of the Church.' M.A. dissertation, Lancaster University.

Gelder, Alison and Phillip Escott. 2001. *Faith in Life: A Snapshot of Church Life in England at the Beginning of the 21st Century*. London: Churches Information for Mission.

Griffin, Wendy, ed. 2000. *Daughters of the Goddess: Studies of Healing, Identity and Empowerment*. Walnut Creek, CA: Altamira.

Hartsock, Nancy. 2000. 'The Feminist Standpoint: Developing the Ground for a Specifically Feminist Historical Materialism.' In Darlene Juschka, ed., *Feminism in the Study of Religion*, London and New York: Continuum. 603–628.

Heelas, Paul and Linda Woodhead, with Benjamin Seel, Bronislaw Szerszynski, and Karin Tusting. 2005. *The Spiritual Revolution: Why Religion is Giving Way to Spirituality*. Malden, MA and Oxford: Blackwell Publishing.

Hervieu-Léger, Danielle. 2000. *Religion as a Chain of Memory*. Cambridge: Polity.

Hochschild, Arlie Russell, with Anne Machung. [1989] 2003. *The Second Shift*. New York and London: Penguin.

Knott, Kim and Myfanwy Franks. 2007. 'Secular Values and the Location of Religion: A Spatial Analysis of an English Medical Centre.' *Health and Place*: 224–237.

Lambert, Yves. 1999. 'Religion in Modernity as a New Axial Age: Secularization or New Religious forms?' *Sociology of Religion* 60: 303–333.

Minow, Martha. 1997. *Not Only for Myself*. New York: The New Press.

Ozorak, Elizabeth, J. 1996. 'The Power, but not the Glory: How Women Empower Themselves through Religion.' *Journal for the Scientific Study of Religion* 35: 17–29.

Roof, Wade Clark. 1998. 'Religious Borderlands: Challenges for Future Study.' *Journal for the Scientific Study of Religion* 37: 1–14.

——. 1999. *Spiritual Marketplace: Baby Boomers and the Remaking of American Religion*. Princeton, NJ: Princeton University Press.

——. 2003. 'Religion and Spirituality: Toward an Integrated Analysis.' In Michelle Dillon, ed., *Handbook of the Sociology of Religion*. Cambridge: Cambridge University Press.

Sered, Susan Starr. 1994. *Priestess, Mother, Sacred Sister: Religions Dominated by Women*. New York and Oxford: Oxford University Press.

Starhawk. 1979. *The Spiral Dance: Rebirth of the Ancient Religion of the Great Goddess*. San Francisco: Harper San Francisco.

——. 1990. *Truth or Dare: Encounters with Power, Authority and Mystery*. New York: HarperCollins Publishers.

Stone, Merlin. 1979. *When God was a Woman*. New York: Harvest/Harcourt Brace.

Strathern, Marilyn. 1984. 'Domesticity and the Denigration of Women.' In D.O'Brien and S.W. Tiffany, eds, *Rethinking Women's Roles: Perspectives from the Pacific*, Berkeley: University of California Press. 13–31.

Taylor, Charles. 2002. *Varieties of Religion Today: William James Revisited*. Cambridge, MA and London: Harvard University Press.

Wuthnow, Robert. 1998. *After Heaven: Spirituality in America since the 1950s*. Princeton, NJ: Princeton University Press.

Chapter Three

Young People's Spirituality and the Meaning of Prayer

Sylvia Collins-Mayo

Alice and Laticia live on an inner-ciy house estate in Manchester. Laticia is 18 and of dual heritage. Alice is 19 and White. Life on the estate is not easy. One evening last summer whilst the girls were out with a friend, there was a shooting. The friend was shot right in front of Alice. In the ensuing drama Alice found herself administering first aid, stemming the blood flow, cradling the lad in her arms and trying to keep him conscious until the ambulance came. When the girls eventually got home and Laticia had fallen asleep, Alice looked out of her bedroom window and started to pray. She prayed that her friend would get better; that he would not die. 'I thought I'd see what God was made of; if it would help', she told a youth worker. In the days that followed Laticia prayed similar prayers, 'God, please help. Don't let him die.' Neither Alice nor Laticia are churchgoers. Neither had a clear idea of to whom or what they were praying, or whether there would be tangible outcomes to their petitions. Nevertheless they prayed.

Alice and Laticia's story is a dramatic one, but it highlights an important topic around the theme of religion and the individual, namely the meaning and place of prayer in young people's lives. As a spiritual practice, prayer can take many forms but it always implies some sort of deliberate act on the part of the individual, however minimal (Mauss 2003; Wuthnow 2003). Consequently, the prayer lives of young people can tell us much about the nature of spirituality as it is understood and lived out in contemporary society – how belief relates to practice and what difference spirituality makes to how young people face the world. The aim of this chapter is therefore to draw out salient aspects of the form, meaning and use of prayer as described by young people. The accounts I use come from the study in which Alice and Laticia participated, the primary focus of which was the influence of Christian youth work on young people's religious sensibility. Prayer featured strongly in the course of the study.

The research began with a survey of young people aged 11–23 years who had contact with Christian youth work projects in England between 2004 and 2006. The projects catered for both churchgoing and non-churchgoing young people. Some were associated with particular churches, others were community-based projects; all offered a provision of informal and social education allied to an element of Christian outreach. A third of the projects were described by the youth workers as overtly Christian, the rest said they had a Christian ethos. In all, 297 young people completed a questionnaire on their religious identity, beliefs and practices, their broader values and their experiences of the youth work projects they attended. Of these, 107 young people took part in qualitative individual or small group interviews with the research team to further elaborate on these topics. The demographic profile of the young people was equally balanced between young men and women but was predominately White (over 90 per cent) and nominally Christian (nearly two thirds claimed a Christian identity); there were only two Muslim boys and the rest described themselves as Agnostic (10 per cent), Atheist (5 per cent) or 'Don't Know' (13 per cent).

After the initial survey and interviews were completed, 40 non-churchgoing young people took part in a series of structured conversations with their youth workers in order to find out how they engaged with the youth work programme and how their ideas on various topics changed over the course of a term. Prayer was one topic included in the discussions and with the permission of the young people I also refer to the content of these conversations as recorded by the youth workers. The sample was balanced in terms of gender; half were White, a quarter Black and a quarter of dual heritage. None had any practising religious affiliation.

Prevalence of Prayer

The prevalence of prayer in the general population has been identified in a number of surveys. Opinion polls suggest around a third of British adults pray weekly outside of religious services, and as many as 20 per cent pray every day (Barley 2006; Mori 2000). It is not surprisingly that frequency of prayer is positively correlated with church attendance (Francis and Brown 2001). Nevertheless even non-churchgoers indicate they pray from time to time. Amongst young people, Francis and Robbins (2006) found 29 per cent of non-churchgoing 13- to 15-year-olds pray at least occasionally and 3 per cent pray almost daily.

In this survey of young people in contact with Christian youth work, the figures for prayer were higher still. Of those who answered the questionnaire 60 per cent said they prayed at least once a month, 22 per cent that they prayed less than once a month but occasionally, and only 18 per cent said they never prayed. The correlation with church attendance was clear. Just over half the young people were frequent churchgoers (that is, they attended church at least once a month) and 91 per cent of them said that they also prayed frequently (at least monthly). Indeed, they may have included church prayers in their tally. Of the remaining infrequent churchgoers (those who went to church less than once a month or never), 24 per cent said they prayed frequently. This is more in line with Francis and Robbins' findings. The qualitative interviews suggested the reason prayer was relatively commonplace was because the young people, even the non-churchgoers, routinely came across prayer activities in the institutional settings of which they were a part. For churchgoers prayer was obviously a routine part of Sunday or midweek worship, but for nearly all of the young people in this study school and/or the youth club also provided opportunities for prayer – and many of the young people chose to participate in them either wholly or partially.

Learning to Pray

There are nearly 21,000 state schools in England, a third of which are church schools (Department for Education and Skills 2006), and all of them are supposed to offer a daily act of collective worship under the Education Reform Act 1988. This often includes prayer. Consequently, school assemblies and in some church schools classroom prayers, were two occasions for institutionalised prayer mentioned by the young people. Given the negative views young people sometimes hold about church and religious education (Rankin 2005), it was surprising that alongside the anticipated comments about school prayers being irrelevant or boring, even some of the infrequent churchgoing young people still said that they willingly joined in with school prayers and found it helpful to do so[1]

Jack:	I don't pray every day, but as a group pray every day.
Int.:	But that's at school?
Jack:	Yeah.
Int.:	But what of your own free will?
Jack:	Yeah, it is our own free will ...
William:	In assembly yeah, well they pray for us, most people don't – but when they say like put your head down [and] think about it, I do think about it. ...
Int.:	Yeah, is that helpful or?
Sue:	When you have like the morning after a major thing, then that helps.

The youth clubs offered a rather different context for prayer midway between the formality of school and the informality of home life. Whilst there is no legislative requirement that youth work includes acts of worship, the projects in this study were all of a Christian nature and 43 per cent of the youth workers said that prayer featured in their programmes. This took various forms across projects ranging from the youth workers openly praying before club meetings through to the provision of a dedicated prayer room and opportunities for structured prayer activities. The young people could join in with these activities if they wanted to. None of the young people interviewed were hostile to this prayer activity. At worst they viewed it with indifference but often they spoke in a reasonably positive way. The lack of hostility was partly down to the young people's recognition of the Christian identity of the clubs and youth workers, which they were happy to respect in a spirit of tolerance because they enjoyed the club and liked the youth workers. As Ashley said, 'It's like, they can be who they want to be and I can be who I want to be.' And partly because joining in the prayers was optional.

Clive:	They've got like a prayer time at the club where people can just go and pray and stuff, and just talk about God and stuff.
Int.:	Do you do that?
Clive:	Umm – but I like the way they don't pressure people into praying and they don't make God like a massive presence at their events and stuff.

---

1   All the names quoted in this chapter are pseudonyms. 'Int.:' refers to 'Interviewer'.

These institutional prayer activities had the function of modelling prayer both in terms of accomplishing a prayer act itself (the content and form it might take) and in terms of prayer being viewed as a valid and valued action.

Family influences were also important in this respect, particularly mothers and grandparents.

Lance: Sometimes, it kinda of comes in my head … cos my grandma's Catholic and that, so sometimes I pray.
Int.:   Right and where will you pray, or what will you do when you pray?
Lance: When my granddad phones me up every night, yeah, he says 'Are you praying on your bed …?'

Karen: … we always pray as a family and my mum, you know, she tries to make us pray on our own, so … one day when we have our own family we can pray a prayer, say a prayer. I find that good as well.

Such modelling provided a template onto which young people could map their own private prayers if they chose to do so. This is important because without such socialisation young people are much less likely to pray. Spiritual practices, like faith itself, need to be taught if young people are going to engage in them as part of their emotional and intellectual repertoire (Francis and Brown 2001).

The fact that these institutional and family prayers largely took place within a Christian framework is important given the decline in church attendance amongst young people nationally (Brierley 2006) and recent discussions in the literature about the rise of new forms of spirituality in wider culture (Heelas and Woodhead 2005). Whilst it is undoubtedly the case that young people's lives are highly subjectivised and institutional authority is much weaker than for past generations, young people are not yet entirely cut loose from established social structures. Furlong and Cartmel (2007) make this clear in their analysis of youth experiences in education, work and leisure. On the spiritual front the same is also true. The great majority of young people in England still inherit the Christian culture, albeit a fading heritage which now competes with other religious and secular worldviews. Consequently Rankin (2005) found young people generally associate the concept of spirituality with religion, and religion with the Church, since this is closest to their experience.

Christianity was therefore the starting point for prayer amongst the young people in this study. That is not to say, however, that they fully engaged with or even understood the wider Christian tradition in detail. Hornsby-Smith described what he called 'customary Christianity' amongst the adult Catholic population in England during the 1980s: 'derived from "official" religion but without being under its continuing control … the beliefs and practices that make up customary religion are the product of formal religious socialization but subject to trivialisation, conventionality, apathy, convenience and self-interest' (Hornsby-Smith 1991, 90).

This description could well be applied to many of the young people in the current study. Whilst Christianity was the starting point in schools and the youth clubs, teachers and youth workers generally introduced prayer with a light touch which meant there was a lot of scope for personal interpretation and selectivity; the young people very much viewed participation as optional. Herein lies some of the subjectivisation of late modern spirituality. The fact that young people continued to refer to a Christian template for prayer may say more about a lack of involvement in the direction of alternative spiritualities than a conscious decision to specifically engage with the Christian tradition. Nevertheless, that Christianity however vaguely understood, did provide the template for both public and private prayers was evident in the standardisation of the accounts given during the interviews. The young people spoke about their prayers broadly falling into three categories: petitionary prayers, confessional prayers and prayers of thanksgiving.

Petitionary Prayer

By far the most prevalent form of prayer amongst both the frequent and infrequent churchgoing young people was petitionary in nature – front-line prayers asking God for help when 'something bad happens' or if difficulties are known to lie ahead. As Russell enthusiastically put it, 'I pray when I want a miracle. When I want to complete a mission of James Bond!'

Personal troubles and challenges, it seems, can still make spirituality a salient aspect of life even amongst quite secular youth. Alice and Laticia's prayers in response to the shooting of their friend were a case in point. Illness, death, arguments, friends having a hard time were all causes for petitions to God. As were exams, worries about the future and generally feeling low. Praying for personal material gain, however, was not seen as an acceptable subject for petitions.

Speck argues that stress causes people to adopt 'culturally acquired methods of coping' (Speck 1978, 116). There is an obvious sense in which prayer is one such method. The young people's prayers held within them an attempt to restore meaning and order to circumstances that would otherwise appear beyond their control, chaotic or frightening. Of course, for some like Alice prayer was something of a last resort after other measures had been tried. Nevertheless, it was still seen as a legitimate practical response to a tough situation, a way to bring hope to difficult circumstances. It was also different from simply thinking, hoping or wishing; prayer overlapped with these patterns of cognition but was regarded as a separate category of behaviour in the young people's minds, which they could identify themselves as doing or not doing:

> I think eighty per cent of what I do when I pray is thinking and talking. It's not actually religious. Praying, I guess, is twenty per cent of the time. I do actually ask God about it. (Faith)

> I don't necessarily pray. But I sometimes hope that things will happen, but I don't see it as praying … just send a hope rather than pray by myself. (Polly)

> … anything that's happened in the day, anything serious, I'll mull it over in my mind and just pray about it. (Amanda)

Prayer, for the young people in this study, involved the work of holding in mind the self, another person or situation, and bringing them into a symbolic relationship with

God or more rarely another spiritual entity. In the words of the young people: Prayer is 'a way of talking to God, one to one', 'a way to ask God for something'. I 'pray to God.' 'I just have a talk with the Big Man upstairs.' Conversely, 'I don't believe in God so therefore there's no need for prayer.' That said, the concept of God did not have to be thoroughly worked out in order to engage in an act of prayer. Most did refer to a traditional view of God as an external male reality, albeit God was more friend than omnipotent being; and a couple of girls suggested prayers might be directed at a guardian angel. Others, however, were quite unsure what they believed but were willing to suspend disbelief for the purposes of helping themselves or somebody they cared about. It was largely because the young people regarded prayer as a benevolent act and associated it with caring relationships that when the youth workers offered to pray for them, they generally took it in a positive light. To pray *with* the young person, however, could be a step too far for those who were not used to praying.

Given that prayers were generally seen as a positive form of action to help others, the scope of the young people's prayers indicated something of their sense of moral connectedness. It was very clear from their comments that local concerns were most important to the young people; family and friends were prioritised. Relatively few mentioned praying for people they did not know or for world issues. Katy was one of the few: 'If I see a poor man in the street I pray for him – Find him a job or some housing.'

Other studies have also found that young people lay great emphasis and value on relationships with family and friends. They are central to young people's sense of happiness and well-being (Collins 1997; nfpSynergy 2007; Savage et al. 2006). Praying for family and friends in many cases seemed to mark out and reinforce these loyalties of their relational networks.

Over time, however, loyalties can change. In one case this produced an interesting dilemma for a youth worker who had just begun to introduce the idea of praying to young people who had little experience of it. A young woman asked the youth worker to pray that Clive, her ex-boyfriend, would die because he had cheated on her with her best friend. The youth worker was left to explain the benevolence of prayer should go beyond immediate loyalties and personal hurts and prayed instead that she would not feel so bad about the betrayal. In this way, the teaching of prayer was used to extend and shape the young person's moral universe as well as to socialise her into what counts as 'acceptable' prayer. Iain and Jack also illustrate the point, this time in the context of school:

Iain:	And in the morning when we go to school ... one person's got to pray every day.
Int.:	Oh right.
Iain:	And everyone does it.
Int.:	Yeah? And how do you feel about doing that?
Iain:	I feel like it's good to do.
Int.:	Yeah?
Iain:	Like when we pray we say intentions like world peace and stuff like that, and that's good.
Int.:	Why is it good to pray?
Iain:	It makes you feel good about yourself, and that.

Int.:	You said it's good too, why's that?
Jack:	You are thinking that you can pray for other people's needs and stuff like that. Pray for people that maybe you don't like, but just pray for them to get on and help everyone around you.
Int.:	People you don't like?
Jack:	Yeah, say you don't like someone, you still pray for them. Tell God to somehow bring them together and make peace or something.
Int.:	Does that make any difference?
Jack:	Yeah, 'cos you start feeling better.
Int.:	Start feeling better?
Jack:	Yeah, start thinking better.
Int.:	Start thinking better.
Jack:	Yeah.

Jack's comments raise an important aspect of petitionary prayer – whether and how it 'works'. Whilst a few of the young people were uncertain if their prayers were answered (Alice, for example, was not sure in retrospect if her friend surviving the shooting was down to her prayers, the prayers of others who definitely believed in God, or destiny), most of the young people who engaged in prayer on a regular basis believed their prayers did have consequences, either directly changing the external situation they were praying for or internally altering how they, or another, felt or thought about the situation. These answers to prayer were always held to be a change for the better. In this respect, the young people often described prayers as having a relaxing and calming effect. However, because the young people associated prayers with God acting for their personal well-being and for the benefit of those dearest to them, failure to realise a change for the better could be seen as unanswered prayer and was enough to put some off praying entirely, either because God was not on their side, or he did not listen to them or because it was 'proof' that God did not exist.

Confessional Prayer

The second most common category of prayer could broadly be called 'confessional'. Traditionally the act of confession is one of penitence, a means by which guilt for moral failings can be acknowledged and repented of before God (mediated by a priest or directly through prayer depending on the church tradition) in order to receive pardon, healing of the soul and reconciliation with the Almighty and the Church. It involves speaking the truth about self and the assurance of salvation. However, Foucault (1990) and others have elaborated on the fact that confession is no longer confined to church but appears in many guises. Indeed, we can now talk of living in a confessional culture where it is commonplace to lay the soul bare before a judging audience and find relief and validation in the telling of self. Counselling and psychotherapy for those who can afford it, chat shows and reality television for celebrities and 'wannabes', problem pages and blog sites for the rest. Of course these forms of confession and the power dynamics within the confessional relationship are different from that of religious tradition. Nevertheless the essential features identified by Foucault are retained – a reflexive self, an assumption of truthful admissions, an authority to listen and respond to the confession (counsellor, audience, reader) and an unburdening of anxiety and emotions leading to restoration of a valid self.

The development of a confessional culture can be seen as an outcome of our increasingly individualised society. When institutional association and group belonging are no longer the main sources of identity, individuals are obliged to engage in self-reflexive projects in order to work out their own identity (Giddens 1991). As Aslama and Pantti argue 'an essential part of the strategies of finding the authentic self is the confession of one's innermost feelings to others' (2006, 107). It is in terms of this culture of self-exploration that young people's prayers can be described as confessional. Questions of identity (Who am I? What should I do with my life?) are key to young people as they make the transition from dependent childhood to independent adulthood. At this stage, however, they are not so much looking for salvation as for self-acceptance and a socially acceptable, coping self. The traditional religious language associated with confession was therefore very limited in the interviews. Paige, Lily and Anthony were in the minority when they talked about sin.

> Sometime when I pray I think I may not have said sorry for the last sin I did – it may not have been counted. (Paige)

> I pray all the time because, like, God created us and everything, and if you sin you go to hell. I don't want to go to hell. (Lily)

> Sometimes like when I'm in trouble ... [I pray to] help me get out of the sin [fighting]. (Anthony)

And Blake's comment to a youth worker on the nature of his confessions after wrong-doing was fairly cursory: 'If he'd done something wrong then he'd kind of just chuck a quick prayer up there.'

However, many of the young people spoke about the need to confess the self in general terms, as a means of dealing with anxieties and concerns, a way of coping and reorienting a failing or struggling self.

> If you're struggling – everybody struggles in life – sometimes you just need someone. Even though you've got your family and friends to talk to, it sometimes just feels [like] you need somebody else to talk to, so you talk to God. (Karen)

> Regardless of whether He exists or not, if you're going through a problem and you're explaining them to whoever you believe in, it's got to be good. (Elvis)

> prayer for me is getting things off my chest. It's talking to God. When you do you feel that you are listened to and not judged. (Eric)

In contrast with traditional religious confessions, the young people's prayers were rarely concerned with guilt for moral transgressions and crucially there was no sense of judgement. God's role was to sooth, calm and nurture, not to point the finger and find the young person wanting. Cox (1990) uses the term 'hovering attentiveness' to describe the relationship between counsellor and client; this seems an apt phrase to describe the young people's perception of God's presence in the context of their confessional prayers too. The young people were looking for a confidant with whom they could share their secrets and things that otherwise they would be too embarrassed or ashamed to talk about with family and friends. The young people spoke about 'getting things off their chest', a 'weight being lifted' and 'getting things out of their system'. They felt 'listened to'. This is important, particularly as the survey results show that, whilst three-quarters of the young people said they would feel comfortable talking to a friend if something was worrying them, only half said they would feel comfortable talking to a parent. Despite the tendencies of modern culture to celebrate confessions very publicly, young people need a safe emotional space and opportunities to be heard in a non-judgemental manner if they are to develop a sense of acceptance. Private prayer, it seems, provides this for some and bypasses the fear of public ridicule or shame.

The private nature of these confessional prayers and their relevance to identity construction was further emphasised by the location in which prayers were most likely to take place – the young person's bedroom, alone, at night. This is where they felt safe and where they could most easily be their 'true self'. Lincoln has noted that the bedroom is one of the few spaces young people have control over. She describes the teenager's bedroom as 'a site of multiple cultural and social articulations and expressions ... It is a space in which their cultural biography can be nurtured' (2005, 400). As such, it is place where young people create and re-create identity and meaning. Confessional prayer can be seen as one cultural expression that allowed the young person to think through the person they are and the person they want to become. In this respect it could be quite motivational:

[I pray] when I've not pulled up to my full potential. (Ashley)

... sometimes God sort of reveals something to you about yourself, what you should be doing, changing and stuff. (Frank)

Rachel explained how she would pray if she had an argument with a friend:

... saying I've had an argument, I'm upset. I'm sure it will work, I don't know – it's up to me. I did say some bad things I shouldn't have, I'm really sorry. Erm, just, I don't know, [give me] the strength to make up with them. ... I believe that it's all my actions but praying gives me comfort, but it's all up to me, it's all down to my decisions.

These prayers allowed the young people to imagine an improved self and to find within that the will to change for the better. The result of these prayers could therefore best be described as cathartic relief, comfort, reassurance and a more positive sense of self. Not quite salvation but personally significant nevertheless.

Prayers of Thanksgiving

The last category of prayer was thanksgiving. This was mentioned less often than petitionary or confessional prayers, but was interesting in terms of the young people's sense of the rectitude of prayer content and in terms of its potential sociological function. It also stands in contrast with the common portrayal of young people as hedonistic, inward-looking and ungrateful souls.

> Oh yeah, I pray. It's not always negative, like if I'm praying everyday, obviously there's not dramas in my life everyday, so when I pray ... like today, I'm happy, so it's going to be about thanking God for today, thanking him for my friends, my cousin. (Cecilia)

> Pray to thank God and asking him for stuff as well. (Iain)

> I try to kinda balance it [the content of prayers] out; just sort of saying thanks and ... things that worry you. (Elvis)

Thanksgiving is part of the inherited template of prayer young people learn in church, school and the youth club, and in some cases appeared to be little more than a polite nod in the direction of God before moving on to the 'real' business of prayer – requests for help. Thus Rachel suggested thanksgiving received less thought than other aspects of her prayers:

> If a bad thing happens I really concentrate on something, but if it's thanking, if it's been a good day then it's just thanking and I don't really concentrate as much as I would if something really bad had happened.

Nevertheless, even if thanksgiving could be quite perfunctory, the fact that some young people still saw it as a part of the prayer act says something about the tenacity of cultural practices. Consumer society of which young people are very much a part does not promote appreciation of, or thankfulness for, things, people or even the planet, despite our growing awareness of ecological issues. Consumerism is based on the principle of being dissatisfied and moving on to the next thing. This, coupled with a growing emphasis on individual rights means that there is little imperative to give thanks anywhere, to anyone, in our society, let alone to God. Yet in these voluntary prayers of thanksgiving the young people have stopped, however briefly, to acknowledge the benefits of life that they enjoy. Indeed, the template of prayer may help to generate feelings of gratitude insofar as it prompts the pray-er to think of things they are thankful for. This in itself could be beneficial for young people. Simon, for example, only prayed when he joined in the prayers at the beginning of youth club football matches; but, much to the youth worker's surprise, he said that he valued those prayers because it 'was a chance to be grateful'. For Linda thanksgiving helped her appreciate life.

> Linda: Just before I go to bed I normally do that [pray]. I say ... how my day's been and thanks for whatever else that's going on in my life, and that.
> Int.:   Oh OK, is that important to you?
> Linda: Yeah, sort of.
> Int.:   Why is that important, what does it do?
> Linda: It makes me feel like I've appreciated my life, what's going on.

The literature on well-being indicates a sense of gratitude is important for enhancing life, both on an individual and on a collective level. Emmons (2001) argues gratitude is a vital civic virtue which motivates and sustains prosocial moral behaviour. Simmel is also very clear about the important role of gratitude in holding society together. He describes gratitude as the 'moral memory of mankind' (1950, 388) which binds people together, even when good deeds have been reciprocated or surpassed. Gratitude forms 'innumerable connections, ideal and concrete, loose and firm' (1950, 389) between people who feel grateful to the same giver. These glimpses of gratitude in prayers therefore hint at something of wider significance, about how the young person sees their place in the world and potentially how they may respond to those around them.

Certainly for some of the young people in this study thanksgiving helped to put things into perspective. For Freddie, gratitude turned his focus away from himself towards the wider world: 'Well, I don't pray for my personal needs. I think there's too much going on in the world for me to be praying for myself. I'm lucky enough to be here in England where I'm able to, you know, speak for myself.'

Similarly, Grant told a youth worker that when he lies in bed at night and realises how fortunate he is compared to other people, he then prays for others and their needs. 'Praying is good,' he said, 'it gets you thinking about those I'm better off than. Gets me thinking about giving to charity and poverty and all that stuff.'

Thanksgiving was also one of the few ways in which the young people demonstrated respect for God, something slightly beyond the intimacy of the confidant. In this respect a couple of the young people indicated that God should not be taken for granted or 'used'. They said that they should take responsibility for those areas of their life which they have control over and not ask God for help. There was no mention, however, of worship being a part of personal prayers. It may be that in young people's minds praise and worship are concepts more restricted to collective religious services.

The Possibility of Prayer

From the young people's comments it seems that prayer is still a valid practice for some despite the apparent secularisation of much of their lives. As might be expected, frequent churchgoers are more likely to pray than those who rarely or never go to church. But even infrequent churchgoers tend to regard prayer as a good thing and may occasionally pray as a way to make sense of their lives and cope with problems and difficulties. Prayer therefore remains a possibility for young people like Alice and Laticia, with the potential to help them build up a positive self-identity, strengthen their sense of moral connectedness and motivate them towards more purposive and confident living.

Bibliography

Aslama, Minna and Mervi Pantti. 2006. 'Talking Alone: Reality TV, Emotions and Authenticity.' *European Journal of Cultural Studies* 9: 167–84.
Barley, Lynda. 2006. *Christian Roots, Contemporary Spirituality.* London: Church House Publishing.

Brierley, Peter. 2006. *Pulling Out of the Nose Dive: A Contemporary Picture of Churchgoing.* London: Christian Research.

Collins, Sylvia. 1997. 'Young People's Faith in Late Modernity.' Ph.D. dissertation, University of Surrey, Guildford.

Cox, Murray. 1990. 'Psychopathology and Treatment of Psychotic Aggression.' In R. Bluglass and P. Bowden, eds, *Principles and Practice of Forensic Psychiatry.* London: Churchill Livingstone.

Department for Education and Skills. 2006. *Making Places in Faith Schools Available to Other Faiths.* http://www.dfes.gov.uk/pns/DisplayPN.cgi?pn_id=2006_0149. October 18. Accessed 11 March 2007.

Emmons, Robert. 2001. 'Making a Science of Virtue.' In *Science and Theology News, Online Edition.* http://www.stnews.org/News-2301.htm. January 1. Accessed 6 March 2006.

Foucault, Michel. 1990. *The History of Sexuality. Vol. 1: An Introduction.* Trans. Robert Hurley. New York: Random House. First published in 1978.

Francis, Leslie J. and Laurence B. Brown. 2001. 'The Influence of Home, Church and School on Prayer Among Sixteen-Year-Old Adolescents in England.' In Leslie J. Francis and Jess Astley, eds, *Psychological Perspectives on Prayer,*. Leominster: Gracewing. 98–107

—— and Mandy Robbins. 2006. 'Prayer, Purpose in Life, Personality and Social Attitudes Among Non-Churchgoing 13- to 15-year-olds in England and Wales.' *Research in the Social Scientific Study of Religion* 17: 123–156.

Furlong, Andy and Fred Cartmel. 2007. *Young People and Social Change: New Perspectives.* 2nd edn. Maidenhead: Open University Press.

Giddens, Anthony. 1991. *Modernity and Self-Identity: Self and Society in the Late Modern Age.* Cambridge: Polity Press.

Heelas, Paul and Linda Woodhead, with Benjamin Seel, Bronislaw Szerszynski and Karin Tusting. 2005. *The Spiritual Revolution: Why Religion is Giving Way to Spirituality.* Oxford: Blackwell Publishing.

Hornsby-Smith, Michael P. 1991. *Roman Catholic Beliefs in England: Customary Catholicism and Transformations of Religious Authority.* Cambridge: Cambridge University Press.

Lincoln, Sian. 2005. 'Feeling the Noise: Teenagers, Bedrooms and Music.' *Leisure Studies* 24: 399–414.

Mauss, Marcel. 2003. *On Prayer.* Trans. W.S.F. Pickering. New York: Durkheim Press. First published in 1909.

Mori. 2000. 'Divine Inspiration is our Speciality!' http://www.ipsos-mori.com/polls/2000/bbc-top.shtml. 14 January. Accessed 11 March 2007.

nfpSynergy. 2007. 'Typical Young People: A Study of What Young People Are Really Like Today.' London: nfpSynergy.

http://www.scouts.org.uk/news/archive/2007/Jan/index.html. 8 January. Accessed 11 March 2007.

Rankin, Phil. 2005. *Buried Spirituality.* Salisbury: Sarum College Press.

Savage, Sara, Sylvia Collins-Mayo and Bob Mayo, with Graham Cray. 2006. *Making Sense of Generation Y: The World View of 15–25 Year Olds.* London: Church House Publishing.

Simmel, George. 1950. 'Faithfulness and Gratitude.' In Kurt H. Wolff, ed. and trans., *The Sociology of George Simmel*, New York: The Free Press. 379–95.

Speck, Peter W. 1978. *Loss and Grief in Medicine.* London: Bailliere Tindall.

Wuthnow, Robert. 2003. 'Spirituality and Spiritual Practice.' In Richard K. Fenn, ed., *The Blackwell Companion to Sociology of Religion.* Oxford: Blackwell. 306–20.

Chapter Four

Who are the Believers in Religion in China?

Xiaowen Lu, Richard O'Leary and Yaojun Li

Introduction

While it is widely accepted that there has been a revival of religious belief in post-Mao China, so far there is still relatively little known about this development. Sociologists and others have documented the changes in the laws and state regulation pertaining to religion (Yang 2006; Leung 2005; Potter 2003) and have provided accounts of religious practices and beliefs based on field research (for example, Dean 2003 on popular religion; Madsen 1998 on Catholics; Hunter and Chan 1993 on Protestants). However, to date there has been a lack of research based on national random sample surveys which could provide a firmer basis for generalization. The development of nationwide survey-based research has been hampered by both the relative underdevelopment of survey research generally in China and the inhibition about conducting empirical research on the sensitive topic of religion. Those survey findings about religion which have recently emerged have tended to lend themselves to superficial, sensationalist media headlines about the number of believers, devoid of critical interpretation. Furthermore, they have been limited to reporting simple percentages and have not proceeded to multivariate statistical analysis. In this chapter we attempt to rectify this by presenting some important new findings about religion in contemporary China that are based on multivariate statistical analysis of national random sample survey data.

Our research focus in on the specific question of who are the believers in religion in China. Our starting point needs to be how we interpret what Chinese mean by the self-description 'believer in religion'. Our initial research finding will be a report on the number of self-reporting believers in religion in China. Our main empirical results pertain to the multivariate statistical analysis which examines the socio-demographic and other individual characteristics associated with believing in religion. We locate this analysis within the broad theoretical framework of modernization and secularization and their application to the study of religion in contemporary China. Before we do this it will be helpful to our readers if we present the context for the study of believing in religion in present-day China. Of particular relevance are the legal status, and the meaning, of believing in religion.

The Legal Status of Believing in Religion

In the post-Mao period, the principal law affecting religion has been the provisions of Article 36 of the 1982 constitution. These state:

> Citizens of the People's Republic of China enjoy freedom of religious belief.

and

> No state organ, public organization or individual may compel citizens to believe in, or not to believe in, any religion: nor may they discriminate against citizens who believe in, or do not believe in any religion. (PRC Constitution 1982)

While the freedom to believe in religion is protected under the law, the state is not indifferent to religious belief as the ruling Communist Party is explicitly atheistic. In accordance with traditional Marxist theory, religion is at best frowned upon and is supposed to gradually disappear as the socialist development progresses. In the view of one academic commentator, the Communist Party policy has privileged the freedom not to believe in religion and has used its control over the educational system to marginalize religious belief (Potter 2003, 14).

The state also distinguishes between what it views as legitimate religious activities and illegitimate activities which disrupt social order; and it only protects what it describes as normal religious activities. The Constitution specifies that no one may make use of religion to engage in activities that disrupt public order, impair the health of citizens or interfere with the educational system of the state. The Religious Affairs Bureau monitors the activities of all religions from the local to the national level. The practice of religion is legally confined to designated public places which can more easily be monitored. The government has suppressed some heterodox Christian and Qigong sects (Yang 2006). However, at times even some Protestant and Catholics centres of worship, their clergy or members have been censured by the Religious Affairs Bureau. This is typically related to unregistered 'house church' Protestants or Catholics operating outside the designated state-sponsored religious organizations. Potter (2003, 11) has summed up the situation for religious belief under the post-Mao government as permitting limited freedom of religious belief, subject to legal and regulatory restrictions on religious behaviour.

The Meaning of 'Believe in Religion'

The freedom to believe in religion described above refers to government-approved forms of five major traditions – Buddhism, Taoism, Catholic and Protestant Christianity, and Islam. This does not include independent groups of these traditions or traditional Chinese folk religion – the latter being viewed by the Communist Party as 'feudal superstition' and unworthy of recognition (Overmyer 2003, 2). In the questionnaire upon which our study is based, the question '*Ni xing jiao ma?*' is translated as 'Do you believe in religion?'. Our interpretation of the responses to this question should consider the issues of the limitations of the Chinese word '*jiao*' to describe religion and the exclusion of folk religion, the imprecision of membership of religions in China and the syncretic nature of much of Chinese religious belief.

Sun (2005, 232) reminds us that historically the term '*jiao*' meant teachings rather than religion and that common references to the three teachings or '*san jiao*' referred to Buddhism, Taoism and Confucianism. Sun elaborates how more recent usage of '*jiao*' as 'religion' began in the twentieth century when *jiao* became a component of the newer term *zongjiao* to describe 'religion'. According to Dean (2003, 32), Western definitions of religion (including Marxist) tend to focus on features of religion which exclude much of Chinese religiosity. These are features such as religious doctrine, institutional organization, a hierarchical priesthood and rites that express particular beliefs. Dean reminds us that in China local communal religion, or 'popular religion' is very diverse in terms of its organization, includes multiple deities and does not always take the form of a clearly recognizable doctrine. In his view the narrow official definition of religion does not readily apply to 'popular religion' as practised by millions of people in China.

There is in any case a difference between Western and Chinese notions of membership of a religion. Some respondents in a survey may not claim to believe in religion but upon further probing may reveal some religious beliefs. Under-reporting of this type has been found in surveys among the Chinese in Taiwan (Zhang and Lin 1992, 102; reported in Lu 2005, 182). Unlike Christianity, which emphasizes clearly defined membership of a single religion and encourages declarations of belief and the rituals of membership such as baptism, the traditional Chinese religions do not emphasize definite and exclusive membership. Not only can Chinese temples house a mix of deities from Taoism and Buddhism but persons may worship at multiple temples (Lang et al. 2005). The syncretism of Chinese religions is such that for many people there is no clear boundary between Buddhism, Taoism and the beliefs and practices of folk religion (Liu 2003). The notion of membership and of believing in religion is additionally complicated for China's ethnic minorities. For example, for ethno-religious minorities such as the Muslim Hui, their Hui ethnic identity is inherited, but not all may choose to describe themselves as believers in religion (Islam).

Individual Characteristics Associated with Reported Belief in Religion

There are now a number of qualitative studies of religious believers in China (see for example, Fan 2003 on folk religion; Aikman 2003 on Protestants; Lozada 2001 on Catholics). A strength of qualitative studies is that they provide valuable ethnographic material and offer some insights into the characteristics of believers in religion, in small localities or among particular congregations. However, there are not in existence – and it is unlikely there ever will be – sufficient local studies to piece together a national overview of believers in religion. Furthermore, small-scale studies which are not intended to be a basis for generalization may nevertheless have coloured our perception of the characteristics of believers in religion. Nationwide research based on random sample surveys can also complement the qualitative research and provide confirmation of or correction to some of the insights.

First, we examine a range of individual characteristics which the literature has suggested may be associated with being a believer in religion in China. We then attempt to make sense of the effect of these characteristics in terms of the framework of modernization and concomitant secularization. This framework has been widely applied to the study of religion in Western industrial societies, and proposes that religion declines with advancing modernization (Wilson 1982; Wallis and Bruce 1992). Modernization is typically presented as a process effecting secularization but this thesis has been hotly debated and criticized (see Bruce 1992; Crockett and O'Leary 2004, O'Leary 2004) including when it is applied to Asian societies (Overmyer 2003,4). There is an additional dimension in China, in that the Christian religion in particular is perceived as being associated with modern Western societies, which may add to its appeal. Nevertheless, despite criticisms, the modernization-secularization framework generates clear hypotheses which can be tested for contemporary China.

The concept of modernization is used to describe a society in terms of economic growth, industrialization, changing occupational structure, and the expansion of education, institutional differentiation and urbanization. The more a society's economy is based on industry rather than agriculture, the better educated its population and the more urban it is, then the more modern that society is considered to be. We can also view individuals in terms of whether they belong to a modern sector of society or they have exposure to modern influences (O'Leary 2001).

The secularization thesis lies within the broad theoretical framework of modernization. As part of this thesis, religious decline is predicted in response to the operation of features of modernization such as rationalization and societalization. Following Weber and his emphasis on the shift to rationality as part of the process of modernization, Bryan Wilson (1982) highlighted how the rational, scientific way of thinking of the modern individual would displace the religious way of thinking, undermining religious belief ranging from belief in the healing power of religious charms to belief in God. At the same time, societalization entails the enlargement of scale in society with a shift from living in small communities, typically the village, to living in cities. For Wilson, the small community, including the agriculturally based, is more conducive to religious belief and practice. In terms of the modernization-secularization perspective we would hypothesize that persons who might be seen as less advanced along the modernization process – that is, older compared to younger, least educated compared to tertiary educated, farmers/peasants compared to white-collar workers, and rural compared to urban – would all be more likely to be believers in religion.

The recent rapid modernization in China and the sharp shift from a state-controlled to a more market-based economy and society in the post-Mao period have brought substantial material benefits to many citizens. However, they have also been accompanied by the break-up of rural communes and mass rural-to-urban migration, high unemployment and involuntary early retirement, the ejection of persons from the universal state health-care system and increased marital breakdown. Social dislocation may generate new spiritual questions (Fan 2003, 65) and quasi-religious healing practices may give meaning to those who are displaced in the new economic order (Chen 2003, 199). Bays (2003, 193) draws attention to how the Christian magazine *Tianfeng* (*Heavenly Wind*) often prints articles or replies to readers advising them how to cope with the stresses of economic change and family problems. Therefore, persons from these dislocated and disadvantaged categories may search for comfort and so we may hypothesize that they will be more likely than persons in the socially advantaged or socially stable categories to be believers in religion.

There are additional categories or persons, such as women and ethnic minorities, who do not so neatly fit into a general designation as less modernized or more socially dislocated. However, in spite of state-sponsored gender equality, women in China tend to be more disadvantaged in socio-economic positions and, even among the city dwellers, they tend to be disproportionately vulnerable to unemployment and early retirement in the wake of economic restructuring, and less likely to find re-employment after being laid off. Ethnic minority groups tend to be concentrated in economically backward interior regions which remain socio-economically disadvantaged or have even declined in comparison with the rapid development witnessed by the coastal areas since the 1980s. Thus, international research on women and on ethnic minorities and ethnographic accounts for China would lead us to hypothesize that these categories too will be more likely to believe in religion.

Methodology

In order to address the research questions as outlined above, we use the China Values Survey conducted by Shanghai Academy of Social Sciences and Beijing University in 2004. This is a national representative sample covering 3,267 respondents aged 18 or over and resident in private households. The sampling instrument employed is that of satellite targeting, a new method increasingly used for government and academic research in China. The geographic coverage includes 65 counties in 23 (out of 30) provinces. The total effective response rate is 75 per cent.

To investigate the patterns of religious belief in China, we use the question '*ni xing jiao ma*?' (Do you believe in religion?), as noted above. This is a dichotomous variable used in descriptive and modelling analysis. We also use a range of socio-economic variables (as earlier discussed) to address the modernization and secularization theses. As some of the explanatory variables such as sex and marital status are self-evident, we give a brief description below of the other explanatory variables as we constructed.

Age

We differentiate three age groups: 18–35, 36–50 and 51–70. The youngest group are those born and educated after China adopted the opening policy after the end of the Cultural Revolution. The middle group were mainly educated during the period after the founding of the new China and prior to the socio-economic restructuring that started in 1978 as a result of the adoption of the reforms. The oldest group was the least educated.

Education

One important determinant of socio-economic attainment and religious belief is the level of education an individual has attained. Given that a very large proportion of people in China are peasants with low levels of formal education, we differentiated four groups: tertiary, secondary, primary and no education.

Class

We use a six-category variable for class to reflect the social realities in China. As is well documented, China has a large agricultural sector. Many city dwellers were forced to take early retirement or were laid off. A large number of people turned to self-employment either as a result of forced redundancy or as a means to economic prosperity. The six categories were based on the occupational status of the respondents at the time of interview: (1) salariat (professionals and managers); (2) routine non-manual or manual workers (the former consisting mainly of junior office clerks or sales/personal service workers in commerce and service sectors, and the latter of manual workers in industry and commerce); (3) retired; (4) petty bourgeoisie (sole traders or small employers); (5) the unemployed/laid off/never worked; and (6) peasants/farmers.

Urban-rural (Hukou)

A unique feature of China is the household registration system (*hukou* in Chinese). Although this system has relaxed somewhat in recent years, it still plays a very important role in people's lives, especially when people with rural *hukou* wish to live and work, and to have their kids educated in big cities such as Beijing or Shanghai. Since the 1980s millions of peasants have migrated to cities to find work. A three-way variable is created: (1) urbanite; (2) migrant worker; and (3) rural.

Results

The Percentage of Believers in Religion

Table 4.1 shows the association between socio-cultural-demographic attributes of the individual respondents and whether they believe or do not believe in religion. At the bottom of the table we see the result that 11.4 per cent reported that they believe in religion. This is a modest percentage and, as we discussed earlier, it is likely to be an underestimation of the percentage that have some religious beliefs, especially beliefs in Chinese folk religion. It is closer to official government figures than to the much higher non-governmental estimates, and the distinction between a narrow and a broader definition of believing in religion may account for much of the discrepancy. The percentage is also much lower than that reported for even the most irreligious of the post-Communist countries of Eastern Europe (Need and Evans 2004).

Table 4.1 Believing in religion by socio-cultural-demographic factors (percentage by row)

	Believe in religion – yes	Believe in religion – no	N
Age			
18–35	12.5	87.6	1,225
36–50	11.3	88.7	1,237
51–70	10.9	89.1	805
Sex			
Male	9.7	90.3	1,574
Female	13.4***	86.6	1,693
Education			
Tertiary	8.8	91.2	350
Secondary	10.6	89.4	1,632
Primary	11.7	88.3	486
None	15.3**	84.7	799
Class			
Salariat (Professional/Manager)	7.5	92.5	290
Routine non-manual or manual	7.6	92.4	530
Retired	7.8	92.2	314
Petty bourgeoisie	11.6	88.4	136
Unemployed	13.2*	86.8	227
Farmer/peasant	14.4**	85.6	1,770
Marital status			
Single	11.3	88.9	427
Married	11.4	88.6	2,650
Separated/Divorced/Widowed	16.4†	83.4	190
Health			
Good	9.3	90.7	640
Fair	11.7†	88.3	2,541
Poor	26.4***	73.6	86
Ethnicity			
Han	8.9	91.1	2,903
Minority ethnicity	33.6***	66.4	364
Urban-rural (*Hukou*)			
Urbanite	8.3	91.7	1,295
Migrant worker	14.5***	85.5	394
Rural	14.1***	85.9	1,578
All	11.4	88.6	3,267

Note: Weighted percentages and unweighted Ns. Each of the other categories in a variable is contrasted with the reference category listed in italics with significance levels shown for the differences in question: †p<0.10; *p<0.05; ** p<0.01; and *** p<0.001.
Source: The China Social Values Survey (2004).

Individual Characteristics Associated with Believing in Religion

Who is more likely to believe in religion? Each of our individual characteristics or variables is presented separately with a test for statistical significance. Categories of a variable are contrasted with the reference category (in italics) and an asterix indicates differences which are statistically significant. These tests allow us to be confident that the differences between categories of respondents are really to be found in the Chinese population and are unlikely to result from sampling error.

We see that there is no significant association between age group and believing in religion. There is, however, a statistically significant association between gender and believing in religion: only 9.7 per cent of males stated they believed in religion, whereas 13.4 per cent of females did. As regards education, only 8.8 per cent of respondents with tertiary education said they believed in religion, compared with 15.3 per cent of those with no education. This difference is substantial and statistically significant. Turning now to class-occupational category, only 7.5 per cent of respondents in the salariat (professionals/managers) said they believed in religion, compared with 13.2 per cent of those who are unemployed and 14.4 per cent of farmers/peasants. These differences, too, are substantial and statistically significant.

For marital status, although a higher percentage of persons who are separated/ divorced/widowed believe in religion than single people (16.4 per cent compared with 11.3 per cent), we cannot be confident that this difference is really found in the entire population as the result is not statistically significant. On the other hand, there is a clear association between self-reported health status and believing in religion. Almost three times as high a percentage of the persons with poor health (26.4 per cent) believe in religion compared to those with good health (9.3 per cent). This difference is highly statistically significant. However, we should note that persons who self-report their health as poor are a very small percentage of all respondents.

The results for ethnic group are clear. Over four times as high a percentage of those belonging to ethnic minorities (33.6 per cent) believe in religion compared to the majority Han Chinese (8.9 per cent). This difference is highly statistically significant. Finally, there is a statistically significant association between type of residence and believing in religion. While the higher percentage of believers among rural dwellers compared to urbanites – 14.1 per cent as against 8.3 per cent – is not unexpected, the large difference between migrant workers at 14.5 per cent and other urban dwellers (with official urban residency) is striking. Migrant workers retained their ideological outlook and their even higher propensity for religious believing than their non-mobile peers in the rural areas might reflect the harsh socio-economic situation they faced in the city and the concomitant socio-psychological dislocation.

Overall, the description of believers which is emerging is that they are disproportionately found among the following categories: females, persons with no education, farmers/peasants or the unemployed, rural dwellers or migrants, ethnic minorities, and those with self-reported poor health. This bivariate analysis is a useful first step in description, but it is inadequate for our exploration of the associations between individual attributes and believing in religion. It may be for example, that the relatively high percentage of believers among the persons with no education is because these are also the persons who are farmers/peasants. To try to unpack these complex multiple associations we now turn to multivariate statistical analysis. However, we will first provide some additional information about the religious composition of the believers in religion.

The Religious Composition of Believers in Religion

Of the 11.4 per cent of our respondents who declared they believed in religion, the largest single category of believing was Buddhism, amounting to 4.4 per cent of all persons in the survey. Less than 1 per cent reported that they believed in Taoism. This obviously underestimates the extent to which people may engage in some Taoist practices. It may also indicate the damage done to Taoism in particular by the suppression of religion (Lai 2003). A total of 2.5 per cent of all respondents reported that they were believers in Christianity (Protestantism). There were far fewer reported believers in Catholicism at 0.5 per cent. This looks about right as it is widely accepted that Protestants are about three times as numerous as Catholics. Finally, 3 per cent of respondents reported that they were Muslim believers. While these simple percentages may be of interest to some of our readers, we recall Chen's observation that there can be an undue interest in simply counting the number of believers (2003, 212). We are even more curious about who the believers are. Therefore, we wish to move on to our multivariate analysis of the characteristics of those respondents who declare they are believers in religion.

Logistic Regression Coefficients on Religion by Socio-cultural-demographic Factors

Logistic regression models are used to assess the relative importance of each of the socio-cultural-demographic characteristics while holding constant the other variables. The models use log odds ratios and therefore we report the coefficients of each category as against the base or reference category, holding constant all other variables in the models. If a category is equally likely to be a believer in religion as the reference category, then the odds ratio would be 1 and the log of the ratio would be 0. Thus a positive coefficient means a greater and a negative coefficient a lesser likelihood of being a believer. The data are shown in Table 4.2, where we present two models.

Table 4.2   Logit regression coefficients on 'believe in religion' by socio-cultural-demographic factors

	Model 1	Model 2
Age		
18–35	.000	.000
36–50	−.199	−.063
51–70	−.332[†]	−.163
Sex		
Male	.000	.000
Female	.280[*]	.336[**]
Education		
Tertiary	.000	.000
Secondary	.017	−.271
Primary	.029	−.412
None	.258	−.153
Class		
Salariat	.000	.000
Routine non-manual or manual	−.019	−.033
Retired	.135	.192
Petty bourgeoisie	.447	.359
Unemployed	.581[†]	.551
Farmer/peasant	.655[*]	.606[*]
Marital status		
Single		.000
Married		.087
Separated/Divorced/Widowed		.412
Health		
Good		.000
Fair		.181
Poor		1.084[***]
Ethnicity		
Han		.000
Minority ethnicity		1.594[***]
Urban-rural (*Hukou*)		
Urbanite		.000
Migrant worker		.756[***]
Rural		.141
Constant	−2.550[***]	- 3.073[***]
Pseudo R^2	.020	.088
Model comparison χ^2		163.440[a][***]
N	3,267	3,267

Note: Weighted percentages and unweighted Ns. Each of the other categories in a variable is contrasted with the reference category listed in italics with significance levels shown for the differences in question: [†]p<0.10; [*]p<0.05; [**] p<0.01; and [***] p<0.001.

Standard errors and 95 per cent confidence intervals are not shown but are available on request.
[a] refers to terms in Model 2 that are additional to those in Model 1.

Source: The China Social Values Survey (2004).

Model 1 in Table 4.2 shows that when age, gender, level of education and class are entered into the model as the independent variables, respondents who are female compared to male and those who are farmers/peasants compared to the salariat are both significantly more likely to report they believe in religion. As in Table 4.1 the asterix is used to indicate statistical significance. It is note-worthy that, while the 'no education' category was shown in Table 4.1 to be significantly more likely than the tertiary educated to believe in religion when no other factors were considered, the significance disappears in this model when age, gender and class effects are taken into account. Similarly, the effect of being unemployed is no longer significant when these other variables are taken into account.

Model 2 adds marital status, health status, ethnicity and type of residency. At the bottom of Table 4.2, we show that Model 2 gives a significant improvement in fit over Model 1. We see that the coefficients for female and for farmer/peasant change only slightly and that both are still significant. We also now see that respondents who report poor health compared to good health, are minority ethnics compared to Han Chinese, or are migrant workers compared to urbanites, are all significantly more likely to report they believe in religion. Again, it is noteworthy that, while the rural category was shown in Table 4.1 to be significantly more likely than the urban category to believe in religion when no other factors were considered, the significance disappears in this model when our other variables are taken into account. It seems that what is important for believing in religion is being a farmer/peasant rather than simply being a rural dweller.

Therefore, some of the patterns suggested in our bivariate analysis in Table 4.1 are no longer present when we consider all the variables simultaneously in our Model 2. The categories of low level of education, being unemployed or being a rural dweller are no longer associated with believing in religion. What still holds is that females, farmers/peasants, those with poor health, minority ethnics and migrants are more likely to be believers in religion. Among these, it is minority ethnicity and health status which carry the greatest relative importance in terms of believing in religion.

Discussion and Conclusion

We turn now to the insights our results may provide us about the possible associations between modernization, social dislocation and disadvantage, and the reporting of believing in religion. We found no association between age group and believing in religion – neither reduced believing among the young which would be consistent with the prediction of both secularization and Marxist theories, nor an increased level of believing among the young consistent with the claims of religious revival and which might be expected given the increased tolerance of religious belief by the Communist Party. The absence of either an age effect or an effect for being 'retired' would also appear to belie the emphasis on greater religiosity among older and retired persons (for example, Luo 1991). We do not attempt to deny that many older people believe in religion, but we cannot claim that they are more likely to believe than younger people. The resolution here may be that there may be less difference between the age groups as regards believing in religion (as narrowly defined) but larger differences may be uncovered when examining religious practice.

A higher percentage of believing was found among the 'no education' category in the bivariate tables. This is consistent with claims of other commentators (for example, Kindopp 2004, 135; reported in Tamney 2005, 8). However, this may not necessarily be attributable to education per se. The association disappeared when other variables, including class, were taken into account in the multivariate analysis. Overall, the findings for level of education do not offer support to the modernization-secularization perspective, which would expect the higher educated to be more non-believing. It is even possible that there is some under-reporting of believing among intellectuals. For example, Bays (2003, 193) advises us that, for intellectuals, to be known to be a religious believer would be detrimental to one's career. Here we should note that there is a difference between public proclamation of religious belief and anonymous response to a survey item.

On the basis of the multivariate analysis, rural dwellers are no more likely than urban dwellers to report being believers in religion, once class-occupational situation is taken into account. The absence of a rural effect would at first appear to belie the numerous ethnographic studies which highlight the association between rural dwellers and religion. While it is the case that there are many more places of worship in rural areas, including folk religion temples, and so *practice* may be higher, the levels of *believing* in religion (as narrowly understood in terms of Buddhism, Christianity or Islam) may not necessarily be higher. What is more relevant is whether or not the respondent is a farmer/peasant. The statistically significant result for farmers is consistent with a modernization-secularization perspective, although, overall, our results are rather indifferent to that perspective since being older and being less educated were not associated with being a believer.

Where we might extend the usefulness of the insight from the focus on modernization is to consider the impact of being in categories which may be viewed as disadvantaged and socially dislocated, and which may be a concomitant of that modernization. There is a positive effect on believing in religion for being a migrant. This is even more important for believing than being rural, once being a farmer has been taken into account. This is an interesting result as it contradicts the expectation under the modernization perspective that migration from the rural to urban environment would diminish religious belief. Given the extent of rural-to-urban migration taking place in China under modernization, this represents a large and growing potential market for religious suppliers.

Having a self-perception of poor health is associated with being a believer. This is consistent with ethnographic studies on Chinese folk religion, quasi religious Qigong and Christianity where the attraction of faith healing is a prominent feature (Fan 2003; Chen 2003). Chen, in discussing healing sects in particular, describes how 'followers were drawn to the messages of inclusion where anyone could participate, especially those who had lost jobs or health care benefits' (2003, 199). If this reflects an appeal of religions more widely, then, as with the migrants, the appeal is to a socially disadvantaged group and their incorporation into the population of believers would shape the social composition of believers. However, we also note that, although we saw in the bivariate analysis that the unemployed were more likely than the salariat to believe in religion, there was no effect in the multivariate analysis once level of education was taken into account. Therefore, the higher level of believing in religion is not evident for all our categories of social disadvantage.

We found that ethnic minority respondents were much more likely to be believers. However, it is also interesting to note that, even among the minority ethnic respondents, only a third report that they believe in religion. This belies a tendency in the literature on religion in China which tends to equate minority ethnicity and being religious. The finding of higher levels of believing for women is consistent with numerous other commentators on a wide range of religions. It is also consistent with Feuchtwang's (2002) observation that there may be a feminization of both Buddhism and Christianity, at least in its congregational forms.

We are aware of limitations of our study – the respondent's own definition of religion available to us through our survey data is narrow. Further analysis for the different religious categories within the believing group is likely to reveal differences between the adherents of the various religions. Nevertheless, our present multivariate analysis has produced important new findings on religion across the entire Chinese population. We have identified particular categories of individual who are associated with believing in religion. These are women, farmers/peasants, ethnic minorities, persons with poor health and migrants. We have not found statistically significant effects for age or level of education and overall our findings do not lend themselves to a consistent explanation in terms of a modernization-secularization perspective. However, there is more consistent support for the view that the believers are disproportionately drawn from some of the socially dislocated and disadvantaged categories in society. This has implications for the future growth and social composition of believers in religion in China.

Bibliography

Aikman, David. 2003. *Jesus in Beijing: How Christianity is Transforming China and Changing the Global Balance of Power.* Washington: Regnery.

Bays, Daniel. 2003. 'Chinese Protestant Christianity Today.' In Daniel Overmyer (ed.), *Religion in China Today*, Cambridge: Cambridge University Press. 182–198.

Bruce, Steve (ed.). 1992. *Religion and Modernization: Sociologist and Historians Debate the Secularization Thesis.* Oxford: Oxford University Press.

Chen, Nancy. 2003. 'Healing Sects and Ant-Cult Campaigns.' In Daniel Overmyer (ed.), *Religion in China Today*, Cambridge: Cambridge University Press. 199–214.

Crockett, Alasdair and Richard O'Leary (eds). 2004. *Patterns and Processes of Religious Change in Modern Industrial Societies: Europe and America*, Lampeter: Edwin Mellen Press.

Dean, Kenneth. 2003. 'Local Communal Religion in South-east China.' In Daniel Overmyer (ed.), *Religion in China Today*, Cambridge: Cambridge University Press. 32–52.

Fan, Lizhu. 2003. 'The Cult of the Silkworm Mother as a Core of a Local Community Religion in a North China Village: Field Study in Zhiwuying, Baoding, Hebei.'

In Daniel Overmyer (ed.), *Religion in China Today*, Cambridge: Cambridge University Press. 53–66.

Feuchtwang, Stephan. 2002. 'Chinese Religions.' In Linda Woodhead, Paul Fletcher, Hiroko Kawanami and David Smith (eds), *Religions in the Modern World*. London: Routledge. 86–107.

Hunter, Alan and Kim-Kwong Chan. 1993. *Protestantism in Contemporary China*. Cambridge: Cambridge University Press.

Kindopp, Jason. 2004. 'Fragmented yet Defiant: Protestant Resilience Under Chinese Communist Party Rule.' In Jason Kindopp and Carol Lee Hamrin (eds), *God and Caesar in China*, Washington, DC: Brookings Institution Press. 122–148.

Lai, Chi-Tim. 2003. 'Taoism in China Today, 1980–2002.' In Daniel Overmyer (ed.), *Religion in China Today*, Cambridge: Cambridge University Press. 107–121.

Lang, Graham, Selina Chan and Lars Ragvald. 2005. 'Temples and Religious Economy.' In Fenggang Yang and Joseph Tamney (eds), *State, Market and Religions in Chinese Societies*. Leiden: Brill. 149–180.

Leung, Beatrice. 2005. 'China's Religious Freedom Policy: An Art of Managing Religious Activity.' *The China Quarterly*. **184**: 894–913.

Liu, Tik-sang. 2003. 'A Nameless but Active Religion: An Anthropologist's View of Local Religion in Hong Kong and Macau.' In Daniel Overmyer (ed.), *Religion in China Today*, Cambridge: Cambridge University Press. 67–88.

Lozada, Eriberto. 2001. *God Above Ground: Catholic Church, Post Socialist State, and Transnational Processes in a Chinese Village*. Stanford: Stanford University Press.

Lu, Paul Yunfeng. 2005. 'Helping People to Fulfill Vows: Commitment Mechanisms in a Chinese Sect.' In Fenggang Yang and Joseph Tamney (eds), *State, Market and Religions in Chinese Societies*. Leiden: Brill. 181–202.

Luo, Zhufeng. 1991. 'A Survey of Christian Retired Workers in a Shanghai District.' In Luo, Zhufeng (ed.), *Religion Under Socialism in China*. London: M.E. Sharpe. 195–202.

Madsen, Richard. 1998. *China's Catholics: Tragedy and Hope in an Emerging Civil Society*. Berkeley: University of California Press.

Need, Ariana and Geoff Evans. 2004. 'Religious Mobility in Post-Communist Eastern Europe.' In Alasdair Crockett and Richard O'Leary (eds), *Patterns and Processes of Religious Change in Modern Industrial Societies: Europe and America*, Lampeter: Edwin Mellen Press. 191–206.

O'Leary, Richard. 2001. 'Modernization and Religious Intermarriage' *British Journal of Sociology*, **52**: 4. 647–665.

——. 2004. 'Modernization and Secularization' In Zhuo Xinping (ed.) *Religious Comparison and Dialogue*, [in Chinese] Beijing: Religious Culture Publishing House. 178–190.

Overmyer, Daniel (ed.). 2003. *Religion in China Today*. Cambridge: Cambridge University Press.

Potter, Pitman. 2003. 'Belief in Control: Regulation of Religion In China.' In Daniel Overmyer (ed.), *Religion in China Today*, Cambridge: Cambridge University Press. 11–31.

Sun, Anna Xiao Dong. 2005. 'The fate of Confucianism as a Religion in Socialist China: Controversies and Paradoxes.' In Fenggang Yang and Joseph Tamney (eds), *State, Market and Religions in Chinese Societies*. Leiden: Brill. 229–253.

Tamney, Joseph. 2005. 'Introduction.' In Fenggang Yang and Joseph Tamney (eds), *State, Market and Religions in Chinese Societies*, Leiden: Brill. 1–18.

Wallis, Roy and Steve Bruce. 1992. 'Secularization the Orthodox Model.' In Steve Bruce (ed.), *Religion and Modernization: Sociologist and Historians Debate the Secularization Thesis*, Oxford: Oxford University Press. 8–30.

Wilson, Bryan. 1982. *Religion in Sociological Perspective*. Oxford: Oxford University Press.

Yang, Fenggang. 2006. 'The Red, Black, and Gray Markets of Religion in China.' *The Sociological Quarterly*, **47**: 93–122.

—— and Joseph Tamney (eds). 2005. *State, Market and Religions in Chinese Societies*. Leiden: Brill.

Zhang, Maogui and Lin Benxuan. 1992. 'The Social Implications of Religion: A Problem for the Sociology of Knowledge.' *Bulletin of the Institute of Ethnology Academica Sinica*, **74**: 95–123.

PART II
Practice

Chapter Five

New Paradigm Christianity and Commitment-formation: The Case of Hope Filipino (Singapore)[1]

Jayeel Serrano Cornelio

Hope Filipino

Hope Filipino is one of the many congregations of migrants found in Protestant churches in cosmopolitan Singapore, and the largest among all the Filipino congregations of Hope of God International that originated in Bangkok, Thailand. Having started in 2000 with only three regular Sunday service attendees, Hope Filipino now has more than 700 – and it fearlessly aims to reach 1,000 by the end of 2007. Approximately 90 per cent are professionally employed while 10 per cent are domestic helpers. Women comprise 70 per cent of the total. Although primarily Filipino, the congregation is open to other nationalities, which accounts for the use of English in all interactions. In fact, a very small but increasing number of non-Filipinos are joining the ranks, most of whom are colleagues in the workplace. Several leaders are also local Chinese Singaporeans. Except for the pastor, everyone else is employed fulltime while involved in the congregation. The other local congregations of Hope Church Singapore (for example, adult, youth, Chinese-speaking), whose overall attendance reaches beyond 3,000 weekly, see the substantial contribution of its Filipino counterpart in bringing more potential members into the church. Currently, there are more than 40 weekly care groups (small communities of less than 20), up from 22 in 2004.

The strength and continuous growth of this congregation occur in light of the fact that Filipinos are mostly Catholics and are generally employed for shift-based and demanding professions in the 24/7 industries of healthcare, shipping, electronics and IT. Hence, the conversion of Filipinos and the development of their commitment are focal to the congregation's activities. What makes the phenomenon more interesting is the fact that Hope Filipino is a growing new paradigm congregation, determined to become a megachurch of migrant professionals whose many members have opted to stay in Singapore with church as decisive factor.

1   My gratitude extends to Professor Bryan Turner, Associate Professor Syed Farid Alatas, and Dr. Abby Day for all the invaluable comments that strengthened this chapter.

Research Purpose

Moving away from the frequently studied large churches in the US, this research looks at the experience of a relatively young migrant congregation in an Asian context where new paradigm churches are increasingly changing the religious landscape. What accounts for lay involvement in the new paradigm environment at Hope Filipino? What subjectivities surrounding commitment are emerging? As contribution to the present volume, my inquiry attempts to enrich understanding of new paradigm Christianity in view of particular subjectivities and practices individuals have about religious involvement. In this chapter, I argue that new paradigm Christianity's determination to be culturally relevant in terms of its openness to new ways of doing church while maintaining an arguably strict position on Biblical standards on behavior and providing opportunities for greater involvement becomes the institutional space for the development of significant levels of commitment. This is a phenomenon that surfaces as Hope Filipino, as a new paradigm congregation, strategically addresses the issues of the migrant Filipino professional. By focusing on the subjectivity, my analysis of commitment-formation deviates from less meaningful conceptualizations of religious involvement in terms of attendance and affiliation (for discussion, see Roberts and Davidson 1984). The chapter ends by presenting a more nuanced theoretical view of new paradigm Christianity.

Because my interest is in the subjectivities concerning commitment, the method is qualitative. I conducted data gathering in early 2006 for my independent research at the master's level. Interviewees have been selected based on a balanced representation of gender, length of stay in church, leadership position, degree of involvement and nationality (local Singaporean and Filipino). A very small number of the key leaders, including the pastor, are Chinese Singaporeans who pioneered the congregation. Participant observations of major evangelistic activities, including an evangelistic Sunday service and an evangelistic care group session, complete the methodology.

Characterizing New Paradigm Christianity

Largely successful in the US and Australia and mostly in the form of megachurch movements, new paradigm Christianity's ability to draw crowds to Protestant conversion foreshadows a new form of contemporary Christianity sensitive to the needs and interests of the modern individual (Miller 1997). In his groundbreaking work, Miller (1997) looks at the massive success of its congregations in terms of their ability to be culturally relevant, which he describes as the new paradigm of doing evangelism. The main target is the modern urbanite, who, as a result of a secular environment, avoids mainstream religion (Balmer and Winner 2002). Relevance is achieved by overhauling many of the traditional practices in mainline Protestantism in light of adopting appealing contemporary culture. This explains why megachurches have thrown out images and rituals that offer any tinge of structured religiosity.

Miller (1997, 1) has identified several defining characteristics of new paradigm Christianity: up-to-date worship style incorporating elements from the music scene, a Christ-centered theology applicable to everyday living and a social organization principally run by the laity. The operative word describing what is also known as new evangelicalism (Balmer and Winner 2002) is flexibility, the openness to new processes in doing church. As a religious movement, new paradigm Christianity not only builds new congregations but also reforms existing ones in the hope of making church appealing. One may typically find megachurches conducting Sunday services in such secular places as auditoriums or function rooms of hotels. The more affluent churches capable of constructing their own buildings reflect nevertheless mall-like architecture and interior.

Although challenging tradition, new paradigm Christianity maintains its ties with Protestantism through its central belief in salvation through Christ. The 'focus is on "inviting Jesus into your heart" and witnessing his transforming love' (Miller 1998, 203). Miller argues that doctrinal persuasions are usually of individual position, depending on one's experience and exposure to the Bible:

> New paradigm Christians are doctrinal minimalists. Their focus is on retelling the narratives of the Bible and seeking analogues to the experience of their members. So long as one subscribes to the basic teaching of Jesus and the practice of the early Christians, there is room for debate on the details of interpretation. The goal is for members to have a relationship with Jesus, not to pledge allegiance to a particular catechism or doctrinal statement. (1998, 203)

Miller's proposition, however, needs to be qualified. Based on my own research, I argue that doctrinal interpretation is never completely malleable. While there might be evangelical congregations more concerned with tolerance for differences and new paradigm Christianity may be deemed so because of the continual reinvention of its practices (Guest 2004), many new paradigm congregations, including Hope Filipino, uphold particular sets of conservative positions about the Trinity, the Scriptures, and salvation, to which its members must adhere before official membership is approved, for instance. My observation turns out to be a response to Percy's (2003) concern about the seeming theological incoherence in global Charismatic Christianity (which, inferring from his definition, includes new paradigm Christianity). At the global level, doctrinal unity may be impossible to ascertain. This is not so at the level of the new paradigm organization where statements of faith and doctrinal positions set the boundaries for individual interpretation. Such negotiation, as presented in this chapter, takes place through socialization processes of discipleship in the congregation. Arguably, what remains central is the belief in the priesthood of believers, and what is subject to cultural relevance is the manner by which the church operates.

Gap in the Literature

Observers providing case studies, mostly of prominent megachurches, have been inclined to look at congregational identity in terms of such institutional factors as entertainment technology and marketing strategies (Connell 2005; Cruz 2006). The proposition is that, because these churches are primarily concerned with gaining numerical strength, nurturing commitment by maintaining a level of strictness among their adherents becomes impossible (Guest 2004; Connell 2005). Connell observes that the buoyant theme is 'Christianity Lite' (2005, 328), referring to new paradigm Christianity's practice of recasting conventionally aloof religion into bite-sized spiritual experience. Supporting this is Balmer and Winner's observation that the use of a music band in worship is 'probably the most visible manifestation of this pandering to popular tastes, but it is evident in everything from interior decoration and seating plans to preaching styles' (2002, 117). I argue, however, that these analyses place more emphasis on the growth of the new paradigm church as a result of its reliance on such consumerist factors as market research and entertainment technology, overlooking the agency of individuals who engage with new paradigm Christianity and how they lead to the formation of congregational identity.

Theoretical Location

In this chapter, I argue that new paradigm Christianity provides a unique space that allows for the emergence of an idioculture wherein the church is focal to membership commitment. Here, Fine's work on idioculture, which he defines as the 'system of knowledge, beliefs, behaviors, and customs shared by members of an interacting group to which members can refer and employ as the basis of further interaction' (1979, 734), proves helpful in understanding community and identity in the context of commitment-formation within the group life at Hope Filipino. The key elements of group life, in this case the congregation itself, are socioemotional orientation (interpersonal relationships) and task orientation (collective objective).

Socioemotional orientation is reflected in Miller's observation that 'individuals gravitate toward communities with some cultural resonance for them' (1997, 79). New paradigm Christianity's flexibility in doing church allows for the adoption of relevant practices that build and reinforce socioemotional orientation with members and new believers. Twitchell (2006) comments, for instance, that men find the megachurch as a hiding place.

Serving as the congregation's task orientation (Fine 1979), the commitment to life-transformation is manifest in the organizational arrangements wherein personal development is cultivated, for instance, the small care groups, and in the case of Hope Filipino, one-on-one shepherding. Miller points out that 'converts are going to maintain loyalty to institutions that rigorously pursue the task of life-transformation' (1997, 79). He also confirms that 'words such as *discipleship* and *accountability* are heard at every turn ... More mature Christians *disciple* younger converts ...' (1997, 76). So, despite the apparent casualness in new paradigm Christianity, the relationships within the institution can be demanding, a critical element in instilling loyalty (Miller 1997; see also Ianaccone 1994). Describing contemporary evangelicals in America, which include new paradigm churches, Shibley (1998, 83–84) points out that, although they are world-affirming in adapting to secular lifestyle, 'these congregations provide a distinct identity and relatively clear guidelines for organizing a new life', the postconversion lifestyle. However, Miller's discussion on the postconversion lifestyle, which I argue informs the congregational identity in new paradigm Christianity, is rather limited. This inquiry on the meaning-making processes of individuals that inform the identity of Hope Filipino locates itself within intrinsic congregational studies (Guest, Tusting and Woodhead 2004).

Commitment at Hope Filipino

In the experience of Hope Filipino, the postconversion lifestyle entails a process of commitment-formation that reorganizes one's worldview concerning individual aspirations and ministerial calling.[2] In the ensuing quote, Allan, an IT specialist in Singapore and simultaneously involved in Hope Filipino, summarizes his mindset in fulfilling his roles as shepherd in mentoring younger Christians and as care leader to one of the many small groups of professionals in the congregation:

> For me, it's about being there all the time. Opportunity, you take every opportunity you can grab. You are committed that through you, the Lord will be able to accomplish what He wants in people's lives. I am always there, even if without enough sleep, even if I lack the time, being always ready to go, to serve, to share what I can in order to be a blessing to other people.

Allan's statement reflects Hope Filipino's understanding of commitment in terms of sacrificial action in order to 'serve in the Kingdom of God'. Although the 'Kingdom of God' is employed to refer to the solidarity of Christians around the world, it is in colloquial terms the church organization, nuanced in Hope Filipino's vision statement: 'To fulfill the Great Commission in our lifetime by building strong and Biblical people to plant strong and Biblical churches in Singapore, the Philippines and all over the world.' This intriguing subjectivity concerning sacrificial action for the congregation is an identifiable ethos among the members and leaders who, except for the local pastor, are lay and currently working as fulltime professionals.

Individuals are socialized into such understanding through discipleship activities done at various levels starting with the care group. Two care groups form one unit, which with other units forms a sub-district. A sub-district is part of a district. Originally, the subdivisions were based on geographic location in Singapore, but today, one big district may be composed of individuals from all parts of the country, who nevertheless share similar professional backgrounds. Lay leaders in the form of the pastor, district leaders, sub-district leaders, unit leaders and care group leaders oversee and facilitate activities. As evangelism is done at the care group level, individuals, both regulars and guests, primarily locate themselves in a particular care group, seen in how, for instance, members and leaders are seated together during the Sunday service. In addition, everyone is being 'shepherded' (if already an official member) or 'followed up' (if a new convert) on a one-on-one basis by a Christian of

---

2 Such reorganization occurs after conversion. In the event that one is already a Protestant prior to affiliating with Hope Filipino, what possibly occurs is 'alternation' in which one embraces a supposedly more meaningful framework for Christian living (Barker and Currie 1985). In my analysis, then, the subjectivity surrounding commitment points to a postconversion (or postalternation) lifestyle.

acknowledged maturity. Opportunities to lead, say, a new care group, or shepherd another individual, arise as membership increases.

Many of the members of Hope Filipino who have now taken up leadership responsibilities have decided to stay in Singapore because of the church. Furthermore, the congregation has seen two of its members give up their profession to become exploratory missionaries to Brazil. Two are in the process of leaving in 2007. The emergence of this kind of commitment becomes an intriguing phenomenon given the existing assessment of new paradigm churches as consumerist and, hence, undemanding.

Underpinning Elements of Commitment-formation

Hope Filipino's ability to facilitate worldview reorganization initially rests on its ability to engage with the issues of the migrant Filipino in attendance. Such sociocultural resonance develops within the flexible institutional space in new paradigm Christianity. Shibley (1998) describes this flexible institutional space as the world-affirming character of contemporary evangelicalism, which arises, according to Miller (1997), out of the countercultural attitude of the founders of new paradigm churches in America in the 1960s. At Hope Filipino, however, there is no historically based anti-establishment attitude pervading the discourse. What emerges is a straightforward engagement with the issues of the migrant Filipino professional.

Hunt (1997, 91) explains that the success of the Anglican congregation he studies in the UK lies in addressing 'the middle class concerns with continual personal growth and fulfillment of spiritual potential' that can be traced back to the influence of Vineyard, which Miller (1997) considers to be a new paradigm movement in the US. For Hope Filipino, the engagement is similarly practical. In discussing this, I employ the two elements essential to group life: socioemotional orientation and task orientation (Fine 1979). To these I add a third element, opportunities for greater involvement in the form of 'serving in the Kingdom of God'. When these three are considered, one gets a richer view of new paradigm Christianity.

Socioemotional Orientation

The local pastor has identified three important matters to help the Filipino cope with the demands of Singapore living: punctuality, as Filipinos are known for tardiness; financial responsibility, as they have the tendency to be debt-ridden; and management of emotions, as they are away from spouses and families. The last two are typical issues of the migrant Filipino professional, although I focus on the last one as it is most strategically addressed by the congregation. The importance of emotional support for new immigrants has also been identified in Korean Christian churches in the US (Kwon, Ebaugh and Hagan 1997).

Kinship relationships formed in the care groups and shepherding arrangements help Filipinos cope with emotional difficulties. For instance, the usual point of entry for guests is the Matthew Care Group gathering, wherein invited friends are introduced to the rest in an atmosphere of games and food. Once they are comfortable with the 'family', the succeeding gatherings conduct a presentation of the gospel. Furthermore, female shepherds are often called 'nanay', Filipino term for mother. Interestingly, family-orientation as a Filipino value is also employed in the formation of social capital in Asian American religions (Gonzalez and Maison 2004).

Jerebel's narrative reflects a typical story among current members who decided to join Hope Filipino because of the available relationships. I quote her narrative at length:

> Actually, back in the Philippines, I was anti-Christian. If anyone would ask me to come to a Christian church, I would readily tell them that best of friends who talk about politics and religion become best of enemies. I respect your religion, you respect my belief. Let's talk about another topic. That was because I saw the Christians in the Philippines singing in the streets, reading the Bible but I felt their actions were hypocritical. But I was a religious person. I would always lead the rosary and prayer. I would go to a Catholic church regularly on top of the Sunday Mass. To the point that I really wanted to be a nun. When I came to Singapore, my housemates met Daphne [a pioneering Chinese Singaporean at Hope Filipino] and other Christians. Then they came to our place. We were actually doubtful of their motives. They were bringing us food and a lot more. When they invited us to attend church [there was no Filipino congregation then], we went with them. After that, when they came back to us, we tried to avoid them. But they still came back. And so I joined them. And I noticed that at Hope, even if I was alone, I felt I already had a family after service. All of a sudden, I knew a lot of people! And during that time, there were people following up on me. They would come to our house to discuss the Word of God – without missing a weekend. I realized that this was the church where I got family, where they helped me grow, read the Bible and know about God.

Task Orientation

Such socioemotional orientations constructed in the group life (Fine 1979) allow for the individual's life-transformation that in effect is a socialization process to establish the behavioral expectations of and affiliation with the congregation, and ultimately membership. Here, life-transformation, in Fine's (1979) framework, comes in as the task orientation at Hope Filipino. Behavioral expectations are adjusted to biblical standards. Miller observes that 'new paradigm Christians believe that they are continually being humbled and transformed and that it is through daily interaction with God's word that they are given direction' (1997, 130).

At Hope Filipino, however, the process is not completely independent. One's understanding of the Scriptures is shaped in the discipleship contexts of shepherding, care group and the Sunday service, where the church's values are reiterated to both member and new believer, whose conversion takes place by 'accepting Jesus'. Maturity is seen in how the individual concedes to the principles and practices of the congregation and how he/she accounts life details to his/her leader, most likely the shepherd and care leader, depends on the constant interaction available in the discipleship contexts. Official membership simultaneously becomes an individual declaration and a public recognition of one's identification with the community.

With socioemotional orientations and behavioral expectations established in the process of life-transformation through constant interaction in the care group and shepherding, possibilities of free-riding is minimized despite the size of the congregation. This substantiates what Miller (1997, 76) considers to be the 'structure of mentoring and accountability'. The pastor explains:

> We want the people to realize that when you become a member, you are saying that you are one of the family. The family matters. It's just the members who can be part of it. Before the person becomes a member, we'd know the character, lives, needs of the people because it's not so much about coming and going [to and from the congregation].

Helen, a domestic helper to an expatriate household, who now serves as care leader to a group of professionals, recounts her experience being 'discipled' at Hope Filipino:.

> When I received Christ in the church, the leaders never stopped from following up on me. Doctrine, 18 lessons, how to grow as a Christian – all these were discussed in shepherding. I was encouraged in shepherding. Also, this might be the church that has most number of meetings and teachings! Seven days a week, if possible. And then there's the informal follow up, as when they call you up on your handphone. When they called me, they shared the word and they rebuked me too because I was quite tactless. So I was also being corrected.

Greater Involvement

As individuals carry on with the life-transformation process at Hope Filipino, they are entrusted greater responsibilities, such as being part of the care leader's core team handling discussion, leading worship, facilitating group dynamics or even shepherding another person. Functional ministries such as Children's Church and Music Team are also available for participation, granted that the interested individual is first involved in his own care group, where discipleship is essential.

As an individual's involvement in the congregation broadens, one's value-orientation encompasses a scope beyond the self. Shepherding, for example, requires that personal attention shifts to another believer, most likely a recent convert in the care group.

Doing evangelism, which is a strong ethos at Hope Filipino, is another form of expansion of one's value-orientation beyond the self. The global outlook of proselytizing articulated in the vision begins locally, usually by inviting outsiders to care group or church service, understood as 'evacs', shorthand for evangelism. Interviewees have enumerated different ways of accomplishing this, depending on their care groups' targeted individuals: introducing themselves to Filipino passersby along cosmopolitan Orchard Road, going from house to house and even playing tennis with them on weekends. Asked how his care group does evangelism, a male leader explains:

> We have many ways of doing evangelism. But we always pray for the place first. At one time, we went from flat to flat. And we even went into one to pray for the people inside, hoping that God will answer the prayer. When there's a big event in church, especially if

it's Christmas, we go to Lucky Plaza [the shopping center famous for being the hangout for many Filipinos] to invite people to church. Then we have sports evangelism designed for one month. First week, we just play tennis and we don't mention anything about religion. Second week, we play, then we mention one thing about God. Third, [we talk] about God and who we are in the church. Fourth, we invite them to care group. Usually, the fourth week is Matthew Care Group, which is non-threatening for people to get to know one another. Sports evangelism caters for those who work in aerospace, men who are uncomfortable when you start talking about Bible, church or religion.

Construction of Worldview

With opportunities for greater involvement, the 'Kingdom of God' then becomes an experienced reality seen in light of the congregation. The local pastor explains:

> The value I impart to the Filipinos about commitment to church is that we are involved in church activities more than we need to go to work. The rest of the time, we are involved in the lives of the people, care group, shepherding ... The value I always teach is that you are first a Christian, then you are a nurse. You are not a nurse and by chance you are a Christian. Because you carry the name of Christ, you serve God fully first.

This clearly exemplifies what Hunt (1997, 80) considers as 'construction of a worldview' which is important in motivating and supporting 'radical attitudinal or behavioural alteration in terms of the movement's goals and priorities'.

The construction of this worldview that privileges the congregation a central position effectively leads to a 'ritualisation of everyday experience' whereby 'practice and experience evident in services are evident in everyday existence' (Coleman and Collins 2000, 324). Members, for instance, rent a flat together and convert it to a 'ministry house' that allows use for discipleship functions such as shepherding and care group gatherings. Consequently, the everyday life distinctions between public religious and private domestic become blurred.

Furthermore, such understanding of commitment leads to restructuring of lifestyle patterns. Testimonies of personal sacrifices are recounted, such as of lay leaders doing shepherding with a health-care attendant even if just at the gate of the latter's nursing home because of curfew restrictions. Arguably, the most manifest example of restructured lifestyle patterns is in how many have opted to stay in Singapore because of the church. In Singapore, work experience is considered merely a career springboard for many health professionals who want to earn higher in such places as the UK and Australia. Francis, a male unit leader, explains:

> Usually, my commitment is being tested when it comes to major decisions in my life. For example, in my career path. Am I going to follow the worldview or the Biblical view? The view of the worldly man or the view of the Christian? In terms of career, I receive less here in Singapore compared to what I will receive in the UK or US. Four-fold, five-fold our salary. But what made us stay? Because we know that what we are doing for the Lord is more valuable. If you love God, you view the things around you differently.

Here, personal ambition is subjected to the greater calling of 'building the Kingdom of God'. With this consciousness, many of the lay leaders recognize the necessity of evangelism beyond Singapore, as when Sheila, who sees herself involved in church-planting in the future, says:

> enthusiasm for evangelism in my unit is incredible. And it will not stop. If your heart is for evangelism, you will continue doing it. So we would saturate all these MRT [train] stations. But granted that you have invited everyone, would you stop? God said, all nations. So one nation after another.

The value attached to personal profitability has clearly been transferred from one's personal economic gain to the life-conversion of another person. Moreover, witnessing behavioral transformation not only motivates older members to carry on. The 'joy of seeing lives changed' refocuses one's response to personal dilemmas. Leaving the congregation, either when tempted by opportunities abroad or when compelled by internal conflict, becomes a costly choice because of the investments made in relationships therein. This, interestingly, is an extension of Kanter's proposition that 'commitment should be stronger ... if investment and its irreversibility are emphasized' (1968, 506). Furthermore, the irreversibility is reinforced in how violations of this norm among leaders do not go unchallenged. A unit leader explains her conviction:

> If they want to leave Singapore for another country, ultimately they need to check their heart motive. Is this really about continuing the work God has placed in their hands or because they want to pursue their career? If they are leading people here and they want to serve God, why do they have to go there? Unless they are going on a mission, and that is the purpose. So when they go there, it's not really for God, it's for their career. And we have a lot of people who did that who eventually turned away from God.

Locating New Paradigm Christianity

The flexibility in doing church, as when one conducts Matthew Care Group or sports evangelism, points to my contention that cultural relevance is an achievement at Hope Filipino. Such openness to new practices explains why Miller (1997) considers new paradigm Christianity a postdenominational movement, in which rigidity gives way to relevance.

It is this flexible environment that provides space for individuals to be comfortable with the process of life-transformation. Eventually, the individual may assume greater responsibilities in the congregation, which leads to the possibility of commitment-formation as reorganization of worldview, whereby lay participation becomes spontaneous and 'commitment to a particular ministry grows out of an individual's personal experience' (Miller 1997, 138). Such postconversion (or postalternation) lifestyle informs Hope Filipino's congregational identity.

For this, I argue that commitment-formation that places the Kingdom of God central value at Hope Filipino serves as its congregational identity or idioculture which becomes a valid outcome within the flexible institutional space of new paradigm Christianity. Hope Filipino's ability to reorganize one's worldview is achieved as a result of its engagement with the practical concerns of the migrant Filipino, the presence of high-demand mechanisms of accountability overseen by lay leaders and the opportunities for participation whereby one's attention is transferred to another, making the Kingdom of God a tangible reality.

The possibility of commitment-formation in new paradigm Christianity highlights the conceptual limitation in Becker's (1999) congregational models, which, as he admits, does not include the phenomenon of megachurches. Arguably, new paradigm Christianity is in itself a unique congregational model in terms of its openness to continuous re-appropriation given different environments around the world. Lyon (2000), for instance, briefly contrasts American churches with Korean megachurches in terms of their perceptions of wealth. To identify congregational idiosyncracies, empirical focus is called for. Although Becker proposes to drop the particularistic view of congregations in favor of identifying institutional commonalities, Guest (2004) argues for a balance by including in the analysis local contexts to understand congregational life. This becomes even more necessary in trying to understand new paradigm churches given unique contexts, as in the case of the present inquiry's newly emerging congregation of overseas workers in an Asian setting.

Commitment-formation at Hope Filipino needs careful analysis. On one hand, one may expect such worldview reorganization only in sectarian religious organizations. Tipton observes that alternative religions such as the millenarian Christian sect he studies in the US unify 'private life, work, and interpersonal relatings within a single system of moral meanings' (1982, 239). Its members who came out of drug addiction, for instance, are building a physical structure where everyone will relocate in anticipation of Christ's Second Coming.

But on the other hand, the continual reinvention of practices in new paradigm Christianity to appeal to contemporary society may be seen as a largely loose spiritual environment that potentially breeds divergence. Guest (2004) argues for this when he observes that in a Church of England congregation that has embraced a contemporary evangelical spirit, sustained attendance is achieved as a result of public tolerance for various evangelical leanings, from the liberal to the conservative. Strict moral discourse is limited in private interactions so as to 'suppress forces which have previously provoked disinvolvement' especially among the 'elective parochials' whose affiliation with the congregation is temporary because of labor force mobility (2004, 83). With this, Guest (2004, 82) reminds the reader that 'beliefs and values are often heterogeneous, even within so-called "evangelical" congregations' among which he includes successful megachurches.

While this chapter does not provide representation of global new paradigm Christianity, I argue that a closer look at new paradigm congregations is necessary to comprehend its distinctiveness as a religious phenomenon. It is rather dismissive to assume, as suggested in Guest (2004), that new paradigm Christianity's propensity for reinvention and its greater concern for tolerance over divergence, are the only bases for its success. Neglected in the local analysis are opportunities for life-transformation and greater involvement, signifying levels of strictness with regards to faith issues that inform behavioral expectations. With this, one may locate new paradigm congregations such as Hope Filipino in the middle of Tipton's and Guest's propositions presented above because of their ability to offer cultural relevance and discipleship mechanisms. The strength and future of new paradigm Christianity, which is arguably an extension of Charismatic Christianity (Percy 2003), lies in its ability to balance strictness and appeal.

One may articulate the uniqueness of new paradigm Christianity through the framework of detraditionalization within the religious milieu. Woodhead and Heelas (2000) describe new paradigm Christianity as less radically detraditionalized in the sense that it balances individual experience with biblical authority. Individual experience speaks of the engagement with the issues of the people. Miller (1997, 184–185) argues that the American new paradigm churches are addressing the deficit in 'human community' largely among the baby boomers whose countercultural values rally against the conventions of mainline denominations. Picking up Guest's (2004) proposition about the importance of local contexts, which becomes more important given the flexible environment within new paradigm Christianity, one sees the distinctiveness of commitment-formation at Hope Filipino.

Bibliography

Balmer, Randall, and Lauren Winner. 2002. *Protestantism in America*. New York: Columbia University Press.

Barker, Irwin and Raymond Currie. 1985. 'Do Converts Always Make the Most Committed Christians?' *Journal for the Scientific Study of Religion* 24: 305–313.

Becker, Penny. 1999. *Congregations in Conflict: Cultural Models of Local Religious Life.* Cambdridge: Cambridge University Press.

Coleman, Simon, and Peter Collins. 2000. 'The "Plain" and the "Positive": Ritual, Experience and Aesthetics in Quakerism and Charismatic Christianity.' *Journal of Contemporary Religion* 15: 317–329.

Connell, John. 2005 'Hillsong: A Megachurch in the Sydney Suburbs.' *Australian Geographer* 36: 315–332.

Cruz, Joseph. 2006. 'A Spectacle of Worship: Technology, Modernity and the Rise of the Christian Megachurch.' Paper presented at the Workshop on Religion and Technology in Contemporary Asia, Asia Research Institute, National University of Singapore, January 19 – 20.

Fine, Gary. 1979. 'Small Groups and Culture Creation: The Idioculture of Little League Baseball Teams.' *American Sociological Review* 44: 733–745.

Gonzalez, Joaquin, and Andrea Maison. 2004. 'We do not Bowl Alone: Social and Cultural Capital from Filipinos and their Churches.' In Tony Carnes and Fenggang Yang, eds, *Asian American Religions: The Making and Remaking of Borders and Boundaries*, NY: New York University Press. 338–359.

Guest, Mathew. 2004. '"Friendship, Fellowship and Acceptance": The Public Discourse of a Thriving Evangelical Congregation.' In Mathew Guest, Karin Tusting, and Linda Woodhead, eds, *Congregational Studies in the UK: Christianity in a Post-Christian Context*, Aldershot: Ashgate. 71–84.

——, Karin Tusting, and Linda Woodhead. 2004. 'Congregational Studies: Taking Stock.' In Mathew Guest, Karin Tusting, and Linda Woodhead, eds, *Congregational*

Studies in the UK: Christianity in a Post-Christian Context, Aldershot: Ashgate. 1–23.

Hunt, Stephen. 1997. '"Doing the Stuff": The Vineyard Connection.' In Stephen Hunt, Malcolm Hamilton, and Tony Walter, eds, *Charismatic Christianity*, London: St. Martin's Press. 77–96.

Iannaccone, Laurence. 1994. 'Why Strict Churches are Strong.' *The American Journal of Sociology* 99: 1180–1211.

Kanter, Rosabeth Moss. 1968. 'Commitment and Social Organization: A Study of Commitment Mechanisms in Utopian Communities.' *American Sociological Review* 33: 499–517.

Kwon, V., H. Ebaugh, and J. Hagan. 1997. 'The Structure and Functions of Cell Group Ministry in a Korean Christian Church.' *Journal for the Scientific Study of Religion* 36: 247–256.

Lyon, David. 2000. *Jesus in Disneyland: Religion in Postmodern Times.* Cambridge: Polity Press.

Miller, Donald. 1997. *Reinventing American Protestantism: Christianity in the Next Millennium.* Berkeley: University of California Press.

——. 1998. 'Postdenominational Christianity in the Twenty-First Century.' *Annals of the American Academy of Political and Social Science* 558: 196–210.

Percy, Martyn. 2003. 'A Place at High Table? Assessing the Future of Charismatic Christianity.' In Grace David, Paul Heelas, and Linda Woodhead, eds, *Predicting Religion: Christian, Secular and Alternative Futures*, Aldershot: Ashgate. 95–108.

Roberts, Michael and James Davidson. 1984. 'The Nature and Sources of Religious Involvement.' *Review of Religious Research* 25: 334–350.

Shibley, Mark. 1998. 'Contemporary Evangelicals: Born-Again and World Affirming.' *Annals of the American Academy of Political and Social Science* 558: 67–87.

Tipton, Steven. 1982. *Getting Saved from the Sixties: Moral Meaning in Conversion and Cultural Change.* Berkeley: University of California Press.

Twitchell, James. 2006. *Where Men Hide.* New York: Columbia University Press.

Woodhead, Linda, and Paul Heelas, eds. 2000. *Religion in Modern Times: An Interpretive Anthology.* Oxford: Blackwell.

Chapter Six

A Peaceable Common:
Gathered Wisdom from Exemplar
Muslim and Christian Peacemakers[1]

Kevin S. Reimer, Alvin C. Dueck, Joshua P. Morgan and Deborah E. Kessel

The Holy Prophet Mohammed came into this world and taught us: That man is a Muslim who never hurts anyone by word or deed but who works for the benefit and happiness of God's creatures.

Abdul Ghaffar Khan

Peace is not merely a distant goal that we seek but a means by which we arrive at that goal.

Rev. Dr. Martin Luther King, Jr.

This chapter reviews gathered wisdom of exemplary Muslim and Christian peacemakers from around the world. At this juncture in Western history it is important to consider the peacemaking practices of notable Muslims and Christians who effect positive change in often difficult circumstances. These people have much to teach us. Together they work for peace with persons of different ethnic and religious backgrounds, pushing through failures in the hope of a greater goal, that of mutuality and trust. Our chapter is about their stories and religious meaning frameworks, following seminal work on moral exemplarity by Anne Colby and William Damon (1992).[2] These authors famously interviewed nominated exemplars given to acts of caring and social concern. Participant narratives revealed coherent purposes directed toward the needs of others, defined as *moral identity*. The Colby and Damon study found that exemplars think about the self in ways that reflect systematic organization of moral knowledge derived from diverse situations and relationships. Following this work, our approach to exemplar peacemakers assumes moral identity in terms of unified knowledge given to specific goals in conflict

1   This work was generously funded by the United States Department of Justice. The *Interfaith Conflict Transformation* grant was awarded to Fuller Theological Seminary and Salaam Institute of Peace Studies.

2   For several decades the work of Lawrence Kohlberg dominated the field of moral psychology, focused on the efficacy of justice in moral reasoning. This paradigm virtually ignored the real-world behaviors of people commonly considered to be morally outstanding. Colby and Damon's (1992) study of care exemplars identified this gap with great effect, subsequently altering the course of investigation for many researchers in the field.

mediation. Exemplar participants were from distinct religious traditions, yet we found their stories to demonstrate a significant number of similarities; a peaceable common of shared moral conviction.

Our main goal was to study how exemplar peacemakers from religious backgrounds understand peace as both attitude and practice. To this end, we implemented a mixed-method research design in two complementary moves. In the first move, we summarize findings from a qualitative analysis of narrative responses from exemplar Muslim and Christian peacemakers (Dueck et al. 2007).[3] For this aspect of the study, we solicited nominations of notable peacemakers from a network of scholars engaged in a project on conflict transformation between Muslims and Christians. Criteria for nomination included demonstrated commitment to exceptional peacemaking practices and open identification with either Muslim or Christian faith. While a few exemplars were involved in peacemaking activity of global prominence, the majority laboured quietly in the trenches with local groups, tribes or parties. A number of participants were engaged in conflict mediation in the Middle East or Asia, including politically volatile regions such as Kashmir.[4] Thirteen exemplars from each faith tradition were interviewed. Questions were open-ended and included items from the Life Narrative Interview (McAdams 1997).[5] Peacemaker narratives were subsequently analyzed using *grounded theory* (Strauss and Corbin 1998). A well-known qualitative research technique, grounded theory is used to identify general themes that emerge from subjective coding of individual response data. This process was undertaken with the assistance of a coding software program, resulting in a total of 163 codes that were distilled into five themes.

The second move used a computational knowledge model known as *latent semantic analysis* (LSA).[6] Combined with two multivariate statistical procedures, LSA was used to provide an empirical analysis of similarity and dissimilarity between Muslim and Christian themes identified through the first move of the study. LSA offered two advantages as a complement to the initial qualitative move. First, the model helped provide an objective check on qualitative themes. If the conceptual process that precedes identification of themes is robustly defined and consistently applied across response data, we expect that themes represent similar meaning

---

3 A detailed report of qualitative findings from the study may be found in Dueck et al. (2007 The qualitative research summary provided in the present chapter is purposefully aligned with a second, quantitative methodology. This mixed-method approach attempts to answer a research question not previously considered in publication.

4 Identifying information was removed or altered for all exemplar participant quotations in this chapter. We are purposefully vague in describing the specific contexts and activities of participating peacemakers in the interest of maintaining confidentiality.

5 The Life Narrative Interview is a qualitative instrument that elicits responses related to personal identity and self-understanding.

6 LSA is one of several programs in the field of computational linguistics that attempts to mimic human knowledge distribution, retrieval and association. The mathematical architecture of the model is similar to factor analysis in multivariate statistics. An excellent preamble to LSA is found in Landauer et al. (1998). Additional information and publications on the LSA method may be obtained at http://lsa.colorado.edu

for Muslims and Christians alike. By providing a similarity comparison between narratives, LSA offers an empirical yardstick to measure knowledge embedded in participant responses. Second, LSA can be used to 'map' distributions of peacemaking knowledge. It is entirely possible that, while much peacemaking knowledge is shared between Muslim and Christian exemplars, there are subtle differences in the way that knowledge is distributed. Differences in meaning distribution may reflect nuanced interpretations particular to religious traditions. In this manner we report integrated findings from two different methodologies applied to the same narrative response data.

Qualitative Analysis of Peacemaker Narratives

Theme 1: Peacemaking Methodology

The peacemaking methodology theme refers to strategies and practices of establishing a lasting peace. In many instances peacemaking methodology appeared as an aggregate of the four themes described below. We quickly discovered that peacemaking methodology is adaptive and fluid, evolving to accommodate impasse situations or moments where misunderstanding threatens constructive dialogue. In one Muslim exemplar's words:

> We hung in there for about a year. The whole idea was to come open-minded, to represent our points of view, to listen to theirs and to find the areas where we disagreed and could not come to agreement, and the areas where we had flexibility. And like I said, we were able to do that up to a certain point, when we got to redline issues for both sides. But we couldn't resolve the redline issues. So we felt that instead of trying to force each other to change views, we would instead just continue in the spirit of friendship and dialogue without trying to resolve these major issues beforehand.

A similar perspective was evident in a Christian peacemaker's narrative:

> I will not say the conflict was resolved, it was just we were able to make one positive step and so in that way it was a success. But in that particular case our strategy was twofold – one was that we wanted to listen to them and have face-to-face exchange. In many Asian relationships this is very important and so we wanted to establish face-to-face relationship and in that setting to listen to them and try to break down some of the stereotypes and accusations which can be made at a distance but which take on a different form when you are face-to-face. The second strategy was that in our earlier talks we had called for a ceasefire among all the indigenous groups.

Peacemaking methodology was readily evident in exemplar ability to take on the perspectives of others. Implementation of peacemaking strategies was sensitized to the needs and perceptions of everyone present. In the above quotation, the Muslim exemplar's peacemaking methodology emphasizes a 'spirit of friendship and dialogue', entering into peace negotiation with malleable goals and the ability to walk away without closure. The exemplar speaks for other participants in that peacemaking methodology conforms to relationships, requiring situational learning and adaptation in addition to technique. The importance of cultural sensitivity in successful perspective-taking cannot be overemphasized. The Christian exemplar insists on methodology that respects local requirements for social courtesy as part of the mediation process, particularly where space is created for everyone to 'save face'.

Theme 2: Ideological Commitment

The ideological commitment theme reflects those perspectives, opinions and beliefs directly informed by the religious faith of exemplar peacemakers. This theme was larger than philosophical anecdotes or existential reflections. Instead, ideological commitment underlined the force of religious convictions directed toward the greater goal of peace. Peacemakers readily integrated ideological language into their responses, suggesting that religion was significant to their continued motivation to work with others. In a Christian exemplar's narrative:

> When people have a conflict about a moral issue that means there is at least two or three different perspectives. Often people are on one side that does not have a good understanding of the other perspective. But they are morally obligated to try to understand the other perspective. In this environment, it is not going to be an easy thing. But I think we have something to offer. As a Christian, I see peacemaking as the core of New Testament teaching with the politics of Jesus as the core of peacemaking.

The deeply personal nature of ideological commitment was evident in a Muslim exemplar's response:

> Being mature in your faith is not worrying about what other people think or say about you. It's that you're at peace with yourself and your relationship with God. And then you can move from that place of peace into bringing that to other people. And then your life is in service of God, seeking the pleasure of God. And the way I look at it, too, God describes faith as light, which is a theme that exists in all the texts of religion and spirituality. You bring that light to the world so that when you've achieved that peace and sense of maturity, you're a source of light in other people's lives. We never get to that point of completion because human beings are not perfect. But you're emerging all the time and moving towards that. When you say mature, it almost sounds like you're finished, but no one is ever finished.

Interestingly, we found that ideological commitment in exemplar responses did not impugn other religious worldviews in peacemaking contexts. In other words, ideological commitment avoided exclusivity, serving instead as an invitation for others to delve into their own belief systems in order to better understand shared values toward successful mediation. The Christian exemplar quotation is modeled on the politics of Jesus while acknowledging that peace is hardly exclusive ideological property of the Christian faith. This stance is probably difficult to uphold in practice, requiring added effort from involved parties. However, the rewards are considerable from a peacemaking vantage where commitment to particular religious tradition makes appreciation of other traditions valid and authentic. This process is beautifully described by the Muslim exemplar on the basis of 'faith' and 'light', those common dimensions of religious conviction that contribute to a meaningful peace dialogue while affirming unique views of transcendence in the conversation. Peace exemplars appeal for dialogue where everyone's ideological commitment is required for the sake of mutual understanding and personal growth.

Theme 3: Pragmatism

The pragmatism theme refers to a realistic appraisal of whether peace interventions are effective or ineffective. Pragmatism emphasizes practicality and consistency in peacemaking. Pragmatism is given to concrete peacemaking interventions with the hope that others will understand issues and potential directions for restitution. For one Muslim exemplar:

> We have a Jewish partner who initiated a play. The children wrote the play. It's a hit here in our city. It's going to go national. Then we're building interfaith homes. We're planning on building homes next year. President Carter is going to come work on it. See, that's where my effort has switched now. Before, it was prayer service and dialogue. Now the effort and focus is doing things together, building homes, doing a play with the kids, doing blood drives, practical things. When we do things, we build confidence; get to know each other better.

A similar pragmatic vision is evident in the response of a Christian exemplar:

> Basically, they try to be a nonviolent presence in the middle of the conflict. They take risks themselves. They make sacrifices for the purpose of trying to reduce the level of violence between the two communities. If they have to physically stand between the two groups they will do that. If they need to accompany a child from one place to another, say from home to school or if they need to accompany a farmer going to his fields, they will do that. They will be a presence to reduce the violence to reduce the conflict.

The Muslim peacemaker illustrates the necessity of incorporating practical issues such as physical and psychological needs (shelter, recreation) into the peace process. Rather than focus on abstract dimensions of interpersonal communication, simple practices are emphasized. The relationships forged around these practices engender trust, anticipating the growth of communities in which peace can flourish. The Christian exemplar provides additional examples such as providing a child with safe passage to school. In both instances it seems clear that pragmatic interventions with the greatest likelihood of success are those that bring people together, forging new pathways for understanding.

Theme 4: Personalization

The personalization theme refers to the manner by which individuals understand peacemaking in relation to the self. Personalization is best captured by the idea of ownership and personal responsibility. A Christian exemplar noted:

> I genuinely wanted to be able to have a more open dialogue with the Jewish people on campus. I do not want them to think I am anti-Semitic. They have told me before that they

think I am anti-Semitic and I want to explain that I do not dislike them, that I have nothing against them. I just have a different view on this conflict.

Personalization was often conjoined with leadership, as in the account of a Muslim exemplar:

Well, as the person who runs the mosque and promotes it, I felt particularly responsible for this guy being allowed in. And I try to advertise so that only people who we know and trust know about the mosque. I felt kind of responsible. But mostly, what was important was the safety of other members and keeping the space safe.

The Christian exemplar feels personal responsibility regarding perceptions of his campus efforts on behalf of Palestinians. The exemplar is typical of interviewed peacemakers in his deep sense of personal investment in the peace process and the manner by which peacemaking efforts are interpreted. In many instances, examples of personalization emerged through accounts of participant efforts to lead others. The Muslim exemplar personalizes his work as a cleric who publicly expounds the value of peace. Reflecting their roles as leaders, exemplars generally favor direct involvement as participants in conflict rather than deferring responsibility to third parties. The majority of exemplars come to define themselves in terms of peacemaking, constructing meaning on the basis of personal experiences undertaken in the interest of conflict transformation.

Theme 5: Community

The community theme indicates relationships and group affiliation that empowers peacemakers to do their work. Community describes the interpersonal environment in which the peacemaker lives, emphasizing the value of a reliable support system. The community theme reflects many groups identified by peacemakers, including faith community, mentor figures, family and peer associations or personal friendships. For one Muslim exemplar, community took on a civic flavor consonant with newly acquired citizenship:

I remember the day I was sworn in to be a US citizen. I was so happy. I had my wife, my child and my in-laws all around me as I raised my hand for the first time in my life ever to be a citizen or to be recognized. I was never a citizen of any country. I was a refugee and now to be a citizen, to pledge to protect the country in non-combatant ways and to be someone, it was something I don't think I can find words to describe; in a simple act of extending citizenship to someone you are restoring human faith and telling that person you are someone not just as a number or known as this, you are somebody, you count and you are one of us. It just was overwhelming to me.

Community looked somewhat different for a Christian exemplar who underlined the importance of therapy and close attachments through a particularly difficult time:

I was very depressed, and I needed to go see a counselor mostly because I had no direction. I did not know where I was going. I realized that God had not called me to church ministry as I had thought. At that time also, I was in between relationships. I had hoped to be dating someone and I was not. Since then I have got married, and that helped a lot. Yeah, I even had some thoughts of suicide at that time. I do not know if there were really a lot of specifics. I guess you could say I have lived somewhat of a boring life that did not have anything positive or negative. I had a couple of close friends at the time that talked me into seeing a counselor. The counseling experience was not extraordinarily good or bad. I guess I was looking for a purpose in my life.

Social support was noteworthy in every peacemaker interview. In the Muslim exemplar's narrative, national identity provides a newfound community that frames peacemaking commitment. Citizenship offered this individual a moral charge to engage others in conflict mediation. On these grounds, community is combined with a larger civic identity on the basis of membership in a pluralistic society. Alternatively, a Christian exemplar relates experiences of vocational crisis to more selective attachments in therapy and close intimates. We wondered if religious and cultural differences were at least partly responsible for somewhat divergent accounts of community in the lives of exemplars. In the main, community identification gave peacemakers hope that their efforts were worth the tremendous frustrations and setbacks that often characterize the conflict resolution process.

In summary, the purpose of the first methodological move was to explore thematic content describing peacemaking attitudes and practices. The richly lived experiences of those Muslim and Christian exemplar peacemakers interviewed for this study suggest that peacemaking flourishes when participants maintain a posture of open-mindedness. Open-minded embrace of other perspectives is modeled by exemplars as both virtue and invitation to peacemaking dialogue. Like the participants from Colby and Damon's work, peace exemplars manage the ambiguities of their efforts with highly practical strategies designed to mobilize the assets of involved parties. This practical bent is designed to garner local ownership of projects that creatively engage individuals in a manner that fosters trusting relationship. Exemplars identify themselves with communities of support that nurture, challenge and reinforce core religious commitments. For the combined sample group, moral identity related to peace and conflict mediation is extended from cherished religious principles. By their own testimony, it appears that exemplars would not likely continue their peacemaking efforts in the absence of their religious convictions.

Latent Semantic Analysis of Qualitative Themes

The second methodological move included the use of LSA to analyze the five themes identified above. It was our intention that LSA would provide an empirical comparison of knowledge reflected in themes outlined through the first move. As a cousin of artificial intelligence, LSA is able to compare the similarity and dissimilarity of knowledge within texts such as peacemaker narratives. Additionally, we wanted to use LSA to map peacemaking knowledge in a manner that would facilitate comparison between religious traditions. We hoped that this additional step would clarify the manner by which exemplars think about their own peacemaking practice. LSA offered an opportunity to assess peacemaking attitudes and practices that are latent or otherwise unobserved in participant responses.

For the present study, we wanted to consider peacemaking knowledge on the basis of similarity and dissimilarity in peacemaker narratives. The analysis was premised upon the five themes as found in Muslim peacemaker narratives and the same five themes in Christian narratives. Taken together, the ten narratives were compared to 77 survey item stems from the Just Peacemaking Inventory, a self-report instrument of peacemaking principles (JPI).[7] The rationale for including JPI item stems was to provide a domain that would serve as a peacemaking 'knowledge yardstick' for comparison of the ten narratives. By triangulating religious peacemaker narratives with a survey of peacemaking knowledge, we expected to gain an understanding of similarity or difference between narratives by religious tradition. Multi-dimensional scaling (MDS) and hierarchical cluster analysis (HCA) were used to map and cluster narrative themes, respectively. The MDS map with HCA clusters are provided as an integrated presentation in Figure 6.1.

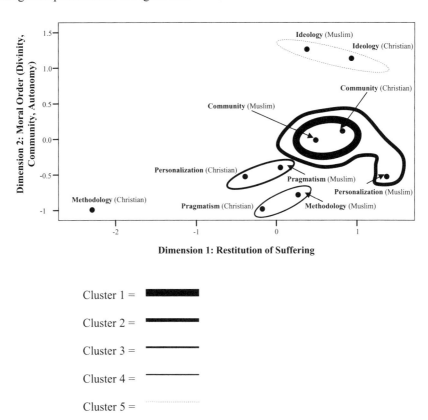

Figure 6.1   Multidimensional scaling dimensions and hierarchical cluster analysis clusters for Muslim and Christian narrative themes

7   See Brown et al. (2008).

Dimension 1: Restitution of Suffering

MDS maps variables in any space where the basis for comparison is unknown or undefined. The interpretation of MDS dimensions is subjective, based on how variables are arrayed from positive to negative poles. Dimension 1 corresponds with the horizontal axis in Figure 6.1. Our interpretation of Dimension 1 is based on the horizontal distribution of theme variables across the map by religious tradition. We found the cross-cultural work of Richard Shweder to be particularly helpful for interpreting MDS dimensions of narrative meaning in peacemaker responses (Shweder et al. 1997).[8] Shweder et al. outline experiences of suffering in the morality of indigenous peoples from India and other cultures. Much peacemaking activity occurs in morally charged circumstances that involve suffering and injustice. Shweder et al. provide a culturally and religiously sensitive appraisal of these issues along with an awareness of local conflicts and moral imperatives to mitigate suffering. Shweder's theory offers a broad horizon for attitudes and practices appropriate to the present sample of Muslim and Christian exemplar peacemakers.

In the MDS map, the distribution of Dimension 1 variables resembled cultural explanations and resolutions for suffering as outlined by Shweder et al. As a result, we labeled Dimension 1 'Restitution of Suffering'. Shweder et al. propose three culturally defined bases for coping with suffering, including (a) moral, (b) interpersonal and (c) biomedical. We trace our discussion of Dimension 1 with the use of these categories spread across arbitrary boundaries for *positive pole* to include points to the right of 0.5, *midrange* to include points between 0.5 and –0.5, and *negative pole* to the left of –0.5. Consonant with the exploratory nature of LSA analyses, our discussion is deliberately suggestive and descriptive.

Positive Pole: Moral Restitution   Shweder et al. outline moral restitution in terms of 'confession' or 'sacrifice' upholding a sense of personal responsibility for suffering. We observed that the positive pole of Dimension 1 included themes in Muslim Personalization, Christian Community and Christian Ideology.[9] The element of personal responsibility is illustrated through several Muslim peacemaker narratives, notably in one individual's concern for the local mosque and its public reputation (Personalization).[10] Similarly, Christian narratives of Ideological Commitment demonstrated moral obligation to understand the perspectives of others, realized in part through the politics of Jesus Christ (Christian Ideology). Finally, Christian narratives reflecting upon community influence described specific moral influences encouraging peacemakers to place personal needs and agendas aside for the sake of the greater good (Christian Community).

---

8   Shweder's (1997) work is interdisciplinary, weaving together cultural anthropology, sociology and psychology in his study of moral functioning.

9   The *ideological commitment* and *peacemaking methodology* themes identified in the first section of the study are abbreviated to 'ideology' and 'methodology' for Muslims and Christians in the second section. This change was made to reduce clutter in Figure 6.1.

10 Because of chapter space limitations we are unable to provide quotations to illustrate.

Midrange: Interpersonal Restitution   Not surprisingly, interpersonal relationship
was a common emphasis in the peacemaking practice of Muslim and Christian
exemplars. Shweder et al. suggest that interpersonal restitution reflects action
intended to repair or improve relationships. Along the Dimension 1 continuum,
midrange themes included Muslim Community, Muslim Pragmatism, Muslim
Ideology, Muslim Peacemaking Methodology, Christian Pragmatism and Christian
Personalization. The position of these themes on Dimension 1 suggests that all make
use of relational knowledge in peacemaking. As examples, relational language was
evident through a civic aspect of interpersonal restitution embedded in the process
of becoming a US citizen (Muslim Community). Others emphasized practical
approaches in building interfaith relationships to promote collective confidence
toward peace interests (Muslim Pragmatism). We found that interpersonal restitution
might also be extended to God, particularly where the divine posits moral expectations
for exemplar relationships with others (Muslim Ideology). Recurrent emphasis upon
dialogue was evident in exemplar efforts to restore and sustain relationships toward
peace (Muslim Peacemaking Methodology). Violence prevention was implied
through interpersonal restitution forming a bridge across a conflict-induced gap
(Christian Pragmatism). Finally, the interpersonal element was explicit in exemplar
desire for broken relationships to be repaired (Christian Personalization).

Negative Pole: Biomedical Restitution   Figure 6.1 depicts an outlier variable in
Christian Peacemaking Methodology. In LSA, the distal position of a variable
suggests that the discourse typical of the narrative in question differs markedly from
knowledge contained in other narratives. We found the Shweder et al. framework
to be particularly helpful in providing interpretation for this surprise finding at the
negative pole of Dimension 1. Shweder et al. identify a third aspect of restitution
for suffering on biomedical grounds, typified by material interventions. Moral
responsibility is often extended beyond individuals to include a global or 'enlightened'
reference to a common enemy. In the biomedical view, physical suffering is the evil
opponent which medical science seeks to defeat. Along the same lines, we found
that Christian peacemakers tended to underline violence rather than any person or
group of people as the moral scapegoat. This subtle difference effectively redirects
culpability for suffering and injustice, emphasizing conflict as an abstraction that
does not jeopardize tacit commitments to democratic pluralism and tolerance.

Dimension 2: Moral Order (Divinity, Community, Autonomy)

A critical question in the cultural study of religion and morality includes the manner
by which people organize moral standards with the guidance of internal and external
reference points. From their intercultural work on the Indian subcontinent, Shweder
et al. arrive at their 'big three' interpretations of Moral Order. These include (a)
divinity, or moral reference to the transcendent realm, (b) community, or moral
reference to group norms for behavior and (c) autonomy, or individual locus of moral
agency and responsibility. We trace the big three aspects of moral order through
our interpretation of Dimension 2. As with the descriptive approach taken with

Dimension 1, we located the *positive pole* to include points above 0.5, *midrange* to include points between 0.5 and –0.5, and *negative pole* below –0.5.

Positive Pole: Divinity   The positive pole of Dimension 2 is anchored by Muslim Ideological Commitment and Christian Ideological Commitment themes. Both religious narratives explicitly reference divinity as a basis for peacemaking. For Shweder et al., the divinity aspect of the moral order refers to natural and metaphysical dimensions of experience that confer a sacred hierarchy of which humans are a part. Muslim exemplars in this instance make note of moral obligations toward peace. To paraphrase their responses, we are to bring light to the world as moral agents in the divine economy. Christian exemplars referenced peacemaking as a moral obligation within the Christian sacred order. Peacemaking is an extension of core New Testament teachings that reflect a political agenda for Jesus. For both religious traditions, divinity is imbued in social and personal ethics that hold peace in the highest esteem.

Midrange: Community   There can be little doubt that group norms and community obligations constrain moral functioning in cultures around the world. Filial duty to one's community and kin is consummated through recognition of hierarchies that promote order. Several themes were distributed across the midrange section of Dimension 2, including Christian Community, Muslim Community and Muslim Pragmatism. We observed that the Christian Community narratives included references to intimate relationships reflecting close support. Several of the Muslim Community narratives reached even further into social bases for moral self-understanding, upholding a morality derived from status as world citizen. Similarly, Muslim Pragmatism narratives emphasized community volunteerism as peacemaking.

Negative Pole: Autonomy   The negative pole of Dimension 2 was interpreted in terms of autonomy in the moral order. This is the language of democratic rights typical of deontological and utilitarian moralities. Autonomy is clearly associated with individual agency. Narrative themes at this pole included Muslim Personalization, Muslim Peacemaking Methodology, Christian Personalization, Christian Pragmatism and Christian Peacemaking Methodology. We noted that the Muslim Personalization narratives often described obligation with reference to guilt, a self-conscious emotion category that in moderation predicts positive moral functioning (Tangney and Mashek 2004). We found that Muslim Peacemaking Methodology narratives were centered on different points of view, discovering each party's personal preferences. To us it seemed that the individual choice and liberty of each person was respected as an explanation of differences. By contrast, the Christian Personalization narratives were replete with first person singular references, grounding responsibility on individual rights. In step with the personalization theme, Christian Pragmatism narratives emphasized the individuality of constituents engaged in peace activity, emphasizing personal risk through choice. Finally, Christian Peacemaking Methodology narratives highlighted a fairly individualized cadre of personal preferences for peace strategy.

Cluster Analysis: Reflections on LSA Findings

A primary reason for using LSA with narrative themes was to provide an unsupervised comparison of Muslim and Christian exemplar attitudes and peacemaking practices. Cluster analysis provides a way to identify latent statistical relationships between variables as identified through LSA. In addition to the visual map provided by MDS, cluster analysis offers an improved picture of what narratives share knowledge (similarity) or represent different knowledge (dissimilarity). For the present study, the HCA solution favored a five-cluster interpretation. Figure 6.1 presents clusters in graded order as indicated by the thickness of boundary lines around variables. Cluster 1 included both Muslim and Christian Community themes. Cluster 2 added Muslim Personalization to Cluster 1. Cluster 3 combined Muslim Pragmatism with Christian Personalization. Cluster 4 enclosed Muslim Methodology and Christian Pragmatism. Finally, Cluster 5 encompassed Muslim Ideology and Christian Ideology themes.

The cluster analysis raised interesting issues in our effort to cross-validate qualitative coding while looking for nuanced differences in Muslim and Christian exemplar responses. First, we note that Cluster 1 and Cluster 5 combined the same themed narratives from both religious traditions. This validates the conceptual robustness of the two themes as understood in terms of latent meaning through peacemaker narratives. When combined with clustering, the LSA move suggests that community and ideological commitment themes are prominent in the shared attitudes and practices of exemplar peacemakers. The dimensional location of the clusters underlines the significance of moral restitution in exemplar attitudes toward the alleviation of suffering in peacemaking practice (Dimension 1), a perspective that potentially originates through moral sensitivities identified in divinity and community (Dimension 2). One interpretation for these findings is that the moral impetus of peacemaking practice is deeply rooted in religious commitments. The relationship between morality and religion is complex, with a truncated empirical history in the psychological research literature (Walker and Reimer 2005).[11] Nevertheless, it does appear that moral exemplarity (of which the Muslim and Christian peacemakers in the present study are a case) is conjoined with religious commitment. If moral functioning grows in and through social cues afforded by context, then the prominence of community and ideological commitment themes in the present study implies that effective peacemaking is larger than any individual. Exemplars approach peacemaking venues and conversations backed by a hidden community of religiously oriented support. Individual exemplars at the negotiating table represent larger communitarian and ideological objectives ratified by their religious traditions. Effectiveness in peacemaking practice affirms a peaceable

---

11 The reluctance of morality researchers to engage religion is somewhat puzzling. Until recently, empirical researchers tended to discount religion as a domain separate from moral functioning. Walker and Reimer (2005) argue that this is an artificial distinction, particularly for exemplars in the present study who demonstrate closely intertwined moral and religious commitments.

common that includes thicker religious particularity (Walzer 1996).[12] This contrasts starkly with the time-honored precept that religion is a divisive influence unwelcome in the public forum where peacemaking occurs.

It would be foolhardy to conclude that exemplars exclusively or even routinely use religious language in peacemaking dialogue or practice. Thin language of democratic priorities and Kantian justice is directly indicated in peacemaker practice. Indeed, cluster 2 suggests that Muslim Personalization is associated with Community (Cluster 1) but is expressed in more autonomous moral language owing to its location on Dimension 2. Clusters 3 and 4 are similarly located at the autonomy end of the moral continuum, reflecting discourse laden with deontological and utilitarian justice ethics. Given the interpersonal location of Clusters 3 and 4 on Dimension 1, we believe that peacemaking critically depends upon deontological and utilitarian moral language in order to facilitate constructive dialogue. Exemplar practice of peace, while founded upon community and ideological commitment motifs reflecting deep religious commitment, is importantly expressed using the language of the democratic public square.

Nuanced differences exist in the manner by which peacemaking interventions are described and implemented. Cluster 3 suggests that Muslim Pragmatism shares considerable knowledge with Christian Personalization. We might conclude from this finding that obligation and personal responsibility are hallmark characteristics of Muslim attitudes toward peace. While autonomous in their moral orientation, both themes are geared toward interpersonal restitution of suffering. Cluster 4 suggests that Muslim Peacemaking Methodology and Christian Pragmatism are also similar in terms of shared knowledge. Again, moral autonomy and interpersonal restitution characterize the peacemaking strategies and attitudes typical of exemplars. The fact that both groups of exemplar peacemakers base their work on cherished religious principles and community means that these differences may be local to tradition, or even further, the personalities of the individual exemplars in question. However, the somewhat odd theme combinations found in Clusters 3 and 4 commend interpretative caution. In the most pessimistic view, the findings suggest that clustered themes may be confounded. At best, the broader implications of similarities and differences reviewed in this discussion should be considered exploratory and tentative pending further quantitative study.

Conclusion

It was our goal to consider how peacemakers from Muslim and Christian religious traditions construct meaning regarding peacemaking attitudes and practices. While participant experiences offer hints rather than prescriptions for effective peacemaking, we do believe that study observations are useful to peace education both within and between religious traditions. Interpreting the complex meanings endemic to

---

12 Walzer (1996) argues that morality is imbued with cultural referents derived from the anthropology of Clifford Geertz. Morality reflects both 'thick' dimensions of ethnic and religious tradition and 'thin' discourse typical of the democratic public square.

peacemaker responses is not an easy prospect. Recognizing the importance of religious and cultural context in this discussion, we offer two summary observations.

First, a peaceable common between Muslim and Christian peacemakers begins with religious tradition and ends with practices characterized by openness and perspective-taking. At one level this suggests that effective peacemakers are comfortable with their own religious beliefs and committed to the practice of religious principles. Belief supports underlying moral commitments inherent to peacemaking. Research on moral exemplarity points to transcendent belief systems beneath the commitments of many exemplars (Colby and Damon 1992; MacIntyre 1991).[13] Yet exemplars do not manifest religious beliefs with the express intent of imposing values on others in conflict dialogue. Instead, religion for these individuals appears to function as a form of moral sustenance. Particular beliefs may play into exemplar peacemaking interventions but only as an invitation for others to resource their own religious traditions toward the goal of building bridges under the auspices of peace. It should be noted that religion is not a necessary prerequisite to moral functioning. Where religion does exist, however, it can be leveraged toward moral goals that are expressed in openness and perspective-taking potentially able to transform previously intractable situations. Exemplars proved to be masters of this complex and socially delicate balancing act.

Second, a peaceable common between Muslim and Christian peacemakers upholds the importance of multi-lingual capability in the public forum of conflict mediation. While exemplars might easily default to their own religiously-informed moral categories in peacemaking discourse, they expend considerable effort to locate ethical language that is commensurable, understood by everyone present. In situations where Western priorities of democracy and individualism are operative, exemplars demonstrate a marked fluency in deontological and utilitarian moral language. Perhaps more impressive, exemplars are able to adjust discourse to fit the particularity and traditions of local groups. This requires an ability to learn and make meaningful associations between exemplar peace priorities ensconced within indigenous rubrics. Exemplars are not only willing to learn local moral dialects but expend considerable energy to this end. In this manner, peacemakers become fluent in many languages of moral sensitivity. We recognize that this may indicate a unique suite of giftedness in exemplar peacemakers that isn't readily transmissible to others. However, exemplars in the present study would be the first to admonish us against an overly individualized interpretation of their activities. The majority of exemplar peacemakers indicate that their primary identity is one of front-line representation for their religious communities. Multi-lingual peacemaking reflects the diverse religious constituencies that animate ongoing efforts of exemplar peacemakers.

We are struck by the fact that peacemaker skills, strategies and attitudes powerfully reflect relational priorities. For peacemakers from both traditions,

---

13 Colby and Damon (1992) noted a surprise finding in that the majority of moral exemplars in their work identified religion as a core framework for motivation and ongoing commitment. It is worth noting that the Colby and Damon study coincided with philosophical arguments for a different view of religious particularity in moral exchange.

relationship seems to be a core religious precept embodied in their view of the world and divinity. Without an authentic commitment to relationship with others, peace is unlikely to become a lasting fixture between tribal leaders or warring political factions. Peacemakers seem to have arrived at this knowledge on their own, through processes we can only indirectly ascertain. Given their narratives, we believe that one way of applying study findings is to consider educational interventions that foster a process of self-reflection such that pragmatic strategies become coherent, personalized schemas resilient to failure. Social support networks are an important complement to the growing wisdom of the peacemaking exemplar, suggesting that interventions should be intentionally situated within communities capable of understanding the purpose and practice of peace. Based on the common wisdom revealed through exemplars, peacemaking arises from within religious tradition-contexts, finding its deepest expression in relationship structures that respect, honor and validate the perspective of the other.

Bibliography

Brown, Steve, Kevin Reimer, Alvin Dueck, Richard Gorsuch, Robert Strong and Tracy Sidesinger. 2008. 'A Particular Peace: Psychometric Properties of the Just Peacemaking Inventory.' *Peace and Conflict: Journal of Peace Psychology*, 14: 1–18.

Colby, Anne, and William Damon. 1992. *Some Do Care: Contemporary Lives of Moral Commitment*. New York: Free Press.

Dueck, Alvin, Kevin Reimer, Joshua Morgan and Steve Brown. 2007. 'Let Peace Flourish: Descriptive and Applied Research from the Conflict Transformation Study.' In M. Abu-Nimer and D. Augsburger, eds, *Conflict Transformation*. Philadelphia: Westminster John Knox.

Landauer, Thomas, Peter Foltz and Darrell Laham. 1998. 'Introduction to Latent Semantic Analysis.' *Discourse Processes* 25: 259–284.

McAdams, Dan P. 1997. *The Stories We Live By*. New York: Guilford.

MacIntyre, Alasdair. 1991. *Three Rival Versions of Moral Enquiry: Encyclopedia, Geneology, and Tradition*. Notre Dame, IN: University of Notre Dame Press.

Shweder, Richard, Nancy Much, Manamohan Mahapatra and Lawrence Park. 1997. 'The Big Three of Morality (Autonomy, Community, Divinity) and the Big Three Explanations of Suffering.' In A. Brandt and P. Rozin, eds, *Morality and Health*. Florence, KY: Routledge. 119–169.

Strauss, Anselm, and Juliet Corbin. 1998. *Basics of Qualitative Research: Second Edition: Techniques and Procedures for Developing Grounded Theory*. Newbury Park, CA: Sage.

Tangney, Judith, and Deborah Mashek. 2004. 'In Search of the Moral Person: Do You Have to Feel Really Bad to be Good?' In J. Greenberg, ed., *Handbook of Experimental Existential Psychology*. New York: Guilford. 156–166.

Walker, Lawrence J., and Kevin S. Reimer. 2005. 'The Relationship Between Moral and Spiritual Development.' In P. Benson, P. King, L. Wagener and

E. Roehlkepartain, eds, *The Handbook of Spiritual Development in Childhood and Adolescence*. Newbury Park, CA: Sage. 265–301.

Walzer, Michael. 1996. *Thick and Thin: Moral Argument at Home and Abroad*. South Bend, IN: University of Notre Dame Press.

Chapter Seven

Autonomous Conformism – the Paradox of Entrepreneurial Protestantism. Spring Harvest: A Case Study

Rob Warner

Introduction

Spring Harvest is the largest contemporary British annual 'Bible week', where the ethos is not only symptomatic of a cultural shift in conservative religion, but has been influential in further reshaping, intentionally and unintentionally, the subculture of those who attend. This tradition of a religious holiday week could perhaps have its origins traced obliquely to the medieval pilgrimage, but is more directly a development from the early nineteenth-century Methodist revivalist camp meetings in the United States. The longest lasting British event of this kind is the Keswick Bible Convention, founded in 1875 (Price and Randall 2000). By the late 1970s, traditional evangelical Bible weeks faced a double cultural dislocation: unsure what to make of the rising prominence of charismatic renewal and hidebound in traditional formalities of presentation and hymnody. In reaction against this increasing subcultural isolation, Spring Harvest held its first annual event at Easter, 1979 and 2,800 attended. Its growth was remarkable: in 1984, 21,000; in 1989, 70,000. From 1990 to 2005 annual attendance was sustained at 60,000–80,000. The venue has been Butlins holiday camps, which are self-contained holiday villages, the first of which opened in 1936. Particularly popular after the Second World War, Butlins provided low-cost family holidays in somewhat Spartan chalets (http://www.butlinsmemories.com/ Accessed 19/12/06).

This wide range of attendance in more recent years is explained by the organisers as a variable plateau, determined by the amount of accommodation that Butlins holiday camps can provide each year. By the early 1990s Spring Harvest had stopped growing, having reached a saturation point – not only for Butlins, but within the evangelical market, according to Alan Johnson, Spring Harvest's Chief Executive, in interview. In 2001, publicity for the event downgraded annual attendance claims from 80,000 to 60,000 (Warner 2007), tacitly indicating either a decline that Spring Harvest's leaders denied in interviews with me, or a greater realism and precision replacing previously overenthusiastic promotion. Moderated claims in publicity may indicate an actual decline in average attendance, masked by being presented as a plateau. Nonetheless, in the first decade of the new century Spring Harvest continued to be, by a significant margin, the largest annual Bible week in Britain.

British Bible week attendance, 2001[1]

Spring Harvest	60,000
Stoneleigh	27,000
Soul Survivor	16,000
New Wine	13,800
Keswick	12,000
Easter People	12,000
Greenbelt	10,000
Grapevine	4,000
Summer Madness	4,000
Flames of Fire	1,000

Among British evangelistic programmes, Alpha (a widely used evangelistic programme that combined conservative apologetics, charismatic experientialism, participative learning and sustained marketing) has become the market leader, and has begun to provoke a growing range of sociological enquiries (Ward 1998; Hunt 2004). Like Alpha, Spring Harvest combines charismatic emphases and a fresh contemporaneity to achieve strong and sustained market dominance. As a highly popular and thereby influential embodiment of late modern evangelicalism that typifies and influenced other reconstructions of that tradition, Spring Harvest, just as much as Alpha, warrants sociological investigation. This chapter is based upon access to Spring Harvest's archives, interviews with senior contributors, and attendance at the event. The sociological interpretation is developed in conversation with key contributors to continuing debates concerning secularisation, cultural transitions and the resilience of conservative religion.

Entrepreneurial Exceptionalism

The long-term patterns of decline in attendance and public influence for institutional Christianity are well documented. (Gilbert 1980; Brown 2001; Bruce 2002; Brierley 2000; Brierley 2006). However, the entrepreneurial type of evangelical, in late-twentieth-century variant typically Pentecostal/charismatic in experiential orientation, has shown a distinct capacity for self-reinvention and resultant durability. As David Edwards (1987) observed:

> ... there will still be a large place in worldwide Christianity for the tradition which can be called Evangelical. Like Roman Catholicism, it changes because it lives ... the Evangelical future will include many Christians who are very simple in their interpretations of the experience of accepting Jesus as Saviour – but the leadership and the theology will be increasingly open to a changing world.

Spring Harvest exemplifies a variant of conservative Protestant Christianity that I have designated *entrepreneurial exceptionalism* (Warner 2007). This proposes a

---

1   Attendance figures cited in *Christianity and Renewal,* May 2002.

distinctive variation to the longstanding debate concerning whether US exceptionalism stands outside the normative secularising trends of Western Europe (and Canada/ Australia), or Western European exceptionalism stands outside the normative United States trend, or indeed whether there is no such thing as a normative trend or a prescriptive model of secularisation. In Western Europe, as in North America, it is sectarian religion – or to use Troeltsch's own alternative terminology 'voluntarist religion' (Martin 1978) – in both its evangelical and Pentecostal expressions, that exhibits a trend in sharp distinction from mainstream Christianity in its institutional forms (Bruce 1996; Davie 2002; Warner 2006).

The rhetoric of entrepreneurial religion aspired in the last quarter of the twentieth century to the acquisition and assertion of political leverage through the demonstration of substantial numerical support. For more than fifteen years a leading influence in British evangelicalism was Clive Calver, Spring Harvest's co-founder and the General Director (1982–1997) of the Evangelical Alliance (EA), the largest pan-Protestant coalition of British evangelicals, founded 1846. Calver emphasised the importance of attenders at Spring Harvest signing up as personal members of the Evangelical Alliance, claiming that a membership of 100,000 would ensure that the political parties could no longer afford to ignore evangelical concerns.

Calver and his colleagues were wary of comparison with the American Right, emphasising a programme of campaigns in favour of social justice as well as defending traditional sexual ethics in terms of restrictive censorship, limited access to abortion, promotion of marriage, and so on. In this, Spring Harvest positioned itself as an heir to the pan-evangelical Lausanne Congress on World Evangelism of 1974, which reconceived global mission for moderate evangelicals as a synthesis of evangelism and social action (Padilla 1976) and initiated a post-colonial re-conception of global evangelicalism (Stott and Coote 1981; Said 1994).

This reprioritisation was more than lip-service: as well as holding an offering each year to promote evangelistic initiatives, Spring Harvest ran an equally prominent fund-raising appeal in promotion of global social action initiatives; and the profits from the music album to commemorate the first ten years were given to international projects supporting people with HIV and AIDS. Similarly indicative of a breadth of missiological understanding, the member organisations of the Evangelical Alliance with the largest annual budgets are the Shaftesbury Society and Tear Fund, respected providers of care, education and personal and community development, in Britain and worldwide respectively. When Calver left EA to assume leadership of World Vision, an American relief and development charity, his career path was consonant with Spring Harvest's longstanding commitment to holistic mission.

Calver often recalled in his preaching a meeting with a senior cabinet member in the then Conservative government. The politician expressed confusion concerning the political orientation of the evangelical coalition: on social justice they appeared left wing, but on sexual ethics right wing. The connection between these disparate and potentially conflictual emphases is the fact that senior British evangelicals like big government. Prominent evangelical leaders tend to take for granted the conviction that government has the right and duty to intervene extensively. The ultimate aspiration of Spring Harvest, according to Alan Johnson, the Chief Executive who was appointed in the final phase of Calver's era, was 'To touch the nation'. It remained unclear when I interviewed him what precisely was signified by this portentous ambition, but it appeared to indicate a Constantinian or Augustinian concept of public life – an emphatic form of 'Christ transforming culture' in H. Richard Niebuhr's typology (1952) – in which the duty of the church is to seek to persuade government to enforce its ethical priorities.

It is difficult to find libertarian traces in senior evangelical leaders' rhetoric. However, as Casanova (1994) has argued, the negotiated return of religious groups to the public square requires recognition of the new context of an established pluralism: churches and other religions may be accepted as one among many contributing voices, but can no longer presume to impose their convictions by decree. Late modern entrepreneurial evangelicals have little appetite for functioning as one minority voice among many in a pluralistic culture, and this inevitably reinforces their perception by others as reactionary, intolerant and thoroughly unrealistic in their socio-political agenda. Even when they explicitly rejected the angry oppositionalism of fundamentalism, notoriously exemplified in extreme fundamentalists' violent and even murderous attacks on American abortion hospitals, their dogmatic absolutism has inevitably invited appraisal in fundamentalist categories (Bruce 2001).

Alongside this impassioned but illusory aspiration to attain decisive socio-political influence (or even Calvinistic control over society), the emphasis of evangelical rhetoric shifted under the influence of the entrepreneurs from the traditional 'the truth that endures' to 'the truth that guarantees success' (Warner 2007). Having embraced a largely unreflexive contemporaneity, many late modern evangelicals inhabited a mechanical universe in which the latest formula for church growth and the advance of the church was championed as failsafe, enthusiastically amnesiac to the failure of previous initiatives launched with similar enthusiasm. Naive importation of the latest methodology derived from a successful church, usually North American, assumed that European church decline could be overturned readily by churches that utilised the latest synthesis of spiritual power and entrepreneurial techniques with a successful track record in other cultures. From the mid-1990s, when the statistics of church attendance first began to indicate slippage among evangelicals (Brierley 2000) even though nowhere near the catastrophic levels of decline at non-evangelical churches, this rhetoric, in preaching and in worship songs, can be shown to have become still more heightened (Warner 2007). Speakers at Spring Harvest commended many initiatives, including seeker services (events designed to be user-friendly to the felt needs of inhabitants of the majority popular culture), purpose-driven churches (seeking to deliver mission through management theory), spiritual warfare (regular prayer to combat dark forces), acts of reconciliation (designed to unlock spiritual potential from the bondage of past offences, personal, corporate or ethnic), church planting (the multiplication of acculturated experiments in gospel communities), the Toronto Blessing (a short-lived, late twentieth-century eruption of ecstatic and revivalistic phenomena) and Alpha as the methodological guarantor. The convertive certainties of the entrepreneurs evidently found it impossible to come to terms with the emergent reality of static evangelical church attendance or even incipient evangelical decline, combined with a continuing diminution in the influence of the Church upon the wider culture. This insistent emphasis upon imminent success, disregarding the failure of previous initiatives, is an exemplary instance of Festinger's 'cognitive dissonance' (Festinger 1957; Festinger et al. 1964).

Dissolving Conservatism

Notwithstanding these overstated, even extravagant and in some cases delusional tendencies found in the sustained rhetoric of imminent advance and conquest, Spring Harvest's considerable and rapid growth makes possible a reappraisal in the late modern context of what kind of conservative religion does best. In an influential study, Dean Kelley (1972) argued that 'traits of strictness' enjoy growth potential. The logic of this analysis would appear to be that the stricter a church, in its dogma and ethics, the greater the potential for growth. James Hunter (1983) built upon Kelley's thesis: when his data revealed moderating tendencies, both doctrinal and ethical, among American evangelicals, he concluded that evangelicals were increasingly distancing themselves from the unreconstructed fundamentalists and were thereby self-propelled towards assimilation into the mainstream of church decline.

Although relatively conservative in faith and sexual ethics, Spring Harvest's pragmatic modernisers were nonetheless consistently deemed unacceptable by British Calvinistic exclusivists, who expressed suspicion of their enthusiastic entrepreneurialism that was unmistakably de-traditionalised, experiential and pragmatic. Arriving early for a Spring Harvest week, I was able to watch on television from my chalet the final evening meeting of Word Alive, a semi-detached affiliate of the main event, representing more conservative strands within evangelicalism. In the sermon, the critique cited above was set within a broad charge of anti-intellectualism levelled against much contemporary evangelicalism. Spring Harvest was not named directly: the charge was that 'many other evangelicals' were subject to these diminutions, but the charismatic and entrepreneurial target was obvious. Notwithstanding the fact that from the perspective of mainstream theology this sermon could hardly have been considered cerebral, the aspirations were emphatically intellectual. This reflects the common device whereby conservative evangelicals have attempted to create clear blue water between themselves and fundamentalists by charging that the latter are anti-intellectual (Edwards and Stott 1988; Calver et al. 1993; Tidball 1994). However, the driving force behind the original publications of fundamentalism was plainly intellectual, and grounded in a foundationalist epistemology derived from Scottish common sense rationalism (Murphy 1996; Harris, 1998). The intellectual pretensions of evangelicals, particularly when allied to unreconstructed conservatism, can therefore be interpreted as potentially indicative of their 'fundamentalising tendencies' rather than their distance from fundamentalism in its classic, early twentieth-century form. Harris's analysis provides a corrective to Barr's tendency (1977) to treat the two categories as synonymous and coterminous. These fundamentalising tendencies have tended to colonise and reconfigure popular Protestant orthodoxy, a pre-critical synthesis arising in the era of the Wesleys, Whitefield and Edwards of pietist and puritan emphases (Bebbington 1989; Noll 2004). As a result, enlightenment-grounded epistemological accretions have come to be interpreted, until the emergence of the post-conservatives, both by evangelicals and their mainstream critics, as symbolic boundaries inherent and intrinsic to the older (and broader) evangelical tradition (Barr 1977; Grenz 1993, 2000; Knight 1997). The Calvinistic exclusivists' critique of Spring Harvest therefore demonstrates the entrepreneurials' distance from unreconstructed conservatism; the entrepreneurial leaders may have espoused overt and unreconstructed conservative theological convictions, but these were being subverted, however unconsciously, by pragmatic experientialism.

The conservative critique of Spring Harvest echoes the characteristic repudiation of Pentecostalism by fundamentalists (Cox 1996; Synan, 1971, 1997). No matter how antiquely conservative the understandings of soteriology and biblical inspiration that have been avowed by Pentecostals (Kay 2000), their experientialism and urgent missiological pragmatism tend to subvert substantively their residual fundamentalising tendencies. Although the symbolic boundaries of their doctrinal framework appear usually to be deeply conservative, Pentecostal subculture's guiding core is pragmatic experientialism, Christocentric and conversionist. British Pentecostals undoubtedly sought mid to late twentieth-century recognition and acceptance from wary evangelicals by emphasising strict tenets of conservative evangelical orthodoxy, but their centre of gravity has continued to be spiritual encounter and conversionist activism, rather than traditional evangelical systematics or foundationalism. Like global Pentecostalism, although with a strongly middle-class market, the entrepreneurial evangelicals of Spring Harvest have assimilated readily to popular culture (Cox 1996), reinventing Christian worship in the idiom of pop songs and stadium rock and adopting enthusiastically the latest multimedia technologies. As the Principal of one liberal Anglo-Catholic college observed to me in 2006, 'We've only just started using PowerPoint in Chapel. There haven't been enough charismatic students to take us there before.' With a market-driven urgency, Spring Harvest pursued an intentional contemporaneity, retaining the traditional in public worship only where it was deemed absolutely essential. Nonetheless, when entrepreneurial evangelical leaders attempted to make a contribution to public life, they remained entrenched in reaction against the 1960s, wanting to turn the clock back impossibly to a former era of sexual regulation (Warner 2007). Moreover, and this was inevitable in the light of the presumption of imminent success, they were in denial faced with the ineluctable and continuing advance of secularisation, and the evidence among evangelicals of incipient, late-onset decline (ibid.). This tendency to denial was reflected not only in their songs of imminent triumph, but in their senior preachers' rhetoric and aspirations. In 1995, for example, the Evangelical Alliance under Calver's leadership announced an aim to double their membership (Evangelical Alliance (UK) Council papers, September 1995): five years later membership had actually dropped by nearly a third (Warner 2007).

Spring Harvest certainly confirms Hunter's thesis that pragmatic and entrepreneurial evangelicals have shifted their ground, in theology and ethics, tending – albeit with glacial slowness compared with liberal traditions – continually to moderate their convictions. Nonetheless, the market dominance of Spring Harvest, that was secured rapidly and sustained for a quarter of a century when almost all its competitors were more conservative, falsifies Kelley's thesis and Hunter's dependence upon it. In the last quarter of the twentieth century, relatively moderate evangelicals have shown a far greater propensity to growth than unreconstructed fundamentalists. 'Traits of strictness' fail to account for their greater success.

Harrington Watt concluded that moderate evangelicals in America were a subculture that was learning to 'fit in' with the majority culture in the period from 1925 to 1975, and this novel (and increasingly post-fundamentalist) cultural fit is central to understanding their relative strength as a religious tradition (Watt 1991). Tamney argued from more recent data that in the United States, moderate charismatics are more closely attuned to contemporary culture than other Christian traditions and therefore more likely to thrive (Tamney 2002). Woodhead and Heelas (2000; Heelas and Woodhead 2005) identified similar advantages for this sector, designated precisely but somewhat inelegantly as an 'experiential religion of difference'. A significant contributory factor to the relative success (in comparison both with fundamentalists and mainstream churches) of the moderate, entrepreneurial evangelicals, usually charismatic or Pentecostal, is found in the way they resolutely combine acculturating and detraditionalised pragmatic experientialism with defiantly optimistic aspirations – albeit sometimes associated, as we have noted, with delusional tendencies and a late modern predilection for proliferating certainties, both doctrinal and missiological. This results in an intrinsically unstable amalgam of a nominally unchanging orthodoxy with a determined pursuit of culturally consonant experimentation, driven by priorities that are pragmatic and missiological. The 'pastoral cycle' of practical theology has emerged into prominence as a neo-Hegelian iterative process of theological rearticulation, particularly within the liberal mainstream (Graham et al. 2005). Nonetheless, the entrepreneurial evangelicals habitually experiment at the level of popular religion with dialectical rearticulations of Gospel and Church, and this trend can be expected to increase within the ferment of cultural change in postmodernity.

Unintended Autonomy

Weber described the promotion of capitalism as the unintended consequence of ascetic Protestantism (Weber 1958). We can now similarly identify an unintended acculturation consequent upon the success and influence of entrepreneurial Protestantism. Bellah argued that the two most dominant and familiar modes of discourse in late twentieth-century American culture were entrepreneurial and therapeutic (Weber 1958). Spring Harvest certainly rearticulated the evangelical tradition in both these categories, even though sometimes in uncomfortable juxtaposition: 'how-to' seminars ran alongside sessions on emotional healing and developing local church pastoral teams. However, Spring Harvest's most decisive reconfiguration of the tradition, implicit rather than overt, was to legitimate, with profound and unintended consequences, a new type of evangelical: the autonomous religious consumer.

As the event grew rapidly, three different styles of main evening meeting emerged. By the mid-1990s these had been defined as 'traditionally charismatic', which meant high-octane stadium rock in the Big Top, 'reflective' and 'experimental/alternative'. In practice these styles were partly defined by generation, with a greater number of older people in the 'reflective' arena, but partly by temperament. The 'experimental' or 'alternative' appeared to attract a small market from across the generations, namely those who preferred intuitive, symbolic, non-linear, and sometimes 'post-evangelical', approaches (Tomlinson 1995).

Similarly, Bible expositions at Spring Harvest have been provided simultaneously each morning in two or three venues. These also make available different approaches – from conventional to moderately progressive, from robustly restorationist to mildly Christian feminist, from formal preaching to interactive, whether in terms of small group discussion or meditative opportunities. In some years, rather than setting aside a time slot solely for biblical exposition, this part of the programme has been provided alongside other seminars and activities. In short, individual participants were given the freedom to choose which style of exposition to attend, or whether to attend at all. The contrast with the subsequent re-contemporisation of Keswick demonstrates a substantive subcultural dissonance. Like Spring Harvest, Keswick has come to provide a wide range of optional seminars on such topics as church, family, work and public life. However, at Keswick there is a single daily Bible exposition and a single evening 'celebration' centred upon keynote preaching, thus maintaining a unitary culture and asserting more unequivocally the centrality of both the Bible and preaching to this more conservative version of evangelical identity.

The logic of the Spring Harvest founders' aspiration to homogeneous mobilisation, subsequently formulated by EAUK as a 'movement for change' (Hilborn 2004), demonstrates that Spring Harvest did not originally set out to promote heterogeneity and evangelical (or even post-evangelical) diversification. Indeed, rigorous conformism suffused the intentional ethos of the event: the 'main seminars' have required the speaking team to deliver a detailed syllabus in their daily sessions – working in small groups rather than presenting on their own – and the guests have been encouraged to buy the 'textbook' for this programme. Although a few speakers were said to have asserted the liberty to make no more than a passing nod to the syllabus, for most, working in partnership with people they have often not known particularly well, the syllabus was followed closely. Curiously, while evangelical ministers have traditionally distanced themselves from lectionary-based preaching, at Spring Harvest the control mechanism of the prescriptive syllabus for the main seminars exhibited a determination to inculcate a new and close conformity. While the speakers were not required to sign a basis of faith, which has been the custom in student Christian Unions affiliated to UCCF (the Universities and Colleges Christian Fellowship, the conservative evangelical student organisation), they were expected to articulate a conformist ethos, doctrinal and ethical, in the main seminars. The official emphasis of the event, therefore, was the articulation and mobilisation of an essentially conventional evangelicalism, albeit with a contemporary, entrepreneurial and charismatic *frisson*. The intentions were conformist and corporate. However, the large numbers attending forced the organisers to provide a multiplicity of simultaneous options.

Spring Harvest's range of options in Bible expositions and evening celebrations therefore ostensibly provides nothing more than disparate emphases within a common ethos of evangelical certainties. On more careful investigation it becomes apparent that entrepreneurialism began to modify, unintentionally but substantively, not merely the cultural packaging but the essential ethos of conservative religion. Herberg's distinction between designated and operative religion (Herberg 1955) remains pertinent: the *designated religion* of those attending Spring Harvest has almost always been Protestant and evangelical and often broadly charismatic; however, the *implicit but operative religion* enshrines the autonomy of the individual consumer. Just as Hammond (1992) demonstrated the priority of autonomy among American churchgoers, inevitably resulting in the reconfiguration of American religion in the late twentieth century, the commodified provision of Spring Harvest elevates individual freedom of choice. The main platform speakers confidently assert the homogeneity of evangelical doctrine, assume a uniform evangelical socio-political agenda, and are obliged to deliver a conformist syllabus in the main teaching programme. However, while the participants appear readily, and often enthusiastically, to assent to the formal rhetoric of religious conformity, they encounter in the huge range of choices integral to the event the operative priority of individual freedom of religious consumption. Here we see the paradox of late modern entrepreneurial evangelicalism: the organisers promoted and sought to mobilise a conformist conservatism (albeit moderated, as the Right's critique recognised), but the delegates nonetheless were empowered to function with the freedom of autonomous consumers.

The paradox of autonomous conformism therefore arises as the result of unintended consequences among entrepreneurial evangelicals. This phenomenon relativises the pluriform certainties of diverse leaders and speakers: not only are their agendas disparate, but the delegates are free to choose among them and even avoid altogether those they find least palatable, while continuing to function as full participants within this religious marketplace. Second, the freedom to choose according to personal taste ineluctably subverts the conformist ethos espoused by some of the most senior evangelical leaders, in their doctrinal, ecclesial and societal aspirations. If, as this analysis has concluded, individual autonomy, normative within the prevailing culture, increasingly becomes a primary aspect of participants' experience at Spring Harvest, then the reactionary sexual ethics of the Religious Right – restricted access to birth control and divorce, severe censorship and the marginalisation of gay and lesbian lifestyles – are likely to possess diminishing plausibility for these insiders, even as these traditionalist mores have already collapsed in wider British society. As Smith (2000) has demonstrated among North American evangelicals, while self-styled evangelical leaders often espouse a rigorously reactionary agenda, this is tolerated rather than enthusiastically supported by many lay evangelicals, for whom the dominant ethical priority is individual freedom of choice. Their ethics may be absolutist in formulation, but their governing principle is voluntaristic individualism.

In an age of militant fundamentalism, when pluralistic cultures may feel under threat from Christian as well Muslim militancy, this study suggests there is nothing of substance for British society to fear from the Christian consumers at Spring Harvest. The event can be designated relatively successful within the internal market of the evangelical subculture, but ultimately inconsequential from the perspective of the wider culture. The entrepreneurial leaders modified conservatism successfully, in particular in response to the Christian existentialism of the charismatic movement and the post-1960s demands for detraditionalised music in worship. One result of their success was the proliferation of competitor events, mostly new initiatives but some reinventions of longstanding programmes, notably Keswick. This proliferation further dissipated the claimed mobilisation of a unitary force, by increasing the range of choices in the 'Bible week' marketplace and demonstrating the ineradicable condition of evangelical pluralism.

At the same time, the experience of functioning as autonomous consumers while at Spring Harvest is likely to have influenced lay perceptions of their local church. Spring Harvest's ethos is essentially post-denominational, with the denominational context of the speaker team rarely emphasised. Having experienced at Spring Harvest a programme that has legitimised the priority of a personal 'religion of preference', the sovereign consumer may return home to appraise and appropriate local church programmes with fresh liberty, more likely to pick and mix rather than feel obliged to attend every available activity, more inclined to experiment with religious consumption from other local providers. This is reflected in Escott and Gelder's (2002) studies of Protestant denominations (Anglicans, Baptists, Methodists, Salvation Army and URC). Those attending Baptist churches considered their denomination much less important than do those attending more institutional churches. My conclusion from examining the practices and underlying ethos of Spring Harvest is that this post-denominational autonomy of the committed but individuated Christian consumer represented a broad trajectory among more moderate evangelicals, rather than being a specifically Baptist distinctive. One delegate explained, 'If my minister says to attend a prayer meeting, I always have, as a matter of course.' Another indicated the shifting pattern: 'We support our village church by attending in the morning – when we have time. But we also attend the city centre Anglican church on a Sunday evening – so long as we are not too busy.'

Constructing Religious Identities

Danielle Hervieu-Léger's (1999) concept of 'religious bricolage' has been questioned by Vassilis Saroglou (2006), who argued that it is precisely the 'centrality, intensity and integrative character' of religious beliefs that is their attraction. However apposite this critique may be with reference to the durability and coherence of occasional consumption of new age spiritualities, Spring Harvest demonstrates a postmodern capacity for bricolage within boundaries. This is, to be sure, far more constrained than the 'Sheila-ism' of Bellah et al. (1996) but is sufficient to provide a functional affirmation of individual autonomy and an appetite for à la carte religion invidious to fundamentalism. Even within the ostensibly safe haven of Spring Harvest as a temporary evangelical village, the participants experience what Anthony Giddens has described as the 'reflexive project of the self'.

> The reflexive project of the self, which consists in the sustaining of coherent, yet continuously revised, biographical narratives ... because of the 'openness' of social life today, the pluralisation of contexts of action and the diversity of 'authorities', lifestyle choice is increasingly important in the constitution of self-identity and daily activity. (1991, 5)

The 'religious bricolage' of constructing an authentic, individual Christian identity, or perhaps a customised fabric of religious recreation, is practised increasingly in the home church (or churches), and not just at an event that has subverted its own conformist ethos with an emphasis upon the autonomous religious consumer. This *bricolage within boundaries* may in time dissolve or at least diminish those boundaries' homogenising plausibility. In a climate of pragmatic acculturation, the subcultural capital of conservative conformism (Thornton 1995), at least among moderate evangelicals, is being dissolved from within.

The implicit elevation of personal autonomy and the consequent relativising of the diverse certainties of preachers with homogenising aspirations combine to establish within Spring Harvest an unintentional climate of heterogeneity and provisionality. In the creative play of the reflexive project of the religious self, the consumer of experiential and therapeutic religion is given freedom, however unintentionally, to nurture ironic detachment from the conformist projects and the impassioned rhetoric of imminent advance on offer in the religious marketplace of the entrepreneurial evangelicals. Implicit hybridity, cultural and theological, emerges for the autonomous religious consumer. Residual conservatism, detraditionalised experientialism, therapeutic individualism and autonomous self-reinvention all coalesce in a transient and contingent provisionality. If early and broad evangelicalism is conceived as a form of pre-critical, conversion-oriented Protestant orthodoxy, the enlightenment foundationalism of the later conservative evangelicals can be interpreted as a form of cultural imperialism. Post-conservative evangelicals, whether departing intellectually from enlightenment-bound presuppositions or departing from traditionalist conformism in the culturally consonant mode of autonomous religious consumption, can thereby be interpreted as an unexpected instance of cultural hybridity (Bhabha 1994), reconfiguring experimental (and, perhaps, often unstable and transient) fusions of the traditional and the contemporary.

The paradox of autonomous conformism exhibits disparate emphases. We have identified the inflated rhetoric of entrepreneurial conservatism, allegedly mobilised for advance, which in its cognitive dissonance becomes a form of illusory consolation for a semi-conservative remnant, a ghetto on holiday. This leads to the conclusion that entrepreneurial conservatism appears constitutionally incapable of facing the realities, however contested, of secularisation, which condemns its larger aspirations to unreality. We have also explored the new religious *zeitgeist* of autonomous consumerism, in which the delegates become purchasers of religious recreation, with the consumerist ethos subverting the residual conformism of modified conservatism, in doctrine and in ethics. The preachers do not express pluralism, contingency and irony: it is the participants who exercise the freedom to choose between competing sets of certainties or to free-float among them. For some religious consumers, it is plausible that an increasing proportion of their religious convictions and emphases may mutate into provisional allegiances from their former status as non-negotiable and permanent, formative and essential.

Contrary to Hunter's thesis (1983;1989), we conclude that cognitive bargaining is symptomatic of a transitional era, rather than the key dilutant within conservative religious transitions. Pragmatic acculturation that legitimates autonomous consumerism inevitably subverts entrepreneurial conservatism and inculcates in its place, however unintentionally, postmodern bricolage and hybridity, nascent and diverse. The durability of these emergent trajectories remains uncertain. Experimental formulations are likely to be contested, tentative and may remain unreflexive in their theological repositioning, while adhering with superficial loyalty, but underlying ambivalence, to the symbolic boundaries, increasingly porous and implausible, of conventional, modernist evangelical orthodoxy.

What we have identified is the accidental postmodernism of entrepreneurial evangelicalism, constructing an ethos that legitimates the autonomous consumer, pluralistic conceptions of contemporary orthodoxy, and the *bricolage within broadening boundaries* of a reconstructed and provisional religious identity. This is ironic and unexpected when the public face of this religious tradition is late-modern, conformist and unitary, insisting upon adherence to a theological framework that is systematic, non-negotiable and permanent, and combining this with a similarly conservative and inflexible socio-political ethic. Spring Harvest may therefore have become the last redoubt of conservative entrepreneurialism, traditionalist and sometimes even pre-critical in its formulaic theology and ethics, but pragmatic and unreflexively contemporary in its praxis. The tail has wagged the dog. Late-modern evangelical leaders, aspiring to neo-Constantinian social influence, have legitimated postmodern quest, liberty and irony among the cohorts they have assembled. Postmodern methods have begun to subvert late-modern ideology. Once the dominant culture of autonomous consumption is endorsed, conformism becomes increasingly nominal, and the rhetoric of imminent advance drifts towards enthusiastic vacuity, or formulaic and even escapist religious entertainment. The entrepreneurial leaders, pragmatic and acculturating, deliberately sought to change 'from above' the external presentation of evangelicalism; the autonomous consumers were thereby legitimated to deconstruct 'from below' conformist allegiances previously considered self-evident and inherent. Under the impact of postmodernity and as a consequence of their own pragmatic experimentation, the subcultural capital that sustained conformism among moderate evangelicals appears to have been breaking down.

Bibliography

Barr, James. 1977. *Fundamentalism*, London: SCM.

Bebbington, David W. 1989. *Evangelicalism in Modern Britain: A History from the 1730s to the 1980s*, London: Unwin Hyman.

Bellah, Robert N., Richard Madsen, William M. Sullivan, Ann Swidler, Steven M. Tipton (eds). 1996. *Habits of the Heart: Individualism and Commitment in American Life* (updated edn) Berkeley: University of California Press. 1996.

Bhabha, Homi K. 1994. *The Location of Culture*, London, New York: Routledge.

Bibby, Reginald. 1987. *Fragmented Gods: The Poverty and Potential of Religion in Canada*, Toronto: Irwin.

Brierley, Peter W. 2000. *The Tide Is Running Out: What the English Church Attendance Survey Reveals*, London: Christian Research.

———. 2006. *Pulling out of the Nosedive. A Contemporary Picture of Churchgoing: What the 2005 English Church Census Reveals*, London: Christian Research.

Brown, Callum G. 2001. *The Death of Christian Britain: Understanding Secularisation 1800–2000*, London: Routledge.

Bruce, Steve. 1996. *Religion in the Modern World: From Cathedrals to Cults*, Oxford: Oxford University Press

———. 2001. *Fundamentalism*, Cambridge: Polity.

———. 2002. *God Is Dead: Secularization in the West*, Oxford: Blackwell.

Calver, Clive, Ian Coffey, and Peter Meadows. 1993. *Who Do Evangelicals Think They Are?*, London: Evangelical Alliance.

Casanova, José. 1994. *Public Religions in the Modern World*, Chicago; London: University of Chicago Press.

Cox, Harvey. 1996. *Fire from Heaven*, London: Cassell.

Davie, Grace. 2002. *Europe: The Exceptional Case*, London: Darton, Longman & Todd.

Dorrien, Gary J. 1998. *The Remaking of Evangelical Theology*, Louisville, KY: Westminster John Knox Press.

Edwards, David L. 1987. *The Futures of Christianity*, London: Hodder & Stoughton.

——— and John R.W. Stott. 1988. *Essentials: A Liberal–Evangelical Dialogue*, London: Hodder & Stoughton.

Escott, P. and A. Gelder. 2002. *Church Life Profile 2001 – denominational results for the Baptist Union*, London: Churches Information for Mission.

Festinger, Leon. 1957. *A Theory of Cognitive Dissonance*, Stanford, CA: Stanford University Press.

———, Henry W. Riecken, and Stanley Schachter. 1964. *When Prophecy Fails: A Social and Psychological Study of a Modern Group That Predicted the Destruction of the World*, New York; London: Harper & Row.

Giddens, Anthony. 1991. *Modernity and Self-Identity – Self and Society in the Late Modern Age*, Cambridge: Polity.

Gilbert, Alan D. 1980. *The Making of Post-Christian Britain – a History of the Secularization of Modern Society*, London: Longman, 1980.

Graham, Elaine L., Heather Walton, and Frances Ward (eds). 2005. *Theological Reflection: Methods*, London: SCM.

Grenz, Stanley. 1993. *Revisioning Evangelical Theology*, Downers Grove, IL: Inter-Varsity Press.

———. 2000. *Renewing the Center: Evangelical Theology in a Post-Theological Era*, Grand Rapids, MI: Baker.

Hammond, Phillip E. 1992. *Religion and Personal Autonomy: The Third Disestablishment in America*, Columbia: University of South Carolina.

Harris, Harriet A. 1998. *Fundamentalism and Evangelicals*, Oxford: Clarendon.

Heelas, Paul and Linda Woodhead (eds). 2005. *The Spiritual Revolution – why religion is giving way to spirituality*, Oxford: Blackwell.

Herberg, Will. 1955. *Protestant, Catholic, Jew: An Essay in American Religious Sociology*, Garden City, NY: Doubleday.

Hervieu-Léger, Danielle. 1999. *Le Pèlerin et le Converti. La Religion en Mouvement*, Paris: Flammarion.

Hilborn, David (ed.). 2004. *Movement for Change*, Carlisle: Paternoster.

Hunt, Stephen. 2001. *Anyone for Alpha? Evangelism in a Post-Christian Society*, London: Darton, Longman & Todd.

——. 2004. *The Alpha Enterprise*, Aldershot: Ashgate.

Hunter, James Davison. 1983. *American Evangelicalism: Conservative Religion and the Quandary of Modernity*, New Brunswick: Rutgers University Press.

——. 1987. *Evangelicalism: The Coming Generation*, Chicago, IL; London: University of Chicago Press.

Kay, William K. 2000. *Pentecostals in Britain*, Carlisle: Paternoster.

Kelley, Dean M. 1972. *Why Conservative Churches Are Growing: A Study in Sociology of Religion*, New York: Harper & Row.

Knight, Henry H. 1997. *A Future for Truth*, Nashville: Abindgon Press.

Martin, David. 1978. *A General Theory of Secularization*, Oxford: Blackwell.

——. 2002. *Pentecostalism: The World Their Parish*, Oxford: Blackwell.

——. 2005. *On Secularization: Towards a Revised General Theory*, Aldershot: Ashgate.

Murphy, Nancey. 1996. *Beyond Liberalism and Fundamentalism: How Modern and Postmodern Philosophy Set the Theological Agenda*, Valley Forge, PA: Trinity Press International.

Niebuhr, H. Richard. 1952. *Christ and Culture*, London: Faber & Faber.

Noll, Mark A. 2004. *The Rise of Evangelicalism*, Leicester: Inter-Varsity Press,

Padilla, C. René (ed.). 1976. *The New Face of Evangelicalism: An International Symposium on the Lausanne Covenant*, London: Hodder & Stoughton.

Price, Charles W., and Ian M. Randall. 2000. *Transforming Keswick*, Carlisle: Paternoster.

Said, Edward W. 1994. *Culture and Imperialism*, London: Chatto & Windus.

Saroglou, Vassilis. 2006. 'Religious Bricolage as a Psychological Reality: Limits, Structures and Dynamics.' *Social Compass* 53: 109–15.

Smith, Christian. 1998. *American Evangelicals: Embattled and Thriving*, Chicago: University of Chicago Press.

——. 2000. *Christian America? What Evangelicals Really Want*, Berkeley and London: University of California Press.

Stott, J.R.W., and R. Coote (eds). 1981. *Down to Earth: Studies in Christianity and Culture – the Papers of the Lausanne Consultation on Gospel and Culture*, London: Hodder & Stoughton.

Synan, Vinson. 1971, 1977. *The Holiness-Pentecostal Tradition*, Grand Rapids, MI: Eerdmans.

Tamney, Joseph B. 2002. *The Resilience of Conservative Religion: The Case of Popular, Conservative Protestant Congregations*, Cambridge: Cambridge University Press.

Thornton, Sally. 1995. *Club Cultures: music, media and subcultural capital*, Cambridge: Polity.

Tidball, Derek. 1994. *Who Are the Evangelicals? Tracing the Roots of the Modern Movements*, London: Marshall Pickering.

Tomlinson, Dave. 1995. *The Post-Evangelical*, London: Triangle.

Troeltsch, Ernst. 1911, 1992. *The Social Teaching of the Christian Churches*, Louisville, Ky.: Westminster/John Knox Press.

Ward, Pete. 1998. 'Alpha – the Mcdonaldization of Religion.' *Anvil* 15: 279–86.

Warner, Rob. 2006. 'Pluralism and Voluntarism in the English Religious Economy.' *Journal of Contemporary Religion* 21.3.

———. 2007. *Reinventing English Evangelicalism, 1966–2001*, Carlisle: Paternoster.

Watt, David Harrington, 1991. *A Transforming Faith: Explorations of Twentieth-Century American Evangelicalism,* New Brunswick: Rutgers University Press.

Weber, Max. 1958. *The Protestant Ethic and the Spirit of Capitalism*, trans. Talcott Parsons, New York: Scribner's.

Woodhead, Linda, and Paul Heelas (eds). 2000. *Religion in Modern Times*, Oxford: Blackwell.

Chapter Eight

Social vs. Spiritual Capital in Explaining Philanthropic Giving in a Muslim Setting: The Case of Turkey

Ali Çarkoğlu

One of the fundamental ways people relate to others is through religious or spiritual lenses. Religions evolve in a community of believers, which brings warmth, belonging and security to its members. Besides purely personal or psychological gains associated with religiosity, there exists a social reward as well. By being active within the social institutions of a belief system or internalizing its rhetorical as well as doctrinal perspectives and by following its worship rituals people do not only derive a subjective individual psychological gain. They also derive a social return to their investment, in a sense into their religion that helps them achieve personal as well as public objectives. My ensuing arguments below are built upon a newly burgeoning literature on religious or spiritual capital which resembles in many respects to the rather well-known social capital literature. Field (2003), Putnam (2000) and Uslaner (2002) provide reviews of the vast literature on social capital. Iannaccone (1990), Stark and Finke (2000) and Finke and Dougherty (2002) present the arguments upon which the religious/spiritual capital concept is built.

One critical element in any religion that exemplifies the cooperative spirit with the community of believers concerns the level and different forms of philanthropic giving. My objective in this essay is chiefly to present an empirical picture of the state of philanthropic giving in the predominantly Muslim population of Turkey. I build my arguments upon a conceptual link between religiosity of individuals and their abilities to relate to other fellow human beings. The main question I want to address is the relative weights of social as opposed to spiritual/religious capital (SRC) in shaping various forms of philanthropic giving. Following a short discussion of conceptual foundations I operationalize the measurements of these rival concepts with the help of nationally representative survey data from Turkey and describe their basic properties. Next, I will use these measurements to explain variations in individuals' support for philanthropic giving.

Social vs. Spiritual/Religious Capital

Social Capital

In its simplest form, the social capital (SC) argument asserts that long-term maintenance of good working relationships geared towards working together for a purpose render many otherwise unattainable objectives practicable with much less difficulty. In their attempts to achieve objectives that are individually difficult if not impossible to attain individuals use their social relationships and networks wherein a series of common values develop and thus render cooperation easier. To the extent that they use these networks as a resource such relationships become a resource or capital (Field 2003, 1).

Several empirical observations that can be generalized for many countries of diverse backgrounds underline the importance of SC. Family meals, a long-time practised ritual, has become one of the national endangered practices in modern times (Feldstein and Sander 2001, 45). since the early 1970s there is also a noticeable downward trend in the percentage of people who report that others can be in general trusted. Less trusting individuals also tend to trust their governments less and less as well. As a consequence of declining trust, people tend to engage in social activities relatively less over the past few decades. Putnam (2000) notes that Americans are 'bowling alone' and are becoming much less active in mainstream civic organizations concomitantly participating in political and organizational activities at a much lower rate. More relevant for our purposes is the estimate that overall share of philanthropic giving as share of the national income has also been declining. In other words, more isolated individuals, who are interacting less and less with one another for a shared objective, less trusting and less caring in general, tend to cooperate and work less with strangers.

The massive empirical regularities from a large number of comparative contexts seem to have necessitated the introduction of a distinction between two forms of SC. The *bonding* type refers to parochial interpersonal solidarity that exists in small localities wherein exclusive long-term communal socialization develops. Bonding is similar to Durkheim's (1915) notion of solidarity and is more likely to occur within homogeneous small communities. Similar to Durkheim's account, bonding acts as SC in so far as it provides emotional support, fellowship and camaraderie. While bonding promotes in-group trust and focuses on members' needs and interests, any one from out-group tends to be viewed with suspicion and mistrust. The *bridging* type of SC is however less intimate and personal. In line with Granovetter's (1973) conception of 'weak' ties, the bridging type of SC is advantageous in building relationships across different groups of heterogeneous nature and thus fostering a larger cooperative society. Wuthnow (2002, 670) notes that 'compared with bonding, bridging is perhaps more difficult to generate and sustain because it requires that people look beyond their immediate social circles and depends on institutions capable of nurturing cooperation among heterogeneous groups'.

Religious/Spiritual Capital

Building on the work of human capital by Gary Becker (1964), for Laurence Iannaccone (1990) the very process of religious practice and the production of religious satisfaction therein creates a distinct new form of social skill accumulation which he calls religious human capital (RHC). His definition of RHC was based on social skills and experiences that specifically originate from one's religion. These religion specific skills and experiences can be gained in the process of obtaining information and be reflected in one's doctrinal knowledge about his or her religion. Or they may be specific to experience in religious rituals and practical traditions.

Iannaccone's RHC concept is intimately linked to the work carried out in the field of religious psychology which views religion as a human response to a series of stimuli from the social and the natural environments. These stimuli may be internal to the psyche of the individual facing the natural and social realities or just as well be external impositions of the natural or social environment. As people age, for example, their reactions to the external stimuli coming in from their own or their loved one's health, or simple disastrous events are inherently different compared to their youth. This observation alone is enough to point out that external and internal are constantly at play in shaping and reshaping the self-conceptualization as well as social imposition of what it means to be religious for a given individual.

The concepts of religiousness or religiosity as opposed to spirituality have often been used interchangeably. Vaughan (1991) and Argyle and Beith-Hallahmi (1975) underline that *religiousness* involves subscription to institutionalized beliefs, doctrines and practices of worship. *Spirituality* on the other hand, is seen as a subjective individual experience with the sacred world. It involves 'that vast realm of human potential dealing with ultimate purposes, with higher entities, with God, with love, with compassion, with purpose' (Tart 1983, 4; quoted in Zinnbauer et al. 1997, 550). It seems that for all practical purposes religiosity is a subset of spirituality which over-encompasses individuals' subjective dealings with the sacred unknown world. Spirituality then need not involve with the organized religions of any form and remain in its nature a mostly individual subjective experience. Putnam's distinction regarding the bonding as opposed to bridging type of SC accumulation also helps us distinguish spirituality from religiousness. While religiousness tends to bonding with its focus on exclusionist identities, spirituality tends towards bridging, by remaining relatively autonomous from organized religion, and thus from social motivations and pressures, and by staying focused primarily on the individual experiences related to the sacred world and its larger questions of purpose and meaning. Such focus on the subjective evaluations of the ultimate questions of purpose and meaning in sacred dimensions of human existence do not necessarily tend towards exclusionist evaluations of identity. Just as there is an inherent tension between bonding and bridging, spirituality and religiousness coexist; one pushing people towards conformity to an exclusionist identity and the other pulling people towards the unknown humble acceptance of an inclusionist divinity.

What differentiates religious or spiritual capital from its rivals or complementary concepts could still be its intimate and direct link to one's fundamental identity definitions. Clues of this perspective on spiritual or religious capital can actually be found in the dark-side interpretations of social capital on which Uslaner (2002, 87–88, 138–139) provides a thorough discussion. While the *bright* side of social capital is all inclusive; that is, it evokes trust in all people irrespective of their race, social class, religion, ethnicity and the like, the *dark* side of social capital underlines its exclusivist nature. If one does not share a common identity with the other, then cooperative links are severed and accommodating and supportive social interaction is then denied to the outsiders. While SC's bright side promotes abolishing the distinction between 'we' and 'they', its darker side underlines it. Almost by definition identities create cognitive distortions about the 'in' as opposed to the 'out' group members. Out-groups are homogenized and approached with prejudice and thus discriminated against, while in-group members benefit from favoritism (Fiske and Taylor 1991).

In short, the 'good' or 'brighter' side of social capital describes the all-inclusive cooperative networking amongst individuals while the darker side emphasizes the exclusionist identity based interaction between members of the same identity group as opposed to between individuals of different identity groups. Since the brighter side is all inclusive by definition, it need not incorporate any notion of identity. However, the darker side is built upon the need for identity formation. Once the need for an identity is justified on rational grounds then the question as to why people cannot possibly live with only the brighter side of social capital becomes self-evident. People form identities that demarcate in-group from the out-group simply because such a demarcation benefits members. If it benefits members then such identity-based capital accumulation deserves investing in for future use of the in-group networks. If such an investment takes place in the realm of religion then religious – as opposed to spiritual – capital concepts become useful.

The central argument in the above discussion for our purposes here concerns the consequences of SC and RHC. It is anticipated that, after controlling for the effects of other relevant factors – such as social capital, income and attitudes towards philanthropy – the impact of religious capital on donations will be expected to be positive. The data used in the ensuing analyses were collected as part of a series of surveys on philanthropic giving conducted in Turkey during Spring 2004 among household members of voting age as well as foundation administrators. The nature of the sample and basic measurement strategies followed for my key variables can be found in Çarkoğlu (2006). Below I present basic characteristics of SC and RHC and formulate a multivariate explanatory model for testing their impact upon philanthropic giving.

Measuring Social and Spiritual Capital

The questionnaire included three interrelated modules that tackle the issue of trust and social capital. The simplest and most widely used index is adopted from a Survey Research Center (1969) module on trust in people and uses three separate questions aggregated in an additive way to form a scale ranging between 0 and 3. In all three questions respondents are asked to choose one of two options, one of which indicates tendency to trust. An individual who chooses the trustworthy responses in all three questions scores the highest score of 3, indicating a high level of trust.[1] We see that nearly 60 per cent of the sample chose non-trusting answers in all three questions and only a small minority of 2.9 per cent chose trusting answers in all three. The relatively low level of the Cronbach's alpha of 0.5 indicates the low reliability for the scale, which suggests that these questions touch on different dimensions of trust phenomena and thus those who give a trusting answer to one question will not necessarily do so to another, so creating low correlations between the three questions.

In operationalizing the concept of spiritual or religious capital it is difficult to attain a distinction between religiosity and spiritual or religious capital unless the measurements were obtained or designed specifically for this purpose. I only attempted to obtain measures of religious capital that reflect the majority Sunni/ Hanefi school in the Turkish context rather than the other minority schools, such as the Alevis, whose religiosity as reflected in their practices need not coincide with the measures used here. I follow my earlier criticism of this approach in Çarkoğlu (2005) and treat the Alevis separately from the Sunnis in the ensuing analyses. I accordingly worked with multi-dimensional religiosity measurements. Following earlier works by Glock and Stark (1965), Hassan (2002), Çarkoğlu and Toprak (2000) and Çarkoğlu (2005), I devised faith, religious attitudes and religious worship or practice dimensions of religiosity. In addition, respondents' self-evaluations of their own religiosity are used in explanatory analyses.[2] For the details of these measures see Çarkoğlu (2006).

These measures only partially succeed in grasping the conceptual needs underlined above. The faith dimension of religiosity clearly reflects doctrinal elements in Sunni Muslim faith and thus reflects little degree of 'spirituality' as we conceptualized it. However, to the extent that they are voiced openly in social life, the attitudinal positions taken should bear some significance in the way our respondents relate to their fellow community members and as such should entail some degree of religious capital. Like-minded individuals with regards to religiously

---

1　The questions used for this index are as follows: (1) Generally speaking, would you say that most people can be trusted or that you can't be too careful in dealing with people? – Can't be too careful, Most people can be trusted*, (2) Do you think that most people would try to take advantage of you if they got the chance or would they try to be fair? – Take advantage, Try to be fair*, (3) Would you say that most of the time people try to be helpful, or that they are mostly just looking out for themselves? – Look out for themselves, Try to be helpful*. (* = Trustworthy responses.)

2　The ideological or faith dimension emphasizes the set of fundamental beliefs with which the individuals are required to comply. A number of core doctrinal beliefs are used to identify this dimension: belief in God, in sin, in heaven and hell, in the existence of spirit, in the afterlife and in the existence of the devil. Attitudinal differences on issues related to religion have been addressed by providing the respondents with statements which they are required to evaluate by providing their degree of agreement with them on a five-point scale. The dimension of ritualistic or religious practice comprises acts of worship through which believers are expected to show their devotion to their religion. Amongst a large number of rituals in Islam, only five were included in the questionnaire – mosque attendance, zekat and fitre payments, lamb sacrifice, making the Hajj.

significant attitudinal positions are expected to form social communities that relate more easily and intensely with one another. One might be tempted to think that such attitudinal positions might be less easily observable in social life compared to religious practices. However, my reading of the above reported results suggests otherwise. While the Cronbach alpha measure of reliability is about 0.6 for the six items of attitudinal evaluations, it remains low for the practice indices. Thus, while it is comparatively easy to predict someone's attitudes on the basis of just one of these evaluations, it is relatively more difficult to predict one religious practice on the basis of another. In other words, while agreement or disagreement on an attitudinal evaluation (say, that an individual approves of closing of restaurants and coffee houses during the month of Ramadan) is a good predictor of evaluation in another (such as objecting to one's daughter marrying a non-Muslim), it is not equally easy to predict someone's practice. Findings about mosque attendance, for example, would not necessarily predict zakat payments or lamb sacrifice. One of the reasons why this may be so is that attitudes expressed in a survey setting are in all likelihood homogenously constrained. Muslim religious practices are constrained first by context (for example, those who do not have to pay zakat or are exonerated from performing Hajj on the basis of their income or wealth) as well as the practicality of community pressures (for example, mosque attendance in devout Muslim communities is less of a matter of choice compared to less religious communities). This complexity renders predictability of practices on the basis of just one religious requirement less likely than it is the case for attitudinal evaluations.

Our wording of the question concerning self-evaluation of religiosity clearly indicates that in answering this question the respondent should leave the level of religious practices aside and concentrate on the remaining aspects of religiosity. As such, we come closer to an individual evaluation of spirituality. Especially in the multivariate context of our analyses below this variable concerning self-evaluation of religiosity should grasp the spiritual influences rather than social or religious capital accumulation processes.

Focusing on Donations

Direct Giving

Respondents were asked whether and to what degree the respondent individually and directly provided help to others in need. About 44 per cent of respondents responded affirmatively. Cash aid is by far the most common form of giving to relatives. Respondents reported giving less in cash assistance to neighbours than to other needy people. Food aid to neighbours is repeatedly more common than other types of aid. This may be because in close-knit family circles of a typical Turkish village or neighbourhood, in-kind aid to relatives, in the form of clothing and food, could very well be situated within tradition, and therefore might not be considered aid per se but part of traditional generosity. It is noticeable that individual-to-individual giving as a share of household income is quite low. However, these figures reflect only the portion of individual giving that is not institutionalized and only partially motivated by religious considerations, therefore constituting only one segment of total giving. Nearly 56 per cent of the total reported direct aid targeted relatives followed by other needy individuals who were not neighbours (31.2 per cent). The fact that the 'other needy individuals' category gathered the second largest sum points to a potential for more diverse forms of giving.

Zakat Payments

Zakat, which originally meant 'purity', is the third of the Five Pillars of Islam and refers to expending a fixed portion of one's wealth for the poor and needy in the society. There are two main types of zakat: zakat on self (*zakat-ul-fitr*) is a per head payment equivalent to a relatively small cost of living attached to the main food of the region (wheat, dates or rice, depending on the place) paid during the month of Ramadan by the head of a family for himself and his dependents; zakat on wealth (*zakat-ul-mal*) comprises all other types of zakat paid as a 2.5 per cent levy on most valuables and savings held for a full year if their total value is more than a basic minimum known as *nisab* (Robinson 1999, 111–16). The rates of zakat are not uniform. Different commodities attract different rates and the computation on various types of properties can be complicated (Denny 2005).

In this study people were asked whether they paid their zakat on self and on wealth (*fitre* and *zekat* respectively in Turkish) over the last year. Nearly 40 per cent reported they had paid their zakat while about 80 per cent reported so for their fitre. Then open questions were asked regarding the recipients of these payments and how much was paid. We found that, when questioned about to whom they made these payments, respondents indicated that needy acquaintances or relatives comprise 28.8 per cent for zakat payments and 40.9 per cent for fitre payments.

Findings

In a multivariate setting I used as dependent variable a dummy dependent variable taking only the value of 1 when the individual makes any payments of the associated category (fitre-zakat payments, donations to associations at large and only non-religious organizations, direct and informal donations and donations to street beggars) and zero otherwise. In order to facilitate comparisons across our dependent variables I use the same set of independent variables for the purposes of control. When the dependent variable is defined as a dummy variable, the conventional ordinary least squares methods are not appropriate. I use a logistic regression which estimates a non-linear model that helps distinguish those who make donations of different types from those who do not.

In differentiating the donors from non-donors only two variables consistently show up as statistically significant at the conventional levels. One of these is the ownership index that reflects accumulated wealth of the individual. As expected, it consistently has a positive impact on the likelihood of making donations of different types. The highest impact of a unit change in the ownership index is observed for the case of giving to non-religious organizations where a unit rise in ownership status leads to a rise of about 33 per cent in the likelihood of making donations over not making any donations. Similar increases in the likelihood of making donations are observed, in declining order, for associations including the religious ones, then for direct donations followed by fitre-zekat payments and, lastly, for making donations to street beggars which appears as an insignificant impact. It is noticeable that likelihood of making donations is most sensitive to ownership status of individuals in the case of non-religious organizations, while the likelihood of donations for religious organizations is relatively less sensitive to changes in ownership status. Income, however, is only significant in the case of associations and appears to increase the likelihood of making donations to associations at a modest level when compared to the effect of changes in ownership status.

The other variable that showed up consistently as significant is the one reflecting religious practice involvement for individuals. As the number of religious practices reported by individuals increases so does their likelihood of making donations. If the respondent has made the Hajj, has sacrificed a lamb and attends mosque (a religious practice score of 3), then the likelihood of fitre-zekat payment rises to about 63 per cent (a 32 percentage points increase from the base scenario). The highest impact of religious practice is observed in the case of direct donations which, as underlined above, are directed predominantly towards close-by neighbours, family members and the like. When an individual reports one additional religious practice his or her likelihood of making a direct donation increases by 73 per cent. This increase is lower for fitre-zekat payments, associations, non-religious organizations and street beggars.[3] Self-evaluated religiosity as a measure of spirituality is only significant in the case of donations to associations.

The social capital indicators included as separate dummy variables for the three standard questions on interpersonal trust are not consistently significant. What is most surprising is that the general trust question is not significant for any one of the donation categories. The helpfulness version of the interpersonal trust question has a positive coefficient and is significant for only the fitre-zekat payments. If the respondent believes that 'most of the time people try to be helpful' then their likelihood of making a fitre-zekat payment rises by 59 per cent compared to those who do not believe in such a generalization. Another surprising finding about the impact of interpersonal trust indicators concerns the fairness version of the standard questions: if the respondent believes that 'most people would try to be fair' then the likelihood of their making direct informal donations or paying their fitre or zekat declines. The trustworthiness index also has a significant and quite low level of positive impact but only upon donations for associations and non-religious organizations.

Religious attitudes turn out to be significant in the case of fitre-zekat payments and donations for associations, but not for informal direct giving or for street beggars. The faith indicator appears, as expected, positively related to fitre-zekat payments but negatively related to donations to associations. The likelihood of making donations to associations declines by about 27 per cent for every additional faith score

---

3   Note here that religious practice does not include any involvement in fitre-zekat payments but it does include fitre-zekat payments for the case of other donations.

increment. This suggests that strict believers in doctrinal aspects of Sunni-Muslim faith are significantly less likely to make donations to associations which may not be close to their ideological standing. The fact that such a negative impact appears after controlling for the expected positive impacts of other religiosity variables is surprising and may be the reflection of a dual approach towards associations on the basis of religious doctrinal differences.

If we look at other types of donations some patterns catch the eye. One concerns the impact of age on donations. It appears that older people are more likely to make donations to associations (20 per cent more likely for every additional 10 years of age); however, the precise opposite is observed for donations to street beggars. One reason for this might be the fact that younger people are tend to spend more time out and about streets and encounter street beggars more often. Rural area residents are also more likely to make donations to street beggars (44 per cent more likely than an urban area resident). Residents from smaller provinces of Inner Anatolia appear to have a significantly higher likelihood of making donations to associations, street beggars and direct informal donations. Level of education is only significant in relation to direct donations and as the level of education increases so does the likelihood of making donations. This might be a reflection that, even after controlling for the impact of income and ownership status, better-educated people face more opportunities and requests to donate, or are more often under pressure to help close-by needy people directly.

Among the significant variables the one that has the highest impact upon the probability of making a direct donation turns out to be evaluation of prospective economic conditions. When an individual expects that the next year will be economically bad for the whole country (not for the family) then s/he is nearly 2.35 times more likely to make direct donations. A similar level of impact is also observed on the non-religious organizations. This is hardly surprising, suggesting that prospective evaluations act as a predictor of need for individuals who respond to such perceptions by making direct informal donations or donations to non-religious organizations.[4] In other words, people seem to make a judgement about the future needs of their community and act accordingly. If their perception of need in the future rises they become more likely to act so as to meet those needs with their own direct donations to the needy.

---

4   Details of the explanatory power of the models are not reported to save space. The explanatory power of the model is not the same across different types of donations. It is noticeable that, for the case of fitre-azekat payments only, the model predicts about 87 per cent of the observed donors. In the case of direct informal donations this ratio is only about 47 per cent, for street beggars 33 per cent, for associations 21 per cent and for non-religious organizations 4 per cent. However, the overall correctly predicted donors and non-donors range between about 69 per cent and 94 per cent. Nagelkerke R-square is 0.29 for fitre-zekat payments, 0.31 for donations for associations, 0.22 for non-religious organisations, 0.28 for direct-informal and 0.15 for street beggars.

Conclusions

The main conclusion to be drawn from these results is that, while religious capital indicators reflected in religious practices, faith and attitude measures appear to be closely linked to philanthropic donations, social capital measures are not as consistently and as dominantly related to donations. Interestingly, individuals who happen to worship more – and who thus invest more in religious capital as Iannacone (1990) would suggest – tend to donate more for all different types of objectives.

Higher levels of, not belief or faith, but rather of practice, or worship seem to be more effective in shaping people's likelihood of making donations for different causes. As suggested, perhaps it is because people tend to put less emphasis on materialistic values and incline towards spiritual or pious ends that they tend to help others by being active in the community and to donate for philanthropic causes (see Rokeach 1973; Lam 2002; Regnerus et al. 1998). The evidence above cannot determine if this is the dynamics of motivation that leads to the observed outcome. However, we do observe that, more than social capital, it is religious capital that shapes donations. This seems very much in line with the Islamic doctrine; believers seem to give of themselves in the form of fitre and zekat. We should note here that the total sum of all donations – that is religious, formal institutionalized as well as informal and direct – is only a tiny fraction of our respondents' reported total household income. Nevertheless those with more religious capital tend to be distinctly more generous and open-handed when it comes to helping others.

I should note at this juncture that, while measurement of social capital has a long established literature, the same cannot be claimed for the case of religious capital. I basically adopted the framework of religiosity dimensions in forming a measure of religious capital. Although it comes close to the conceptual discussions of Iannocone and others, we still have little knowledge of the meaning people attach to their religious investments. Our questions do not address, for example, the issue of whether or not, and to what extent, people tend to function in their social lives within the religious networks that they form and maintain. To what extent are these networks all-inclusive or alternatively closed and exclusive? Unless such information is collected we have very little basis for judgement as to the bridging or bonding nature of religious capital accumulation.

The only piece of information about this actually comes from an indirect observation. I have underlined above that, in the Turkish case at least, donations tend to be predominantly directed to close-by needy. I called this parochial giving. As noted, such giving is directly influenced by religious capital. If religious capital shapes the philanthropic giving in a parochial, thus bonding nature, then little can be found in these activities that suggest a series of interactions that may lead to the brighter side of the social capital literature. As such increasing religiosity that would be expected to bring about a higher level of giving to the needy will not also lead to increased levels of social capital in Turkish society.

The anecdotal evidence for the darker-side interpretations of social and religious capital can be found in the most recent natural disasters of the 2004 tsunami in Indonesia and the neighbouring areas of Thailand and India, and the 2005 earthquake in Pakistan and India. Despite Turkish government efforts to stimulate a mass response to the call for assitance in the disaster-stricken areas, the philanthropic aid that could be gathered from Turkey for these areas remained quite low. In spite of the openly religious rhetoric adopted in these fund-raising efforts, only very limited amounts came to flow and most strikingly this flow predominantly was directed towards the Muslim areas. A strictly bonding-type exclusionist aid-giving seems to have arisen in this situation.

The question is still with us: do religious people tend to isolate themselves from the 'others' who are more likely to be infidels, disbelievers? Such bonding at the expense of the bridging type of social and religious capital accumulation may depend on the degree of religious homogeneity and the way state relates to religion in a given setting. In the Turkish case, for example, individuals are very unlikely to meet non-Muslims in their daily lives. Infact, there are many more non-Muslim tourists in the country than non-Muslim native minorities. The only element of heterogeneity brought into the Turkish religious scene originates not from outside Islam but from within. The sectarian minorities such as the Alevis, as opposed to the Hanefi-Sunni majority, help shape the religious identity of the masses and divide them into categories that mimic the Muslim-non-Muslim divide in other settings. As I argued elsewhere, overlapping with the Alevi-Sunni divide to a great extent is the pro-Islamist vs. the secularists divide (see Çarkoğlu 2005). To what extent do these apparent sectarian and political cleavages tend to be reflected in the fundamental perceptions of the people concerning other fellow human beings who may be of the same sect as themselves or may not be strict observant Muslims as they see themselves to be? To what extent are people from the other sect seen as 'sinners' and thus to be avoided? Given perhaps a common sect, do people perceive the believer pro-Islamists, as opposed to the secularists, from a political perspective as clear signals of moral decay embedded in their representatives and thus as people not to be trusted and rather to be avoided? Such questions need further examination at both the conceptual and the empirical levels.

Bibliography

Argyle, M. and Beith-Hallahmi, B. 1975. *The Social Psychology of Religion*, London: Routledge & Kegan Paul.

Becker, G.S. 1964. *Human Capital: A Theoretical and Empirical Analysis*, New York: National Bureau of Economic Research.

Beith-Hallahmi, B. and Argyle; M. 1997. *The Psychology of Religious Behavior, Belief and Experience*, London: Routledge.

Çarkoğlu, A. 2005. 'Political Preferences of the Turkish Electorate: Reflections of an Alevi-Sunni Cleavage', *Turkish Studies*, 6: 273–292.

——2006. 'Trends in Individual Giving and Foundation Practices in Turkey', in *Philanthropy in Turkey: Citizens, Foundations and the Pursuit of Social Justice*, İstanbul: Third Sector Foundation of Turkey Publications. 81–160. (http://www.tusev.org.tr/content/detail.aspx?cn=236)

—— and Hassan, R. 2005. 'Giving and Gaining: Philanthropy and Social Justice in Muslim Societies', working paper.

—— and Toprak, B. 2000. *Türkiye'de Din, Toplum ve Siyaset* (Religion, Society and Politics in Turkey), in Turkish, Istanbul: Turkish Economic and Social Studies Foundation (TESEV) Publications.

Denny, F. 2005. *An Introduction to Islam*. Upper Saddle River: Prentice Hall.

Durkheim, E. 1915. *The Elementary Forms of Religious Life*, Glencoe, IL: Free Press.

Feldstein, L.M. and Sander, T.H. 2001. 'Community Foundations and Social Capital', in P. Walkenhorst (ed.), *Building Philanthropic and Social Capital: The Work of Community Foundations*, Gütersloh: Bertelsmann Foundation Publishers. 41–62

Field, J. 2003. *Social Capital*, London: Routledge.

Finke, Roger and Kevin Dougherty. 2002. 'The Effects of Professional Training: The Social and Religious Capital Acquired in Seminaries', *Journal for the Scientific Study of Religion*, 41: 103–120.

Fiske, S.T. and Taylor, S.E. 1991. *Social Cognition*, New York: McGraw Hill.

Glock, C.Y. and Stark, R. 1965. *Religion and Society in Tension*, Chicago: Rand McNally.

Granovetter, M.S. 1973. 'The Strength of Weak Ties', *American Journal of Sociology*, 78: 1360–1380.

Hassan, Riaz. 2002. *Faithliness, Muslim Conceptions of Islam and Society*, Oxford: Oxford University Press.

Iannacone, L. 1990. 'Religious Practice: A Human Capital Approach', *Journal for the Scientific Study of Religion*, 29: 297–314.

Lam, P.Y. 2002. 'As the Flocks Gather: How Religion Affects Voluntary Association Participation', *Journal for the Scientific Study of Religion*, 41: 405–422.

Putnam, R.D. 2000. *Bowling Alone: The Collapse and Revival of American Community*, New York: Simon and Shuster.

Regnerus, M.D., Smith, C. and Sikkink, D. 1998. 'Who Gives to the Poor? The Influence of Religious Tradition and Political Location on the Personal Generosity of Americans Toward the Poor', *Journal for the Scientific Study of Religion*, 37: 481–493.

Robinson, N. 1999. *Islam, A Concise Introduction*, Washington, DC: Georgetown University Press.

Rockeach, M. 1973. *The Nature of Human Values*, New York: Free Press.

Stark, R. and Finke, R. 2000. *Acts of Faith: Explaining the Human Side of Religion*, Berkeley, CA: University of California Press.

Survey Research Center. 1969. *1964 Election Study*. Ann Arbor: Inter-University Consortium for Political Research, University of Michigan.

Tart, C. 1983. *Transpersonal Psychologies*, El Cerrito, CA: Psychological Processes Inc.

Uslaner, E.M. 2002. *The Moral Foundations of Trust*, Cambridge: Cambridge University Press.

Vaughan, F. 1991. 'Spiritual Issues in Psychotherapy', *Journal of Transpersonal Psychology*, 23: 105–119.

Wuthnow, R. 2002. 'Religious Involvement and Status-Bridging Social Capital', *Journal for the Scientific Study of Religion*, 41: 669–684.

Zinnbauer, Brian, Pargement, Cole, Brenda, Rye, Mark S., Butter, Eric M., Belavich, Timothy G., Hipp, Kathleen M., Scott, Allie B., and Kadar, Jill L. 1997. 'Religion and Spirituality: Unfuzzying the Fuzzy.' *Journal for the Scientific Study of Religion*, 36: 549–564.

PART III
Identity

Chapter Nine

Development of the Religious Self: A Theoretical Foundation for Measuring Religious Identity

David M. Bell

In the emerging globalized world, the pooling together of cultures has left in its wake the increasingly enigmatic task of defining one's own identity (Erikson 1975; Lifton 1999). 'Who am I?' has become an archetypal quest for Westerners lost in a sea of replicated interstate exits and branded chain stores. Consumerism has certainly not squelched the desire for a meaningful identity. Despite century-old predictions that religion would fade away, most individuals still report that religion is one of the most important parts of their identity. If so, how does it become so important? This chapter highlights the need for greater precision in the conceptualization and possible measurement of religious identity with the goal of offering a formative beginning for researchers and scholars with what has long been a relatively unknown aspect to religion.

Erik Erikson's original emphasis on the ego's achievement of identity highlighted the importance for each individual to be able to make meaning of one's own self. He located this task in the adolescent years as part of a psychosocial framework in which the sociocultural milieu (*ethos*) is integrated with the biological development of the human being (*soma*) (1950, 1968, 1997). Erikson's concept of identity first sparked the interest of his college students in the 1960s and helped stimulate a 'discursive explosion' in identity research through the ensuing decades (Friedman 1998; Hall 1996). As part of this movement, James Marcia developed one of the most popular research models in identity in which he described four identity statuses in the process of identity formation – identity diffusion, foreclosure, moratorium, and achieved (1966); since then, his work has established an empirical foundation for psychometric measures of identity.

Two important developments have since characterized identity research. First, this 'explosion' in identity research has been plagued by a lack of conceptual clarity as in both the humanities and the social sciences scholars use the term 'identity' in widely varying models (Coté 2006). Researchers from multitudes of backgrounds and theoretical assumptions have amassed nearly 20,000 research articles dealing with identity in just the last decade (research database PsychINFO). Secondly, within the research on identity development, there is good evidence that a person is composed of identity *domains*, such as ethnic, sexual, or religious – each with their own potentially differing identity statuses (Griffith and Griggs 2001; Pulkkinen and Kokko 2000; Bartoszuk 2003; Meeus 2002; Hunter, 1999; Pastorino et. al. 1997; Kroger and Green 1996; Robertson 1995). Both of these developments are significant in the conceptualization of religious identity. Out of the exponential attention to identity, the term 'religious identity' has increasingly appeared, especially in work rooted in the humanities. However, it has lacked theoretical precision and empirical validation. Ethnographic scholars of religion may employ religious identity to describe isolated phenomena in small cultural groups, and social statisticians may refer to religious identity as social capital. Rarely do these researchers consider religious identity beyond a one-dimensional labeling of one's self. Within psychological circles, the growing understanding of identity domains and differing identity statuses has stimulated research per each domain; yet, the scholars have been reticent to work with the domain of religious identity. In fact, although dozens of psychology research articles have been published measuring the separate identity domains of vocation, gender, and ethnicity, none have considered religious identity as a potentially separate and measurable cognitive domain. The first presentation for the possibility of a psychological construct for religious identity (empirically measurable and separable from other identity domains) was given at the 2006 American Psychological Association's Division 36 Conference (Bell 2006). In this vein this chapter argues for a theoretically sharper understanding of religious identity development – one that necessitates a reframing of the research, moving from the question of how religiosity influences identity to the question of how religious identity is an empirically unique component of identity and should be included as an important measure in sociological and psychological measures of religion.

The lack of attention to religious identity within psychological research has been somewhat surprising. Among domains of identity, religious identity seems to be the most unstable in our current sociocultural context. More than ever, individuals are aware of their own choice and possibility within a relative marketplace of religious identities. In America, it is common for people to refer to themselves as 'shopping' for a church and denomination. Despite this instability, individuals consistently rank religiosity very high in their own sense of purpose and subjective well-being. From my experience in teaching the psychology of religion to college students, the domain of religious identity appears to be of great concern and anxiety. 'Who am I?' is inextricably related to 'What do I believe?' This chapter details the theoretical background to a research project that is constructing a psychological measure of religious identity. It is hoped that the project will benefit researchers in the social sciences and humanities, as well as clinical practitioners and religious educators. By offering greater precision to the religious identity domain, researchers may better understand the process of identity development, domain interaction, and religious development. Further, psychologists of religion may be able to discern a facet of religiosity that has been overlooked and falls outside of the common psychological measures for extrinsic and intrinsic religiosity. In practice, such a construct could inform the clinical use of Life Review therapy popularized by pastoral counselors; likewise, religious educators would be able to use a construct of religious identity to investigate which types of behavior facilitate development of the religious self.

Reviewing Identity and Religiosity Measures

Conceptualization and Models of Identity

Erikson's original model of eight psychosocial stages laid the foundation for future work with the conceptual notion of identity (1950). As the primary ego task of adolescents in the fifth stage of identity vs. role confusion, individuals reshape their simpler identifications from childhood by bringing them into a coherent whole marked by internalized integration. Evidenced by the groupish nature of adolescents, Erikson saw teenagers struggle by challenging previous identifications and trying on new identity roles in order to have a sense of balance between the self and the other. However, this is not a fixed achievement, and this integration could be unraveled later in life. In Erikson's clinical work with war veterans, he witnessed a disintegration of ego identity – a breakdown of one's ability to incorporate a role and purpose that was and is incomprehensible, such as in battle for soldiers (1950). Unfortunately, a precise definition of identity eluded Erikson. In one of his more concise statements, he described a 'sense of identity [as] the accrued confidence that the inner sameness and continuity prepared in the past are matched by the sameness and continuity of one's meaning for others …' (1950, 261). As part of an epigenetic model of development, Erikson (1997) described the organic biological development of the person (*soma*) in relationship to the cultural organization (*ethos*) needing to be organized by ego synthesis (*psyche*). In this way, identity is related to the bio-evolutionary breaking away from parents with the integration of both social roles for production and biological needs for intimacy and procreation. Snarey and Bell (2003) mapped out this framework as a functional developmental model, as opposed to structural models (focused exclusively on cognitive structure) on one side and sociocultural models (focused on the cultural construct of developmental age periods) on the other side. The theoretical balance between the biological/ structural development of identity with the sociocultural influence on identity roles and expectations has also been similarly described as developmental contextualism (Lerner 1993). In essence, the psychological study of identity must always keep in mind the essential functional nature of people as biological needs for self-definition can only be met in historically relative cultural contexts. Thus a fuller picture of religion and the individual is encapsulated when both the cognitive structure of identity and the sociocultural contexts of religion are theoretically integrated.

Overall Identity Statuses

Stemming from Erikson's psychosocial conceptualization of identity, Marcia sought to demonstrate construct validity of Erikson's theory of identity achievement through an Identity Status Interview (ISI). From his qualitative and quantitative research, Marcia describes four statuses of overall identity formation – identity diffusion, foreclosure, moratorium, and achieved (1966). Beginning with several open-ended interviews, Marcia found two forms of committed individuals. Subjects referred to as 'identity achieved' had gone through crises and identity explorations which questioned earlier indentifications and had formed a significant commitment.

Other individuals in 'foreclosure' had formed an identity commitment without any process of exploration and one that largely mimicked the commitments of childhood. Marcia also described two forms of uncommitted identities. The identity status of 'moratorium' describes subjects who were in the process of identity exploration and were striving to achieve some direction. Finally, individuals in 'identity diffusion' were not concerned with their lack of direction. Typically, individuals start off in identity diffusion and either move towards foreclosure, or they go through moratorium and then into identity achievement. Although developmental stages have been deconstructed for their simplistic and uniform assumptions about varying cultures, these developmental statuses (not stages) do not assume unidirectional movement. Instead they offer scholars a theoretical map to plot the many cognitive transitions that people make as they struggle with identity.

Marcia's work has established an empirical foundation for psychometric measures of identity with more than 500 published research articles on the process of identity formation. The interview was last revised in 1993 and is characterized by a qualitative nature (approximately one hour in length) with open-ended questions whose answers are then coded (Marcia et al. 1993). The content of the ISI mostly surrounds the subject areas of vocation, religion, politics, and sexuality. Despite this popularity in Marcia's statuses, it should be noted that there also exists a large group of detractors who offer critiques from different theoretical sides. First, Marcia's close proximity to Erikson's work puts his own theory of statuses in jeopardy. As Erikson's model was an outgrowth of Freud's psychoanalytic school, it was largely devoid of empirical research and quantification. Today, many research psychologists beholden to statistical quantification give little credit to Erikson's model as more than an unproven narrative. From the other side, the mere attempt to formulate and measure an overall identity status that is presumed to be universal among the world's many cultures is preposterous to many sociological and ethnographic scholars. Indeed, trying to fashion a model of identity development which is necessarily embedded and functional brings these two different sides to a scholarly battleground.

One of the primary problems with Marcia's model has been entirely overlooked, and serves as the central prompting for this present research in religious identity. Marcia's identity paradigm includes a significant proportion of content regarding religion, and the model values moving towards the fourth and final status of achieved identity. Here, one of the internal problems with the overall identity status paradigm quickly becomes apparent. Marcia's original conception of identity diffusion status implicitly values a growth beyond this status, moving at least to identity foreclosure or moratorium. If a young adult does not move beyond the identity diffusion status, then they could demonstrate psychopathological symptoms (Kroger 2004). Further, identity diffusion is correlated with relatively low pre-conventional or conventional levels of moral reasoning (Skoe and Marcia 1991). Of course, identity questions with religious content are part of the measure and computation of identity. Yet, one can imagine several scenarios in which religious identity in particular should not be related to low moral development, nor to psychopathology. For example, an individual who is brought up within a religious belief system may deconvert, or simply become non-religious. The fact that some individuals choose to be non-religious, or to deconvert, may not be due to a lack of overall identity maturity. Furthermore, in different cultural contexts, religion may not be a predominant resource for identity formation, such as in largely non-religious societies or even in microcosms of family systems that are largely nonreligious. Marcia's original identity trajectory functions, in effect, as a sort of religious propagator by favoring those who are religious and confounding identity development with other domains resulting with a fallacious correlation between non-religious people and poor mental health. This is partly corrected by separately studying religious identity development.

Recent Empirical Work in Identity Statuses

One of the problems with the ISI has been the difficulty of having trained coders and blind coders for the interviews. In response, Adams remodeled the ISI into a 64-item scale with no need for interview coding. The Measure of Ego Identity Status-II (EOMEIS-II) breaks down Marcia's four identity statuses and has been validated through comparison with the ISI (Adams 1999; Adams et al. 1989). The EOMEIS-II includes eight items on religion, but only as a component to the overall identity status with little ability to tease out different levels of analysis per dimension. In another effort, the Ego Identity Process Questionnaire (EIPQ, 32 items) (Balistreri et al. 1995) measures the separate dimensions of commitment and exploration in eight areas: Occupation, Religion, Politics, Values, Family, Friendships, Dating, and Sex Roles. The coadjuted identity domains were not methodologically constructed for separate statistical analysis but extensive validity analysis may support such results. Both of these measures were designed to analyze a 'global identity' – a sense of overall identity formation in each individual. But over the last decade, researchers have challenged the notion of just one identity and have moved towards measuring the identity status of different identity domains.

This is the most important development in identity research to date. Reflecting a postmodern turn with a thicker description of identity complexity, many scholars are now seeing global identity as a collection of different identities which may not coalesce within the same identity status for one person. In other words, an individual may have an achieved sense of vocational identity, and yet a diffused sense of the ethnic or cultural self (De Hann and Schulenberg 1997; Skorikov and Vondracek 1998). In response, dozens of articles have pursued isolated domains of ethnicity, gender, and vocation. But, as mentioned previously, the domain of religion has been completely overlooked. However, some promising research has pointed to this possibility. For example, a recent study included religious identity as a separate domain with measures of Marcia's four statuses (Fadjukoff et al. 2005). Working with Finnish adults, the authors found religious identity to commonly be diffused for men and foreclosed for women, even when the individuals were rated as identity achieved overall. The authors concluded that neither political nor religious identity seemed to be salient in the overall achievement of identity. While still assuming that an individual has a sense of overall global identity achievement, the authors saw the identity domain of religion as unimportant since it did not match their measures and results for the overall identity status. Yet, this also suggests that religious identity may be understood separately from other domains of identity.

There are two further caveats to this study. As the authors point out, Lutheran religion in Finland is not perceived as an important entity in that cultural context. How would North American adults differ in their perception of the importance of religious identity? In the functional framework presented in this chapter, it is not claimed that religious identity is important in largely non-religious cultures. Although it is of scholarly interest to consider alternative responses to possible transcendental and spiritual needs in nonreligious societies, the purpose of this essay is to sharpen the notion of how we perceive religious identity when it is an accessible and readily available resource in one's culture. As a second caveat, the research was conducted through an open-ended question: 'Do you have a personal relationship to religion?' This method lacks a theoretical sharpness that a carefully constructed religious identity scale may be able to provide.

In another study, De Haan and Schulenberg (1997) found that political identity formation does not commonly reach an achieved status until the mid-twenties, whereas religious identity was often achieved in the late teens and early twenties. Further, adolescents in junior high school were typically in foreclosure in the religious identity domain, moving through diffusion in high school, and then moratorium or achieved statuses in college. This would be unique among identity domains, since other identity domains typically begin in diffusion and move towards the other three statuses. The typical pattern of religious identity formation moving from foreclosure towards diffusion is complemented by a general decline in religiosity from early to later adolescence (Francis and Pearson 1987). This generates several questions. Why is the religious identity domain so unique? Is religious identity formation affected by different religious backgrounds, such as Protestant vs. Catholic? Is there an increased anxiety for individuals who are in religious identity moratorium or diffusion? De Haan and Schulenberg's findings were limited by using the EOMEIS-II which only asks eight questions in the religious identity domain; thus only two questions are asked per the four identity statuses of religious identity. Further, the authors understood religiosity as fairly uniform and did not break down results for religious backgrounds, even though the sample was nicely divided (49 per cent Protestant; 36 per cent Catholic). The only other study that has measured religious identity status independently from overall identity found that religious identity lagged behind vocational identity among adolescents (Skorikov and Vondracek 1998). This leaves researchers and counselors with a plethora of unanswered questions. How do denominational factors influence religious identity formation? Is religious identity achievement as stable in adulthood as in other identity domains?

Religiosity Measures

In regard to identity, scholars in the psychological study of religion have most often been interested in how established and measurable variables of religiosity (that is, 'extrinsic' and 'intrinsic' religiosity, 'quest' measures) interact with an individual's overall identity development status (Allport and Ross 1966; Gorsuch and McPherson 1989). The most common measure in religion is for (I) intrinsic religiosity (inwardly motivated) and (E) extrinsic religiosity (outwardly motivated, possibly for social gain) (Allport and Ross 1966). The measures are not on a continuum, and you could score high on both I and E, low on both, or mixed scores. Using these measures, researchers have investigated how they influence the status of an overall identity. Intrinsic religiosity has been linked with identity achievement and extrinsic religiosity with identity diffusion (Fulton 1997). Identity foreclosure has been associated with indiscriminates (low I and E, or high I and E) and extrinsics (Markstrom-Adams and Smith 1996). Differing from some of the assumptions in identity research, many of these research projects find religious orientation to be quite salient in the statuses of identity development. Overall, religion has been positively associated with identity achievement but researchers know little of the mechanism or specific interaction in this positive association. King (2003) has suggested that religion uniquely provides a rich nexus of ideological, spiritual, and social resources which prove quite helpful in reaching identity achievement. A significant problem with this correlational research is that many identity status scales are confounded by their amount of religious content (Adams et al. 1989). Thus, the higher one's religiosity (I or E), the more likely an individual has explored his/her own religious identity. Given the domain uniqueness and the confounding religious content in identity scales, Spilka et al. (2003) suggest that researchers should construct an independent measure for religious identity.

Reframing Religious Identity

The ongoing research at Emory University proposes that religious identity be reframed, moving from the question of how *religiosity* influences overall *identity* to the question of how *religious identity* is an empirically unique, potentially separable component of identity (qualitatively different per religious identity statuses) and how *religious identity* should be included as an important measure when investigating degrees of religiosity (quantitatively different in salience to an individual).

With the lack of conceptual clarity in scholarly articles, researchers have loosely presumed 'religious identity' to be an easily understood, self-reported labeling of one's religious affiliation. However, it is much more unique, complex, and significant than has been previously assumed. In the American marketplace of religion, individuals who refer to 'shopping' for a religious home or see themselves as spiritual 'seekers' are looking for more than a religious label. The postmodern tension between religious homogenization (lowest-common-denominator theology) and religious splintering has resulted in a great deal of angst and internal mistrust for persons seeking religious identity. Furthermore, identity is more than a theoretical concept. It begins with a real cognitive component located in the neurological structure of the mind.

Religious Identity Development

Cognitive Foundation and Social Context

The above proposal suggests that religious identity may be measurable by both qualitative complexity and quantitative salience. By using the descriptive 'qualitative', what is meant is that religious identity does not just quantitatively increase as a child emerges into adulthood. Instead, there are qualitative aspects of religious identity in which one's relationship with the outside-religious-world/ religious-other is fundamentally different in each of the proposed religious identity statuses. Are there conceptual reasons to understand qualitatively different statuses of religious identity? Identity, as a whole, is indeed cognitively unique; we know it has specific and multiple neurological locations and functions. A necessary condition for an identity achieved status is the ability to remember and integrate one's own remembered experiences. You can lose your identity – and only your identity – through brain trauma or neurological disease. More specifically, different components of identity are formed when episodic memory, encoded in the hippocampus and stored in the temporal cortex, is selectively retrieved and narratively available as autobiographical memory. This storehouse of memories may be conscious or unconscious patterns of self-definition and understanding. As stated above, such identity motifs may operate uniquely per identity domains and may show patterns of likely development as a child grows into adulthood. Also demonstrating cognitive specifity, Marcia's four statuses are statistically correlated with Piagetian cognitive development in childhood and adolescence (Marcia et al. 1993). Further, the statuses reflect real resources of autobiographical memory and patterned identity motifs that are significantly different per each status.

In the functional description of identity, it is important to note that these neurological entities (also known as 'individuals') pull upon dramatically different cultural resources in order to construct identity. Although there is a cognitive foundation to identity, identity domains are not necessarily, cognitively unique. For instance, domains can blend per individuals and contexts, for example, a minister's vocational and religious identity; or, sociocultural contexts may not offer options per some domains, for example, some societies or families may offer no religious/ spiritual domain of identity content. These domains are historically relative and shaped by one's own experiences and cultural contexts. But that does not free them from their cognitive roots. It is likely that identity domains naturally pull from significantly different regions of the brain. For instance, when individuals are prompted in a functional magnetic resonance imaging (fMRI) study, vocational identity uses different areas of the brain than sexual identity. Although untested, it is probable that religious identity is likewise characterized by unique neurological modularity. Given this relationship between cognition and social context, identity domains should be understood in a functional model which incorporates both.

If one accepts Marcia's four identity statuses (as much of identity research has done) and the domain specificity of identity, then we may begin to see the helpfulness of studying identity statuses for religious identity. How might religious identity be different from gender or ethnic identity? It is potentially the least stable identity domain in Western societies and is the one domain that pertains to transcending the self. By instability of an identity domain, what is meant is that one would be able to switch between different religious identity statuses through the lifespan – that is, an achieved religious identity status could be unraveled. Further, religious identity is psychosocially unique in that it is the only domain which is so closely related to transcending the self. In the domain of religious identity, identity is drawn from individual and social/institutional allegiance to an unseen, outside-of-me god/s, cosmic force – it is the most imaginative identity domain. A popular phrase among evangelical Americans is 'being lost in Jesus'. Since identity is an integration and balance between self and other, a religious identity is peculiar in that its trajectory, in some religions, is towards transcending the self in some manner. This could be understood as an internalized/integrated sense of sacred Other, or even a third 'other' as identity is potentially triangulated.

Religious Identity Statuses Measure

In developing a Religious Identity Status Scale, four statuses of religious identity (see Figure 9.1) are offered as the first step in seeing the qualitative complexity of how an individual integrates his/her transcendent sense of a relationship with the sacred and the surrounding religious community into a coherent sense of self.

Position on religious identity	**Religious identity moratorium**	**Religious identity foreclosure**	**Religious identity diffusion**	**Religious identity integration**
Crisis	Present	Absent	Absent	Present
Commitment	Absent	Present	Absent	Present

Figure 9.1   Religious Identity Status Measure

A 28-item questionnaire has been designed, using the eight previous questions from the EOMEIS-II, and adding twenty more questions (a total of seven per religious identity status), in order to better get at the complexity and formation of religious identity. Results are being correlated with demographics, religious backgrounds (including denominational differences), and religious practices and beliefs. Construct validity is partly established by consistency among status questions, test-retest variation, and statistical similarity to the previously validated EOMEIS-II questions. The questionnaire is constructed for the internet, and results will be weighted to consider selection biases (those with a computer may be younger, ethnically homogenous, and better educated). The n goal is 1000. In general, as with other identity domains, it is expected that individuals will typically move developmentally from religious identity diffusion (RID) and foreclosure (RIF) towards religious identity moratorium (RIM) and then to religious identity integration (RII) through the adolescent years into early adulthood. However, it is also expected that adults may have situational events and cultural factors that could unravel RII into RIM at any point in the lifespan, or they may become non-religious and move into a RID status. One major problem with developmental models is the presumption that people should end up at the end of the model. This Religious Identity Statuses Scale is not a measure that esteems one status over another, saying how individuals *should* integrate religion into their identity. Instead, it is understood that each of the four statuses, albeit reflecting development, may move in any direction and that each status is perfectly acceptable. One goal of the research is to see these patterns of movement and to correlate them with age, religious practices, and cultural contexts.

Religious identity diffusion (RID)   It has been assumed that children inherently begin in identity diffusion. Prior to adolescence, they have little psychological need for constructing identity. They are not interested in defining themselves. RID would not only describe children, but also adults who are disinterested in religion, and possibly those who are extrinsically oriented towards their religion (self-serving motivation for religious involvement[1]) (Griffith and Griggs 2001). They have made no commitment to a religious community or set of beliefs, nor have they felt any crisis in regards to this lack of commitment. Thus, RID includes two sets of people. One group is largely disinterested in identity overall and have not yet experienced any search for internal meaning. A second group has searched for meaning and may have found purpose in identity resources other than religion.

Religious identity foreclosure (RIF)   This status reflects individuals who have made a commitment to a religious tradition and its set of beliefs and practices. RIF's are distinguished from RII individuals by their lack of flexibility and their strong desire for conformity. Overall foreclosed individuals tend to be authoritarian and need the approval of their peers. They can quickly become defensive about their faith and are correlated with conventional moral reasoning (Kroger 2004). They are marked by a pattern of accommodation and inherit their religious identity with little critical reflection. As stated above, De Hann and Schulenberg (1997) reviewed findings that showed early adolescents in the RIF status, and then moving into a RID status – opposite of more typical patterns of other identity domains. In highly religious societies, it may be that teenagers have ample opportunities to unquestionably adopt a religious identity for sake of ease and comfort. If we had data for pre-adolescents, we may find that they move from diffusion earlier than other identity domains, as many adopt a solidified style of religious identity (RIF) by the age of 13. That this is out of sync with other identity domains establishes further evidence that religious identity functions in cognitively unique ways for many individuals. Are religious symbols and belief systems more salient resources for identity commitments at an earlier age than other identity resources? If so, why has some research pointed to a move from RIF to RID as the teenager gets older? Further, in that some churches encourage critical reflection on their beliefs and others renounce such efforts, we could imagine that denominational backgrounds would be strongly influential in moving masses of people into RIF, or towards RII.

Religious identity moratorium (RIM)   Individuals characterized by an RIM status do not demonstrate a commitment to a religious tradition, and they may either feel

---

1   Although overall identity diffusion is related to extrinsic religiosity, Allport and Ross's (1966) measures of intrinsic and extrinsic religious orientation are problematic in that the measure applies negative value to extrinsic religious motivation. Thus, those more motivated by the liturgical practices and fellowship in a religious community are deemed less religiously mature than those who are more intrinsically motivated by personal belief systems.

some anxiety about their religious identity, or may simply be reflective and attentive to this identity domain. They have a strong sense of willfulness and self-esteem while resisting demands for conformity. These are the religious seekers, those who are open to different religious identities and score high on the Quest measure of religiosity. Their religious identity is in flux and may stay in this status for weeks or for a lifetime. From clinical experience, these are the individuals who feel greater stress and seek out pastoral counselors and clinical psychologists. In regards to those in overall identity moratorium, individuals report that Marcia's identity status interview gives them insight into their situation (Kroger 2004). Such clinical application could be sharpened with a clearer perspective on the individual domain of religious identity, especially for spiritual caregivers and pastoral counselors.

Religious identity integration (RII)   The word integration is used instead of Marcia's word achievement in order to remove the implicit valuing of different theologies and traditions of religious identity formation. Those who are foreclosed can be quite satisfied with their religious identity; it may serve them and their tradition well. Erikson (1950) used the terminology 'identity vs. role confusion' to describe this stage in which an individual takes previous identifications (labels) and integrates them into a coherent sense of self. Building on Erikson's original conceptualization, integration better describes this process in religious identity formation in which a person critically reflects upon his/her culture's religious belief systems and traditions. They then choose for their own sake, and not just for others, to integrate a particular faith system into who they are and how they define themselves. Having made a commitment to a religious identity, RII individuals have a strong sense of self-esteem and autonomy. However, they also remain flexible, even playful, with religious practices and beliefs.

These four qualitative statuses of religious identity are a first offering towards a conceptually sharper understanding of religious identity and religious identity development. Given the recently understood complexity of identity domains, there is ample evidence that individuals negotiate qualitatively different religious identity statuses. This taxonomy could provide religious educators and clinical practitioners with a helpful tool to better understand how religion works in the mind. In clinical practice, such a scale could help determine more specific and informed interventions (per domains) which could (1) offer validation and allow room for religious identity moratorium status, (2) prompt possibly delayed individuals (diffused religious identity in adulthood) with presenting symptoms into some integrated sense of and search for religious identity, (3) enable foreclosed religious identity clients with related presenting problems to become less religiously stagnate via an earned religious identity. And as stated before, it could enable theory and practice in religious education as statuses of religious identity could be correlated with types of religiosity (denominations, faith practices, religious orientations).

Religious Identity Salience Measure

The second component to the measure of religious identity is the Religious Identity
Salience Scale. This simpler Likert-type measure will ask individuals to self-rate
the importance of different identity domains. With potential sub-domains of implicit
and explicit religious identity, the individuals will not be aware at first that the scale
is aimed specifically at religious identity. If added to comprehensive psychometric
inventories of religiosity, it could help understand the social psychological *predictors*
and psychological *effects* of an individual's high or low salience in religious identity.
When psychologists of religion employ measures of overall religiosity and religious
orientation, the measures overlook the very important psychological role of religious
identity. One anecdotal illustration: an adult subject raised in a Catholic home who
currently does not practice (low extrinsic religiosity) and is not internally motivated
by a belief system (low intrinsic religiosity) would be labeled non-religious.
However, the individual may explicitly consider her/himself as Catholic, a religious
identity; this identity may actually be very important to the subject and hold more
value than a simple labeled identification. How does this religious identity operate?
Why, if it does not influence daily internal decisions nor external behavior, is it still
important to an individual? Some scholars have dismissed such religious identities
as not really 'religious.' However, it is likely that this religious identity satisfies
some need for a transcendent identity – a 'fall-back', if you will, providing security
and the ability to pull from internalized resources which are paradoxically outside
of the self.

When conducting psychological research in religion, scholars should not only
analyze extrinsics, intrinsics, and questors (the most common measures), but the
degree of salience of religious identity, both implicitly (not prompted for religion)
and explicitly (subsequently prompted for religion and ranks identity domains
including religion) held by the subject. An explicit religious identity refers to an
individual who consciously identifies with a religious community and/or supernatural
entity. A person who has an implicit religious identity may be largely unaware of the
attachments to a religious community. For instance, a young adult who has moved
away from her/his family's religious background and consciously assumes little
connection to this religious tradition may still harbor strong unconscious identity
attachments to this religion. Neurologically, identity works both in the explicit and
conscious construction of the self, and in the unconscious long-term autobiographical
memories stored in the temporal cortex and cerebellum. Likewise, an individual
may show little implicit religious identity, and yet explicitly (likely for contextual
approval) state that religious identity is important to her/his sense of self. The
research model is designed to look at religious identity which may operate separately
and yet importantly in the subconciousness. The first results of the Religious Identity
Salience Scale are being statistically compared with Allport and Ross's measure for
extrinsic and intrinsic religious orientation. A cross-tabulated taxonomy shows such
possibilities in Figure 9.2

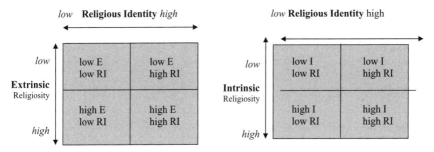

Figure 9.2   Taxonomy of Religious Identity Salience

In practice, a scale for implicit and explicit religious identity salience may show how religious identities tend to sustain individuals through periods of dissonance. For instance, an implicit religious identity may be the primary factor sustaining overall religiosity when an individual is confronted with conflicting belief systems and observed reality, or when an individual's religious community encounters a crisis (the individual relies on religious identity until a new community is found, or returns to the previous one). In short, individuals may not practice religion nor even hold salient religious beliefs, and yet their religious identity may continue to push and pull upon them throughout adulthood.

Conclusion: A First Step

The search for identity is rooted in finding meaning. As adolescents, we often find meaning in *not* being our parents. As we turn to peers and institutions, we are given to unwavering ideological allegiance. Soon, however, in early adulthood, we may learn to question our allegiances and may struggle with the ways in which these questions and doubts upset what we thought we knew. After some time, we form and re-form commitments into patterns that best fit our identities. Erikson first wrote about this pattern and found his most favorable audience in his own college students (1950; 1968). It helped them articulate their experiences. Marcia's four identity statuses attempted to measure this patterned growth of identity. However, by including religious content, the statuses confounded those who chose to be non-religious and privileged only those who struggled with their belief systems.

Identity research is now being revolutionized with the new tools of neurological modularity and identity domain specificity. This research in religious identity development uses a functional model which balances cognitive foundations of autobiographical memory with the contextual reality in which religion operates. There is growing evidence that religious identity develops in a way unique to other domains of identity. However, the research is likely to prompt many more questions than it answers.

The importance of sharpening our understanding of religious identity cannot be understated. As forms of globalized modernity settle across distant countries, individuals undergoing the normal process of identity formation are confronted with contrasting belief systems for the first time in their cultural history. Interestingly, the religious beliefs and religious actions appear to be secondary to the importance of the religious identity. For many, a radicalized and unquestioning allegiance (religious identity foreclosure) to a religious identity provides personal stability at the cost of ripening the likelihood of distanced conflict. This conceptualization of religious identity is one that both offers insight into one's own religious self and may garner even more important insights into cultural movements.

Possibly the most interesting aspect of the research has been the growing evidence that religious identity may form the core of religiosity for individuals. Once an attachment or commitment have been made, religious identity seems more fundamental than religious beliefs or religious practices. Individuals can stop going to religious services, stop reading sacred texts, and possibly even stop believing in core tenets of their faith tradition, and yet their religious identity still remains with them across their lifespan. With the weight of most research in religious beliefs and practices, it may be that religious identity research unlocks a key to understanding religion and the individual.

Bibliography

Adams, G.R. 1999. 'The objective measure of ego identity status: a manual on theory and test construction.' Unpublished manuscript, University of Guelph, Ontario, Canada.

——, L. Bennion and K. Huh. 1989. *Objective measure of ego identity status: A reference manual.* 2nd edn. Logan, UT: Utah State University.

Allport, G.W. and J.M. Ross. 1966. 'Personal religious orientation and prejudice.' *Journal of Personality and Social Psychology*, 5: 432–443.

Balistreri, E., N.A. Busch-Rossnagel and K.F. Geisinger. 1995. 'Development and preliminary validation of the ego identity process questionnaire.' *Journal of Adolescence*, 18: 172–192.

Bartoszuk, K. 2003. 'The influence of family structure and family functioning on identity development.' *Dissertation Abstracts International Section A: Humanities and Social Sciences*, 63: 4106.

Bell, D.B. 2006. 'Religious Identity: Conceptualizing a measure for research and practice.' Unpublished paper presented at APA Div. 36 Mid-Conference, March 3–4, 2006.

Coté, J. 2006. 'Identity studies: How close are we to developing a social science of identity? – An appraisal of the field.' *Identity: An international journal of theory and research*, 6: 3–25.

De Haan, L.G. and J. Schulenberg. 1997. 'The covariation of religion and politics during the transition to adulthood: Challenging global identity assumptions.' *Journal of Adolescence*, 20: 537–552.

Erikson, E.H. 1950. *Childhood and society.* New York: Norton.

——. 1968. *Identity, youth, and crisis.* New York: Norton.

——. 1975. *Life history and the historical moment.* New York: Norton.

——. 1997. *The Life cycle completed.* New York: Norton.

Fadjukoff, P., L. Pulkkinen and K. Kokko. 2005. 'Identity Processes in Adulthood: Diverging Domains.' *Identity*, 5: 1–20.

Fivush, R. 1994. 'Constructing narrative, emotion and self in parent–child conversations about the past.' In U. Neisser and R. Fivush (eds), *The remembering self: Accuracy and construction in the life narrative.* New York: Cambridge. 136–157.

Francis, L.J. and P.R. Pearson 1987. 'Empathic development during adolescence: religiosity, the missing link?' *Personality and Individual Differences*, 8: 145–148.

Friedman, L.J. 1998. *Identity's architect: A biography of Erik Erikson.* New York: Scribner.

Fulton, A.S. 1997. 'Identity status, religious orientation, and prejudice.' *Journal of Youth and Adolescence*, 26: 1–11.

Gorsuch, R.L. and S.E. McPherson. 1989. 'Intrinsic/Extrinsic measurement: I/E-revised and single-item scales.' *Journal for the Scientific Study of Religion*, 28: 348–354.

Griffith, B. and J. Griggs. 2001. 'Religious identity status as a model to understand, assess, and interact with client spirituality.' *Counseling and Values*, 46: 14–24.

Hall, S. 1996. 'Introduction: Who needs identity?' In S. Hall and P. Du Gay (eds), *Questions of cultural identity.* London: Sage, 1–17.

Hunter, J. 1999. 'Social identity, domain specific self-esteem and intergroup evaluation.' *Current Research in Social Psychology*, 4: 160–177.

King, P.E. 2003. 'Religion and identity: The role of ideological, social, and spiritual contexts.' *Applied Developmental Studies*, 7: 197–204.

Kroger, J. 2004. *Identity in adolescence: The balance between self and other*, 3rd edn. New York: Routledge.

—— and K. Green. 1996. 'Events associated with identity status change.' *Journal of Adolescence*, 19: 477–490.

Lerner, R. 1993. 'A developmental contextual view of human development.' In S.C. Hayes, L.J. Hayes, H.W. Reese and T.R. Sarbin (eds) *Varieties of scientific contextualism.* Reno, NV: Context Press.

Lifton, R.J. 1999. *The Protean self: Human resilience in the age of fragmentation.* Chicago: University of Chicago Press.

Marcia, J.E. 1966. 'Development and validation of ego identity status.' *Journal of Personality and Social Psychology*, 3: 551–558.

——1967. 'Ego identity status: Relationship to self-esteem, general maladjustment, and authoritarianism.' *Journal of Personality*, 35: 118–133.

——, A.S. Waterman, D.R. Matteson, S.L. Archer and J.L. Orlofsky. 1993. *Ego identity: A handbook for psychosocial research.* New York: Springer.

Markstrom-Adams, C., and M. Smith. 1996. 'Identity formation and religious orientation among high school students from the United States and Canada.' *Journal of Adolescence*, 19; 247–261.

Meeus, W. (2002). 'Commitment and exploration as mechanisms of identity formation.' *Psychological Reports*, 90: 771–785.

Pastorino, E., R. Dunham, J. Kidwell, R. Bacho and S. Lamborn. 1997. 'Domain-specific gender comparisons in identity development among college youth: Ideology and relationships.' *Adolescence*, 32: 559–577.

PsycINFO, computerized database operated by the American Psychological Association. www.psychinfo.com

Pulkkinen, L. and K. Kokko. 2000. 'Identity development in adulthood: a longitudinal study.' *Journal of Research in Personality*, 35: 445–470.

Robertson, G.M. 1995. 'Forming the faith: Religious identity development in adolescents.' *Dissertation Abstracts International: Section B: The Sciences and Engineering*, 56: 2338.

Skoe, E.E. and J.E. Marcia. 1991. 'A measure of care-based morality and its relation to ego identity.' *Merrill-Palmer Quarterly*, 37: 289–304.

Skorikov, V. and F. Vondracek. 1998. 'Vocational identity development: Its relationship to other identity domains and to overall identity development.' *Journal of Career Assessment*, 6: 13–35.

Snarey, J.R. and D.M. Bell. 2003. 'Distinguishing structural and functional models of human development: A response to "What transits in an identity status transition?"' *Identity*, 3: 221–230.

Spilka, B., R. Hood, B. Hunsberger, and R. Gorsuch. 2003. *The Psychology of Religion: An Empirical Approach*, 3rd edn. New York: Guilford.

Chapter Ten

Accommodating the Individual and the Social, the Religious and the Secular: Modelling the Parameters of Discourse in 'Religious' Contexts

Peter Collins

Introduction

In this chapter I consider the continuing presence of two recurring and apparently antipathetic terms, ontologies, means of understanding, in the history of religions: the individual and the social (or 'agency' and 'structure'). I begin with an interrogation of the dominant meanings of these terms and the uses to which they are commonly put in *religious contexts*. Apart from representing what is probably the archetypal dualism in the social sciences, together they continue to express perhaps the most vital tension present not only in the history of religions but also in accounts of the quotidian, of the vernacular, of the religious faith and practice experienced by adepts in their daily lives. However, my primary aim here is to present, through an examination of the faith and practice of Quakers in Britain, an alternative approach to the social/individual dichotomy, an approach which eschews any account which represents social interaction in inherently dichotomous terms, whatever those terms might be. Building on earlier work in which I have attempted to model religious faith and practice, in terms of individual, vernacular and canonic narrative, I introduce a complicating factor, the plane of 'secular discourse'. I show how the terms 'religious' and 'secular' represent a second dichotomy which, if we are not careful, contributes fundamentally to our misunderstanding of *religious contexts*. The point of this paper is not to argue against the social and structural in order merely to revert to its opposite – methodological individualism, but rather to restore the balance and make room for the individual agent. Fortunately, individuals experience the world with little regard for the dichotomous theorizing of social scientists. I intend to show that the dichotomies individual/society and religion/secularity damage our attempts to understand the everyday experience of individuals by chronically underestimating the complexity of human life.

The First Dichotomy: Individual/Society

The theme of the conference at which I presented a first draft of this paper – 'religion and the individual' – is teasing. The social sciences (and I would argue the study of religion) rarely considers the individual apart from society: the formulation is almost always presented in fundamentally binary terms: agency /structure, micro/ macro, individual/society, congregant/congregation. In fact, the individual is often marginalized in accounts of religious faith and practice and sometimes entirely invisible as a source of agency. It is also the case that the social (structure) has tended to overwhelm the individual (agency) in accounts which attempt to accommodate the two and I would argue that this is equally true of anthropology, sociology, religious studies (and, for what it's worth, theology). It is this dualism that characterizes all major theoretical paradigms in the social sciences: functionalism, structural functionalism, French structuralism, post-structuralism, symbolic interactionism, ethnomethodology and so on and so forth. And it is both interesting and somewhat perplexing theoretical edifices which have achieved the greatest success in terms at least of academic influence have been those which look first to social structures in attempting to explain social phenomena.

In the study of religion, the emphasis has always been on social structural factors, in explanations of human life. In sociology and anthropology this is mainly a result of the influence of three extraordinarily influential theorists: Marx, Durkheim and Weber. Marx had little to say about religion, but what he did say has had major social and theoretical repercussions. Marx (Marx and Engels 1957) placed religion securely within the realms of ideology: it has been religion perhaps more than anything else that has enabled the powerful in each society to retain power and dominance (Giddens 1970, 206–16). In Medieval Europe, for instance, it was never a matter of the feudal lord foisting religion on the peasantry with the clear and conscious idea of subjugating it. No, the crucial facet of ideology is that it is understood as the God-given truth by all classes, regardless of their place in the social hierarchy. The function of religion, throughout the ages, is to maintain the status quo –- 'the rich man in his castle, the poor man at his gate'. Religion is dealt with in entirely structural terms.

However, individuals have sought, throughout the ages, and with considerable success, to differentiate, diverge and diversify. For instance, although Roman Catholicism endured for many centuries as the orthodox European worldview, individuals, alone and together in groups, have perpetually found ways to invent alternatives. Taking the European case, think, for example, of the Mozarabs, Templars, Vilgard, Leutard, the 'apostolic movements' of the twelfth century, the Petrusians, Humiliati, Tondrakians, Paulicians, Messalanians, Waldenensians and Cathars in Medieval Europe; the Ranters, Fifth Monarchists, Muggletonians and Quakers on the brink of the modern in England; and the dizzying diversity of New Religious Movements in the contemporary world.[1] These groups, sometimes led

---

1   For medieval sects see Lambert (2002); for the Ranters and other English mid-seventeenth-century religious sects see Morton (1970), McGregor and Reay (1984). For a brilliant case study dealing in depth with the faith and practice of a single individual dissenter

by charismatic individuals and sometimes not, themselves demographically and theologically diverse, called into question the pervasive worldview – often in the certain knowledge that persecution would follow. Sometimes this questioning led to schism, sometimes not. And, of course, the Roman Catholic Church has itself never been entirely unified and homogeneous: because people act as though they believe the same thing that does not mean that they believe the same thing.

Social structural approaches, such as that delineated by Marx, ignore such accounts, even though they date back at least to Augustine's *Confessions* (written in the seventh century). There is plenty of evidence that indicates the tendency of pre-modern people to question the validity and viability of their inherited faith and practice, to escape the determining power of structural factors. While Marx admits that religion has some positive use – in nursing the industrial proletariat through exceedingly hard times for instance – on the whole it was a Very Bad Thing, which all good Communists should work to eradicate (though no communist society has managed this completely). Durkheim (1995 [1912]) has an altogether more positive attitude towards religion: in worshipping God, the group is consolidating society – but once again the individual is entirely lost in his theoretical framework, brilliant though it may be. Durkheim (1984 [1893]), the reader will recall, posits two forms of society (or 'the social'): characterized by either mechanical or organic solidarity. In the former, the presence of religion is centrally important in ensuring the successful functioning of society. It is in religion, and more specifically in religious ritual, that the conscience collective is generated – this being the very glue that holds society together. In such cases, far from being the scourge of the downtrodden (as in Marx) it is their saving grace. Where a society demonstrates an organic solidarity, connectedness is not due to the alikeness or replication of composite units (whether individuals, groups of institutions) but to their difference. In modern society it is specialization that connects us – because we each become expert in one small part of the economy. Think of the production line – one person places the nut on the line, the next person fits it onto the correct bolt, the next tightens it, and so on – we depend on each other to ensure our continued well-being. Peasants are generalists – when one ceases to function another will simply take their place. In modernity, we are all specialists – when one fails to function, the process grinds to a halt. But organic solidarity generates only a partial sense of belonging. Religion is both a cause and an effect of the march of modernity – because religion ensures the continuance of the conscience collective – the result of its diminution and eventual disappearance is anomie and a sense of disconnectedness. But the religious life has not disappeared. 'Institutional religion' diversifies in ever more interesting ways, and, while mainstream Christian churches decline, non-Christian faiths thrive. Clearly, individuals respond in various ways to the march of modernity, but the faith and practice of individuals remain of little interest to Durkheim and his followers. Mention of 'decline' brings us, appropriately, to 'secularization' – and Max Weber.

---

see Ginzburg (1980). For the Mormons see Cornwall, Heaton and Young (1994), and for the Shakers see Stein (1992); for New Religious Movements see Arweck (2006) and Dawson (2006).

Weber (1930; 1965) takes an exceedingly pessimistic view of modern society. Weber argues consistently throughout his writings that the world is steadily becoming a more rational place: rather than one class coming to dominate all others, it is the steady advance towards an ever more bureaucratic society that causes his gloomy prognostication. In modern society we are, whether we like it or not, in thrall to the Enlightenment. Science comes to replace religion as the dominant ideology and efficiency becomes our daily watchword. There is no place for the religious, the mysterious, the intangible in modern society – and apparently equally little room for individual agency. In order to increase our efficiency we need to be able to quantify the outputs of our actions. This poses an interesting challenge for British NHS hospital chaplains, some of whom are experiencing a sense of double bind, resulting from the clash of religious beliefs and occupational responsibilities. Different chaplains respond to this challenge in different ways – largely depending on their own, personal trajectory. Certainly, some manage to resist the encroachment of 'rational systems' on their role with extraordinary inventiveness.[2]

It is true to say that the 'masters' have influenced sociologists and anthropologists alike. The dominant paradigm in anthropology has been structural functionalism – deriving primarily from Durkheim and developed ingeniously by figures such as Radcliffe-Brown, Evans-Pritchard and Mary Douglas: despite their strengths, all contributed to the eclipse of the individual in favouring social structural 'forces'.

However, merely arguing whether one should foreground *either* the individual *or* the social is largely fruitless. There are scholars, however, who have made concerted attempts to transcend individual/society dualism. Although these developments have explicitly eschewed the temptation to foreground one or other of the terms – their authors tend merely to claim their demise while inadvertently inviting one term or other in through the back door. For example, the earlier synthesis of Talcott Parsons, Norbert Elias's figurational sociology and, more recently, the development of structuration theory by Giddens and others. It is likely that Goffman was attempting to build the same kind of bridge in developing his idea of the 'interaction order'.

Probably the most energetic and compelling attempt to transcend the obstructive duality individual/society is to be found in the work of Pierre Bourdieu, who strove throughout his long career to provide analytical tools which are 'good to think with'. And in carrying out this mission he develops a series of concepts which, he claimed, generate a theory which obviates the need for unhelpful dichotomies: doxa, symbolic capital, strategy, practice and habitus. While he was extraordinarily persistent in his use of these terms, Bourdieu's consistency in their use was less apparent and this is especially true in the case of his central concept: habitus. The habitus, he argues, is a 'structuring structure', which is embodied, that, is located squarely in the material body of the individual. This would seem to be the epitome of a thoroughgoing structural determinism: individuals think and act as they do entirely because they are entirely socialized, –that is, the individual is the society writ small. Each one does what s/he does because it is what everybody else does. However, although Bourdieu would seem

---

2   These comments are based on as yet unpublished findings from an NHS-funded project on hospital chaplaincies in a multifaith society, in which I am currently engaged.

to foreground the structural to the extent that the agent is lost from sight, he redeems the situation by emphasizing the centrality of temporality to social interaction, which, in turn enables him to introduce the interesting notion of strategy. Indeed, it is true that habitus functions as an 'automatic setting' which enables individuals to get through the day without having to think about every thing they might do, but there is an alternative to this default setting, we have the option of switching from 'robot' to 'strategist'. Individuals as strategists, confronted by a number of choices, select what they considers to be the most appropriate course of action. It is in strategy that Bourdieu hopes to locate a measure of individual agency. But disappointingly, it is the individual who has most perfectly assimilated 'the rules of the game' (for example, in relation to education, work, Culture or religious faith and practice) who is likely to execute the most profitable strategy) – once again, 'structure rules'.[3]

Although it is increasingly difficult to understand 'the individual' and 'the social' as discrete entities, I am inclined, for a number of reasons (moral, methodological, epistemological, ontological, autobiographical), to foreground the individual in my own understanding of social life. The British anthropologist Nigel Rapport is foremost among those who have argued the case for the transcendent individual. He contends, cogently, that individuals are responsible for making their own worlds through acts of perception and interpretation. This means that social milieux cannot be understood apart from the (perceptions of) individuals who compose them – both alone and in relationship (2003, 70–71).

I agree in principle with Rapport's position to the extent that only individuals can make meaning. But then again, I do not wish to reify the individual – the social is implicit in every act of individuality. As social scientists we can only understand the social if we understand the individual: in order to understand the complexity of institutional religion we need first to appreciate the complexity of the individual's faith and practice (Cohen 1994). On the other hand it seems feasible to me to talk *as if* organizations (for instance) have agency. This seems reasonable, *so long as* we recognize the many and varied contributions by individuals to the decision-making process which defines the organization. If we are to understand religion (in any place and at any time) we need to take seriously the faith and practice of individuals.

Let us turn now to the empirical. This paper is part of a continuing attempt to describe and understand a Quaker Meeting in 'Dibdenshaw' in the north of England.[4] During

---

3   Bourdieu's most accomplished account of habitus is found in Bourdieu (1977) Ch. 2, but more accessible texts include Bourdieu (1990; 1998) and Bourdieu and Waquant (1992). See Jenkins (1992) Ch. 4, for a clear and concise critique of 'habitus'. King (2000) argues that the strength of Bourdieu's theory lies in his development of the concept 'practice', which largely escapes the determinism of habitus. See also Collins (in press).

4   'Meeting' refers both to 'meeting for worship' – the Quaker act of worship roughly equivalent to a church service which involves arriving at the meeting house, sitting for an hour in more or less silent worship and for most participants lingering in the meeting house for a chat over a cup of tea; it also refers to 'the meeting' that is the local congregation. It will be obvious from the context which meaning is intended.

'Dibdenshaw' is a pseudonym.

my fieldwork in the early 1990s, I was especially intrigued by its evident continuity (unbroken since the seventeenth century) and by the countless ways in which participants contributed to that continuity. As Van Gennep observed:

> The greatest charm of ethnography is, perhaps, that once its simplest rudiments have been acquired and its specific methods grasped, one's daily life takes on a new aspect. Some trifling little isolated fact, or some chance remark overheard in passing, because one perceives its links with an entire network of beliefs and customs, can conjure up a whole world of analogies and memories. (cited in Belmont 1979, 58)

The isolated little facts with which I was bombarded during fieldwork became increasingly meaningful as I discovered that they comprised networks, that they could always be contextualized within *a narrative framework*. It is worth spelling out what I mean here. First, I propose a strong theory of narrative: we are storied beings in a storied world. Jerome Bruner (2002) has argued persuasively that our very selves are constructed through and of narrative. He writes:

> A self-making narrative is something of a balancing act. It must, on the one hand, create a conviction of autonomy, that one has a will of one's own, a certain freedom of choice, a degree of possibility. But it must also relate the self to a world of others – to friends and family, to institutions, to the past, to reference groups.[5]

Second, it is important to remember that, although narrative analysis was founded in the study of language and is still thought of primarily as a way to understand talking and writing, narrative can be achieved through any sign system: talking and writing for sure, but also through gesture, music, art and design, architecture, dress, and so forth. The 'peace testimony narrative' involved a sequence of many forms of talk, writing, gesture, artwork or graphic representations, movement and so forth. This narrative extends unbroken through five centuries. Thirdly, narrative discourse can be more or less explicit:

More explicit: Two Quakers meet in the meeting house on Sunday morning:

Jonah: hello there – where on earth have you been?
Clive: oh, didn't you know – we've been to France ... [then long account of trip]

Quakers often blatantly told one another such stories, which are easy to spot (at least in conversation) with a bit of practice. They become a part of extended narratives, in this case relating to holidays (and simultaneously to other narrative threads no doubt).

Less explicit: Two Quakers look out over the meeting house garden:

Cynthia: it's great to see the crocuses out ...
Serena: yeah, I can't think what's happened to mine this year ...

---

5   For more on Bruner's influential mode of narrative analysis see also Bruner (1986, 1991).

This short exchange forms a part of a narrative thread on gardening, developed over the years by several participants in the Meeting. Identifying implicit narratives such as these is challenging and requires long-term participant observation. As Carrithers argues, 'narrative thought can be evidenced and conveyed in forms of speech which are not marked as stories at all' (1995, 261). Harder still to identify are those narratives that develop beyond the realms of speech and are made material: the cherry tree planted to celebrate the birth of a new child, the small watercolour painting near the entrance, the table in the library. The difficulty in identifying narrative threads is due partly to the intermittent character of narrative. The plot ('gardening', say) is made manifest, brought to life as it were, on occasion, and continued most often and obviously by particular individuals who have developed a talking relationship (Rapport 1993). One has to be among the same group of people over a long period before one can identify such story lines.

Finally, the narratives I recorded in and around the meeting house can be thought of as implying three 'spheres' – as represented in Figure 10.1.

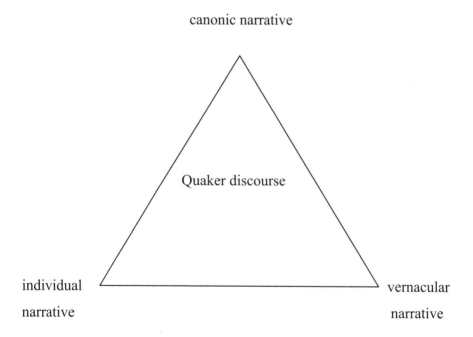

canonic narrative

Quaker discourse

individual narrative

vernacular narrative

Figure 10.1   A two-dimensional model of Quaker discourse

Looking through my field-notes I found that all social interaction in and around the Quaker Meeting could be plotted within this triangular space – which is, in fact, a model of that social interaction. The model suggests that (Quaker) discourse can be understood entirely as narrative: the model emphasizes meaning-making and temporality – present discourse develops from previous discourse; and that there are three spheres of narrative (individual, canonic and vernacular). It also indicates that social interaction can only be understood in composite terms, that is as a precipitate of the prototypical, the canonic and the vernacular.

In talking about narrative spheres I am primarily describing the scale (or 'reach') of social interaction – either real or imagined. Exemplar cases are marked by the points of the triangle and represent discourse relating entirely to the individual (individual or protypical narrative), to the vernacular (local narrative), or to the canonic (national narrative). It is probably impossible to locate any discourse precisely at these points; I found that Quaker meeting narratives always contained something of the individual, the vernacular and the canonic, though one sphere or other might predominate (Collins 2003).

This model effectively occludes dualisms such as 'individual/social' or 'agency/ structure'. It remains true, however, that individuals make meaning. This is an assumption I can make at least in relation to the Quaker Meeting, because it is an expectation that Quakers themselves take for granted, summed up in the canonic question put by George Fox who is reported to have said, whilst preaching in the parish church in Ulverston in 1652, 'You will say, Christ saith this, and the Apostles say this; but what canst thou say?' (*Quaker Faith and Practice*, para 19.07).

What canst thou say? The question assumes that we are all conduits of the Spirit but are necessarily *interpreters* of that Spirit. Just to add, that there must have been a moment when Fox uttered these words or experienced their meaning in some more direct sense, and at that point the narrative was predominantly 'individual'; the question at the moment it was uttered became a part of local or vernacular discourse. Later, Fox went on to write the question down and circulate it among Friends, and it became increasingly canonic (its audience grew) as the decades and centuries passed. It is regularly quoted in published 'introductions' to Quakerism, as well as appearing in the widely read *Quaker Faith and Practice*.[6] The point here is that narrative threads can take various forms at different times and in different places. In these terms, there is no point in attempting to conceive of discourse entirely in terms of either 'the individual' or 'the social', of agency or structure.

The Second Dichotomy: Religion/Secularity

Presented as 'sacred/profane', here is a dualistic assumption that secured its place in social scientific theory by Durkheim (1995 [1912]). In my fieldwork among British Quakers I found this dualistic outlook unnecessarily constraining. Here are a few summary headings taken from my field-notes which, in each case, exemplify 'the practice of meeting':

---

6   *Quaker Faith and Practice* (1995) is the current version of the Quaker Book of Discipline, a volume of extracts from Quaker writing. The Book of Discipline was first published in the eighteenth century and is revised every 25 years or so. The book is available in every meeting house, it is often presented to new members, and is widely cited during spoken ministry and in various other contexts.

during meeting for worship, there is a group of older women who always sit in the same chairs ... (belonging, faith and practice, sharing gender, age, beliefs, friendship, place, etc)

Sunday morning handshakes upon entering the meeting house, everyone receives a handshake from the door-keeper even toddlers and babies

establishing a 'green concerns' group

selecting good causes for Sunday collection

the issue of attenders (non-members) on committees

nail varnish

the subtleties of bringing worship to a close

a long conversation about football

the joys and sorrows of bringing up children

Each of these stand as 'headings' for exchanges involving particular individuals at particular times and in particular places. My field-notes are full of such headings – and in each case the 'drift' of the conversation was not obviously either secular or religious. Let us take 'nail varnish' as an example. This was a conversation between Simon, Serena and Dora which took place in the concourse of Dibdenshaw Meeting one Sunday morning in the Spring of 1992. Friends do not generally wear nail varnish and it is very rarely worn at meeting. The conversation went as follows:

Serena	(Looking down at Dora's hands): Nice nail varnish!
Dora:	Oh yes, divine decadence! (quoting the character from the film *Cabaret*)
Simon:	Oh dear, you'll be drummed out of the Society [of Friends]!
Dora:	I know; I was invited to a rather posh 'do' yesterday and had not time to take it off this morning.
Serena:	Good, it adds a splash of colour.

Why does Serena make her opening remark here? Serena is a friend of Dora's and knows that her bluntness is likely to be tolerated and might even be found amusing. The two have, over the years, developed a 'talking relationship' (Rapport 1993), which is more often than not a joking relationship. Dora's reply to Simon, who is married to Serena, contributes a further joking comment alluding to the Quaker testimony to the plain (and implying that nail varnish is not 'plain' and therefore not 'Quakerly'). Serena concludes the conversation by apparently denying the relevance of the testimony to plainness, preferring to celebrate her friend's boldness and individuality. Despite what might be assumed to be an obviously 'religious' context, such storied discourse transcends accepted dualist analysis: here is social interaction which is simultaneously religious *and* secular, sacred *and* profane. As such, it typifies meeting house discourse.

During fieldwork, the countless 'little isolated facts' and 'chance remarks' that I recorded remained an awful muddle until the penny dropped that these were not isolated phenomena, just the opposite of that, they were moments in a temporal sequence. The continuity of Meeting, I suggested, amounted to a weave of narrative threads. This is what I recognized first and foremost – not that this data was sacred (or religious) and that, secular. Indeed, my point here is that the distinction cannot be made with reference to the practice I recorded.

As I indicated in Figure 10.1, all meeting house talk can be plotted within a triangle the points of which indicate the discursive limits of the canonical, the vernacular and the individual. Given that the meeting house itself demarcates 'Quaker space' and that attendance at meeting similarly demarcates 'Quaker time' (Dandelion 1996: xii), all discourse enacted within this specific, temporalized place will to some degree be constituted by each of these modes of discourse. A remark might be interpreted (by any or all of the actors – including the participant-observer) as more or less grounded in the canonic, the vernacular or the individual and it is important to understand that *none of these categories of discourse is ontologically or epistemologically prior to the others.* To simply cleave 'the religious' from 'the secular' is an entirely artificial dichotomization of practice that does not recognize such a process.

The kind of questions one might legitimately ask at this point might be: is this religion? Are we dealing here with the religious or the secular? Rather than attempting an answer, I would argue that these are misleading questions – they are not the right questions. I mean by this that such questions cannot properly be answered and that furthermore they lead us down a blind alley. This is one of an almost infinite number of conversations undertaken by Friends in meeting houses up and down the country every Sunday morning. In some cases they will engage in explicitly canonic discourse, as represented, for example, in the book *Quaker Faith and Practice*, referring, perhaps to a paragraph dealing with prayer, clerking a business meeting or the sacraments. Or they might refer primarily to what we might call 'the life of the Meeting', that is, vernacular concerns such as the need for a new roof, relations with the parish church or the health problems of a member's daughter. Or the talk might revolve around the individual speaker's own concerns and interests: their attempts to grow a particular type of rose, their involvement in a local choir, their inability to pray. What is 'secular' here and what is 'religious'?

Discussing how to reduce the cost of a weekend retreat, Chris commented:

> What about pledges? [Several people nod and mumble agreement] You know someone agrees to offer some work and the recipient contributes to the Weekend Away fund ... I heard about this on the Archers [one or two whispered conversations about the Archers]

I have become more aware of a crucial limitation of the model represented in Figure 10.1. This was a model applicable to an enclave, to a group that I have characterized as rather too neatly bounded. A useful development of the basic model would be to include a further dimension to Quaker discourse – genre

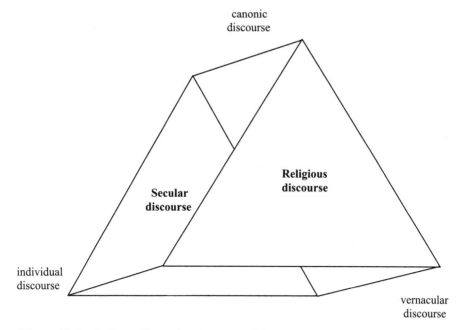

Figure 10.2   A three-dimensional model of Quaker discourse

Based on observations presented above, the second (revised) model (Figure 10.2), accommodating 'genre' as a further dimension, allows for the impossibility of finally distinguishing the sacred (or religious) and secular in Quaker discourse. This three-dimensional model is bounded by two planes: the front plane representing the notional limit of 'religious discourse' and the rear plane the notional limit of 'secular discourse'. All 'meeting house talk', for example, can be plotted within this three-dimensional space, defined now by not one but two criteria: the 'reach' of the discourse (canonic/vernacular/individual), and the genre – toward the 'religious' or toward the 'secular'. The key implication of this model is the fundamental complexity of all discourse.[7] All 'religious' discourse has elements of what we think of as the 'secular' and vice versa. All discourse has elements of the canonic, the vernacular and the individual – though weighting or emphasis will vary – and it is this weighting or emphasis that the model allows us to plot. Plotting Quaker discourse is always bound to be approximate and more or less contentious. I recorded interaction in the Quaker meeting that could not easily be forced into the essentializing categories 'religious discourse' or 'secular discourse'. Quakers will construct (and reconstruct) narratives which cannot easily be understood either as 'religious' or even as specifically 'Quaker'; and at the same

---

7   Note that the model appears static due entirely to the limitations of print media – discursive acts are dynamic and processual. Narrative threads may be in perpetual development – though this is not a necessary condition – they seem to wax and wane and may lie dormant for shorter or longer periods of time apparently disappearing until brought back to life, as it were, by a chance remark, for example.

time, these narratives will, on occasion, be taken up by those who are non-Quakers ('others') and subsequently retold or reframed as primarily secular stories.

Envoi

I have tried to show the theoretical limitations of accepted dichotomies which are pervasive in the study of religion and particular those of 'individual/social' and 'religion/secularity'. Drawing on my analysis of social interaction in a Quaker meeting house, I suggest a model of discourse that frees the analyst from the oversimplification and latent determinism of such crude dichotomies.

A significant theoretical gain in adopting the model in Figure 10.2 is that it encourages the posing of old questions in new ways. For example, are Quakers more likely to draw on 'other discourse', during some periods rather than others? What might this tell us about the permeability of boundaries? Are there times (and or places) when the narratives of individuals are accorded greater practical authority than, say, canonic narratives? So long as we remember that narratives are dynamic, the model can be used to map the trajectory of narratives in a particular context and thus help us gain a purchase on changing loci of power and authority. Furthermore, it can be used to generate comparisons between faith groups, or between different manifestations of the same faith group.

The model I have presented avoids the misleading dichotomous analysis, perpetuated in the dualisms identified at the start of this chapter. Narrative necessarily incorporates what we think of as the individual and the social, whilst at the same time bringing into focus the vernacular or local – too often omitted in analyses of religion. Furthermore, in suggesting that Quaker discourse can be further plotted within a space bounded by two planes, the religious and the secular, and in this way we avoid essentializing either genre. The model suggests that no discourse is 'religious' without being to some extent 'secular' – and vice versa. Islam is sometimes described not as 'a religion' but as a 'way of life' – a claim which neatly obviates the religion/ secularity dichotomy. Quakerism is not simply 'a religion', either, but whether or not it is a 'way of life' is a problem that can only be solved by attending to Quaker discourse. The question is whether a model which appears to work well in relation to Quakerism can be applied more broadly.

Bibliography

Arweck, E. 2006. *Researching New Religious Movements: Constructions and Controversies*. London: Routledge.

Belmont, N. 1979. *Arnold Van Gennep*. Chicago, IL: University of Chicago Press.

Bourdieu, P. 1977. *Outline of a Theory of Practice*. Cambridge: Cambridge University Press.

——. 1990. *In Other Words: Essays Towards a Reflexive Sociology*. Cambridge: Polity.

——. 1998. *Practical Reason*. Stanford, CA: Stanford University Press.

—— and Waquant, L.J.D. 1992. *An Invitation to Reflexive Sociology*. Cambridge: Polity.

Bruner, J. 1986. *Actual Minds, Possible Worlds*. Cambridge, MA: Harvard University Press.

——. 1991. *Acts of Meaning*. Cambridge, MA: Harvard University Press.

——. 2002. *Making Stories: Law, Literature, Life*. New York: Farrar, Strauss and Giroux.

Carrithers, M. 1995. 'Stories in the Social and Mental life of People.' In E. Goody, ed., *Social Intelligence and Interaction: Expressions and Implications of the Social Bias in Human Intelligence*, Cambridge: Cambridge University Press. 261–76.

Cohen, A.P. 1994. *Self Consciousness: an Alternative Anthropology of Identity*. London: Routledge.

Collins, P. 2002. 'Both Independent and Interconnected Voices: Bakhtin Among the Quakers.' In. N.R. Rapport, ed., *British Subjects: The Anthropology of Britain*, Oxford: Berg. 281–98.

——. 2003. 'Storying Self and Others: the Construction of Narrative Identity', *Journal of Politics and Language*, 2: 243–65.

——. 2004. 'Congregations, Narratives and Identities: a Quaker Case Study.' In M. Guest, T. Tusting, and L. Woodhead, eds, *Congregational Studies in the UK: Christianity in a Post-Christian Context*, Aldershot: Ashgate. 99–112.

——. 2006. 'Reading Religious Architecture.' In E. Arweck and P. Collins eds, *Reading Religion in Text and Context: Reflections of Faith and Practice in Religious Materials*, Aldershot: Ashgate. 137–56.

——. In press. "The Practice of Discipline and the Discipline of Practice.' In N. Dyke, ed., *Exploring Regimes of Discipline: The Dynamics of Restraint*, Oxford: Berghahn.

Cornwall, M., Heaton, T.B. and Young, L.A. (eds). 1994. *Contemporary Mormonism: Social Science Perspectives*. Urbana: University of Illinois Press.

Dandelion, P. 1996. *A Sociological Analysis of the Theology of Quakers: The Silent Revolution*. Lewiston, PA: Edwin Mellen.

Davie, G. 1994. *Religion in Britain since 1945. Believing Without Belonging*. Oxford: Blackwell.

Dawson L.L. 2006. *Comprehending Cults: the Sociology of New Religious Movements*. Oxford: Oxford University Press.

Durkheim, E. 1984 [1893]. *The Division of Labour in Society*. London: Macmillan.

——. 1995 [1912]. *Elementary Forms of the Religious Life*. New York: Free Press.

Giddens, A. 1970. *Capitalism and Modern Social Theory*. Cambridge: Cambridge University Press.

Ginzburg, C. 1980. *The Cheese and the Worms: the Cosmos of a Sixteenth-Century Miller*. Baltimore: Johns Hopkins University Press.

Jenkins, R. 1992. *Pierre Bourdieu*. London: Routledge.

King, A. 2000. Thinking with Bourdieu Against Bourdieu: A "Practical" Critique of the Habitus', *Sociological Theory*, 18: 417–433.

Lambert, M. 2002. *Medieval Heresy*. Oxford: Blackwell.

McGregor, J.F. and Reay, B., eds. 1984. *Radical Religion in the English Revolution.* Oxford: Oxford University Press.

Marx, K. and Engels, F. 1957. *On Religion.* Moscow: Progress Publishers.

Morton, A.L. 1970. *The World of the Ranters: Religious Radicalism in the English Revolution.* London: Lawrence and Wishart.

Quaker Faith and Practice: the Book of Christian Discipline of the Yearly Meeting of the Religious Society of Friends (Quakers) in Britain. 1995. London: British Yearly Meeting.

Rapport, N. 1993. *Diverse Worldviews in an English Village.* Edinburgh: Edinburgh University Press.

———. 1997. *Transcendent Individual: Towards a Literary and Liberal Anthropology.* London: Routledge.

———. 2003. *I am Dynamite: an Alternative Anthropology of Power.* London: Routledge.

Stein, S. 1992. *The Shaker Experience in America.* New Haven and London: Yale University Press.

Van Gennep, A. 1960. *The Rites of Passage.* London: Routledge and Kegan Paul.

Weber, M. 1930. *The Protestant Ethic and the Spirit of Capitalism.* London: Allen and Unwin.

———. 1965. *The Sociology of Religion.* London: Methuen.

Chapter Eleven

Religion and the Individual: A Socio-legal Perspective

Russell Sandberg

Introduction

The question of whether and how religion ought to be defined has long engaged both sociologists and lawyers (see, for example, Idinopulos and Wilson 1998; Platvoet and Molendijk 1999). Weber and Durkheim put forward contrasting views as to the usefulness of a preliminary (or working) definition of religion. Whilst Weber contended that 'definition can be attempted, if at all, only at the conclusion of the study' (1978, 399), Durkheim argued that a preliminary definition was required in order to 'avoid focusing by mistake on ideas and practices that are not religious or conversely overlooking genuinely religious phenomena' (2001, 25). Durkheim's rationale for a preliminary definition is as persuasive for the practising lawyer as it is for the scholar (Sandberg, 2006b; forthcoming). In both cases, a definition serves as a basis of inclusion and exclusion. Certain groups are not studied by the scholar or denied legal protection on the grounds that they are not religions.

Whilst lawyers and sociologists have often wrestled with the question of defining religion, most work has been done in isolation. There has been very little sociological commentary on the various definitions and conceptions of religion found in law. This is despite the obvious sociological importance a legal definition of religion has. Legal definitions of religion are often used as filtering devices: they are used as the means by which the State determines which groups and which activities are to receive the certain legal benefits and burdens. The juxtaposition of legal texts with sociological material may reveal the often implicit presumptions and prejudices present in the law. Furthermore, a social scientific approach is required so that definitions and conceptions of religion enshrined in law remain in step with the role, status and position of religion in contemporary social life.

This chapter examines one definitional attribute of religion identified by Durkheim in *The Elementary Forms of Religious Life* by reference to state laws on religion. This examination will begin with the most important of these laws: human rights guarantees common to many jurisdictions and constitutional provisions unique to specific jurisdictions. This will be followed by a discussion of particular laws in England and Wales. This chapter will constitute an exploratory examination of how sociological works, such as those of Durkheim, may enable a greater understanding of legal texts on religion. It is part of an emerging discipline, a synthesis of the law on religion, the sociology of religion and the sociology of law, which may be styled a 'sociology of law and religion' (Doe 2004; Sandberg forthcoming).

Durkheim's Definition

As is well known, in *The Elementary Forms of Religious Life* Durkheim defined religion as 'a unified system of beliefs and practices relative to sacred things, that is to say, things set apart and surrounded by prohibitions – beliefs and practices that unites its adherents in a single moral community called a church' (2001, 46). Durkheim thus puts forward a two-stage definition. The first stage is that there needs to be 'beliefs and practices relative to sacred things'. However, this is not sufficient since it does not distinguish between religion and magic. The second stage of Durkheim's definition seeks to make such a distinction by stressing the collective nature of religion (2001, 42). This is the definitional attribute of religion which this chapter seeks to explore from a socio-legal perspective. Do legal definitions and conceptions of religion share the Durkheimian view that religion is something 'eminently collective' (2001, 46)?

For Durkheim, the collective nature of 'religion' was a central definitional attribute. He contended that historically religion had not existed without what he called a 'church' (by which he meant simply a social group who shared a common perception of the sacred translated into common practices – see 2001, 42–43). Durkheim argued that the presence of a church can distinguish religion from mere magic since social and moral bonds are not formed between the magicians and their followers. (2002, 42–43). However, this focus precludes individual religiosity. Writing in 1912, Durkheim conceded this and noted that some of his contemporaries had wondered whether individual religious belief would become the dominant form of religious life. Asking readers to leave such speculation for the future, Durkheim did comment that such individual cults did not constitute a different type of religion but rather shared the same ideas and principles and simply differed in their focus upon the 'life of the individual' rather than the 'collectivity as a whole' (2001, 45). This question remains a subject of intense debate almost a century later: does it remain the case that religion is by definition a collective activity or whether it is now a private individual affair? (see, for example, Hill 1973; James, 1982). However, reference to law is non-existent in this debate. The purpose of the present piece is to attempt to correct the balance.

Religion as an International Human Right

As Edge (2002, 29) notes, throughout the twentieth century, international law evolved beyond the nineteenth-century focus on the relationship between states to the elucidation and protection of international human rights guarantees, which invariably included provisions on religion of various different kinds (see Little 2002, 35). Of these provisions, Article 18 of the Universal Declaration on Human Rights 1948 (UDHR) may be seen as a watershed in that it was the first international treaty which did not conceptualise religion under the umbrella of minority rights (Evans,

1997, 172–173). Rather, religion was protected as a general human right. The Article provides:

> Everyone has the right to freedom of thought, conscience and religion; this right includes freedom to change his religion or belief, and freedom, either alone or in community with others and in public or private, to manifest his religion or belief in teaching, practice, worship and observance.

Religion became seen as primarily an individual right. For Evans, under Article 18, freedom of religion became 'bound up with the development of the concept of individual human rights as an object of international legal concern' (1997, 172–173). There are two separate rights under Article 18. The first right is the internal freedom of freedom of thought, conscience and religion – known as the *forum internum* – this includes the right to hold a religion or belief and to change it. Martínez-Torrón (2002, 104) contends that, like other human rights, this internal freedom is primarily an individual right. The second right is the external freedom to manifest religion or belief in worship, teaching, practice and observance – known as the *forum externum* – this may take place 'either alone or in community with others and in public or private'. This appears to be recognition of a collective right to religious liberty. However, it can be argued that all this affects is the exercise of the rights: the right to manifest is an individual right which may be exercised individually ('alone') or collectively ('in community with others'). The Article simply recognises the choice of the individual; it does not recognise a collective right to religious liberty as such.

This perception of religion as primarily an individual matter has been further elucidated in relation to Article 9 of the European Convention on Human Rights (ECHR). Article 9(1) is almost identical to Article 18 UDHR. Evans (2001, 72) contends that Article 9(1) is an individual right since 'the emphasis in the interpretation of Article 9 is on the internal: the private thought, conscience and religion of the individual'. It does not provide a collective right for religious groups acting as such to manifest their religious liberty (see Evans 2001, 103). However, despite this, the European Court of Human Rights has heard cases brought by religious groups. For example, the Church of Scientology in Sweden claimed that publication of criticism of their Church violated Article 9 and the International Society for Krishna Consciousness (ISKCON) in the United Kingdom claimed that planning restrictions were contrary to religious freedom (see *X and the Church of Scientology v Sweden* [1979]16 D&R 68 and *ISKCON v United Kingdom* [1994] 90 D&R 90). Both cases were heard by European institutions, though the claims proved unsuccessful.

For Taylor (2005, 225–226), this does not indicate that Article 9 includes a collective right; rather when such cases are brought it is actually the individual members who are exercising their individual rights collectively. The European Commission for Human Rights has held that Churches are entitled to protection under Article 9 but only through the protection afforded to its individual members, and based upon their either identical or at least substantially similar views. In *X v Denmark* [1976] 5 ECHR 157, the European Commission noted that organised religious communities are protected in their right to manifest religion through worship, teaching, practice and observance through the right granted to its members under Article 9 (see Taylor 2005, 138–139). Collective religiosity is only protected to facilitate the individual's manifestation of religion. Thus, denying legal recognition entirely to certain religious groups has been held to violate freedom of religion (*Metropolitan Church of Bessarabia v Moldova* [2002] 35 EHRR 306). However, whilst some commentators have claimed that this means that Article 9 also has a very significant 'collective dimension' (see Martínez-Torrón 2002, 14), it is difficult to reconcile this view with the jurisprudence of the international bodies. The way in which Article 9 is framed – as an individual right that which may be exercised with others – means that any collective dimension derives from the individual right.

Other human rights provisions echo Article 9 ECHR and Article 18 UDHR in seeing religion as an individual right which may be manifested collectively. For instance, Evans (2000, 46) contends that Article 18 of the International Covenant on Civil and Political Rights (ICCPR) 'permits individuals to act in a fashion which is in accordance with their beliefs if it is linked to a form of worship, teaching or observance'. However, the Human Rights Committee in 1993 commented that 'acts integral to the conduct by religious groups of their basic affairs, such as, *inter alia*, the freedom to choose their own religious leaders, priests and teachers, the freedom to establish seminaries or religious schools and the freedom to prepare and distribute religious texts and publications' were also protected by the Article (Human Rights Committee General Comment 22 of 1993, paragraph 4). Similarly Article 6 of the Declaration on the Elimination of All Forms of Intolerance and Discrimination based on Religion or Belief 1981, in providing a list of freedoms that are included in the general right to freedom of religion, outlines a number of derivative rights which benefit collective religiosity. In all these instruments, certain collective rights originate from the individual right on the face of the Article. However, at an international level, the legal conception of religion is that of an individual phenomenon. Religion is a private affair and it is up to the individuals how to manifest their religiosity. If free practice and exercise of religion is constrained, it is largely up to the individual whether legal redress is sought.

Religion as a Constitutional Right

The perception of religion as an individual right in international law invariably influences the corresponding provisions in national constitutions. For example, in Finland, section 11 of the 2000 Constitution, which protects freedom of religion, is clearly focused on the individual, bestowing upon individual citizens a number of individual rights and freedoms in language similar to international human rights guarantees. However, this is not always the case. Some national constitutions go further than international instruments and also recognise collective religious liberty. The Constitutions of Spain and Italy, for example, protect freedom of religion as both an individual and a collective right. Article 16 of the Spanish Constitution of 1978 proclaims that, 'Freedom of ideology, religion and worship of individuals and communities is guaranteed, with no other restriction on their expression than may be necessary to maintain public order as protected by law'. The Italian Constitution 1948 protects individual religious freedom under Article 19 (which bestows upon every citizen the right to 'profess faith freely' and to 'exercise worship in public or private, provided that the rites involved do not offend common decency') and collective religious freedom under Articles 7 and 8.

The same is true in England and Wales. Despite the absence of a formal written constitution, legal provisions protecting religion recognise both individual and collective religious freedom. By virtue of the Human Rights Act 1998, the individual right to religious liberty found in Article 9 ECHR is now part of English law. However, section 13 of Human Rights Act 1998 also includes a special provision recognising the Convention rights of religious organisations. This was the result of lobbying by religious groups during the passage of the Human Rights Bill through Parliament. Evangelical Christians, joined by the Roman Catholic Church, the Chief Rabbi, the Church of Scotland and the Plymouth Brethren, feared that the way in which the Bill was framed meant that human rights would only be used as a sword against religious groups and not as a shield. Whilst religious groups would be expected to act in compliance with the Bill, being subject to civil courts in the case of a breach, they would not themselves enjoy enforceable Convention rights (see Cumper 2000b, 72; Edge 2002, 85). Section 13 thus serves as a 'specific recognition of religious group autonomy' (Ahdar and Leigh 2005, 327); it involves only collective, and not individual, religious liberty (Rivers 2000, 138). It reads:

(1) If a court's determination of any question arising under this Act might affect the exercise by a religious organisation (itself or its members collectively) of the Convention right to freedom of thought, conscience and religion, it must have particular regard to the importance of that right.

(2) In this section 'court' includes a tribunal.

Section 13 seems to recognise a collective right to freedom of thought, conscience and religion, which courts should have 'particular regard' for. However, commentators seem divided as to the significance of the section. For Rivers (2001, 227), the section means that a collective religious liberty will prevail over competing interests, but Cumper (2000a) contends that section 13 is merely a symbolic political statement designed to placate religious opponents. Judicial decisions to date suggest that Ahdar and Leigh (2005, 359) may be accurate in calling the provision 'rather mild'. Further, in addition to this formal recognition of the human rights shield, English courts have also diminished fears that human rights will become a sword to use against religious groups. A historical reluctance to interfere with the regulation of religious bodies seems likely to continue (Hill 2001). In *Aston Cantlow Parochial Church Council v Wallbank* [2003] UKHL 37, the House of Lords conclusively determined that a parochial church council of the (established) Church of England was not liable under the Human Rights Act 1998: enforcing a lay rector's obligation for all necessary repairs to the chancel of the local church under the Chancel Repairs Act 1932 did not breach his human right to peaceful enjoyment of his possessions.

The Human Rights Act 1998 aside, there are other examples of how English constitutional law may regard religion as a collective right. By dint of the established status of the Church of England (for details, see Doe 1996; Hill 2001a; Sandberg, 2006a), certain rights are enjoyed by virtue of being resident in a Church of England parish. In the words of Say (1991, 152), 'every citizen resident in the parish has, regardless of their own religious commitment or lack of it, a rightful claim upon their parish priest'. This extends to a broad right to attend public worship, to receive Holy Communion unless there is a lawful excuse for denial, and to be married and buried in the parish church (see Sandberg 2006a; Hill 2007). It is unclear whether such rights are individual rights attached to individual parishioners or collective rights in that they arise by virtue of collective residence in a parish. It is clearer that the exercise of these rights is collective: the resulting rites are all exercised in groups. The fact that English law effectively provides for public access to these rites infers that it sees religion, at least in the guise of the established church, as something that is exercised collectively.

Such collective rights are common in countries where there is a State Church. For example, Article 4 of the Danish Constitution of 1849, as amended in 1953, states 'The Evangelical Lutheran Church shall be the Folk Church of Denmark, and as such shall be supported by the State'. This provides a collective right to the Church for special treatment. Moreover, in some jurisdictions, the constitution may favour the State Church by imposing a collective burden upon members. An example of this may be found in section 7 of the Church of Sweden Act 1998, which states, 'Members of the Church of Sweden shall pay a local and a regional church fee'. Such provisions clearly indicate a perception that religion is a collective phenomenon: the collective practice of religion is recognised by the State and the State imposes upon members a duty to finance it. By contrast, other constitutions reveal a view that freedom of religion is neither a collective nor an individual right. Article 13 of the Greek Constitution states, 'Freedom of religious conscience is inviolable. The enjoyment of civil rights and liberties does not depend on the individual's religious beliefs.' This infers that the right is not directed to religious believers as individuals or religious groups as collectives; rather, the right is free–standing and simply exists.

The recent history of the Irish Constitution shows a move from a collective right to a right which, although individual in part, is actually directed not at human individuals or collectives but rather at the divine. Article 44 of the 1937 Constitution formerly provided a collective right in that it provided that 'the state recognises the special position of the Holy Catholic Apostolic and Roman Church as the guardian of the Faith professed by the great majority of citizens'. However, Article 44(2) now provides an individual right, stating that 'Freedom of conscience and the free profession and practice of religion are, subject to public order and morality, guaranteed to every citizen'. This is preceded by Article 44(1) which casts freedom of religion not as a human right but rather as homage to God, providing, 'The State acknowledges that the homage of public worship is due to Almighty God. It shall hold His Name in reverence, and shall respect and honour religion.' Although the Constitutional Review Group in 1996 called for Article 44(1) to be replaced by the phrase 'The State guarantees to respect religion', this has not been put to the people (Colton 2006, 97). If the change was implemented, it would be uncertain whether the phrase 'The State guarantees to respect religion' sees 'religion' as a collective phenomena, a private affair or a duty to the divine. The current trend, however, is that the view that religion is a collective phenomenon is more grounded in national constitutional provisions than in international human rights guarantees. The public and private aspects of religiosity tend to be recognised in national law.

Religion as Collective Phenomena in England and Wales

Focusing on the law of England and Wales, there are several other areas of law which rely on a conception of religion as primarily a collective affair. There are a number of laws in England and Wales which extend legal protection to religious groups. On the surface, these laws suggest a perception of religion as a collective activity. An obvious example would be laws which provide special treatment for religious groups and organisations. Legal preference is awarded to the collective manifestation of religion. There are a number of criminal offences which outlaw hostility or hatred towards religious groups. Under the Crime and Disorder Act 1998, a crime is 'racially or religiously aggravated' (and consequentially punished by a tougher sentence) where there is 'hostility towards members of a racial or religious group based on their membership of that group'. A defendant is guilty of an offence under the Racial and Religious Hated Act 2006 if he stirs up 'hatred against a group of persons defined by reference to religious belief or lack of religious belief' (see Hare 2006 for details). In both cases, the criminal law only protects religious individuals if they are members of a collective. A further example can be found in the exemptions religious groups enjoy from discrimination law. For example, under the Sex Discrimination Act 1975, it is illegal to discriminate on grounds of sex. However, there is an exemption under section 19 where the employment is made for the purposes of an 'organised religion': such an organisation may lawfully discriminate by requiring employees to be of a particular sex, for example, if that requirement is imposed 'so as to comply with the doctrines of the religion', or 'because of the nature of the employment and the context in which it is carried out, so as to avoid conflicting with the strongly-held religious convictions of a significant number of the religion's followers'. This is clearly a collective right; although if it is exercised for the second reason, it is a collective right exercised on behalf of a 'significant number' of individuals who belong to the collective. Either way, this right is exclusively the privilege of a religious collective: the individual believer is bound by the general law; an organised religion in certain circumstances is not.

A further example of how the law recognises religion as a collective force can be found in the preferential legal treatment for places of worship. Such privileges for places of worship cannot be read as rights for individual members or for individual citizens since the preferential treatment of such buildings does not give rise to an individual right to use such buildings as places or worship or as buildings of historical or architectural interest. However, the legal protection of worship does not infer a perception that religion is a collective force since English law does not distinguish between collective or individual worship; the House of Lords has recognised that worship may be communal or personal (*R v Secretary of State for Education ex parte Williamson* [2005] UKHL 15). A final example of legal protection of religion as collective phenomenon may be found in legal statements that underline the perceived societal benefits of religion. However, although some charity law cases seem to suggest the collective nature of religion by emphasising the public benefit of religion, this is not necessarily evidence that the courts see religion as a collective phenomenon since other decisions have stressed that the public benefit derives from the fact that it beneficial for individuals to have a religion (see, for example, *Gilmour v Coates* [1949] AC 426). Although the black letter of the law seems to be recognising the collective nature of religion, a closer examination shows that it is simply the recognition of the individual right to religious liberty expressed in close association.

Religion as Individual Phenomena in England and Wales

In addition to these laws, which seem to protect religious groups, there are also numerous laws in England and Wales which protect religious believers and seem to infer that religion is an individual matter. Indeed, a recent House of Lords decision explicitly characterised religion as an individual matter. In his judgment in *R v Secretary of State for Education ex parte Williamson* [2005] UKHL 15, Lord Nicholls commented:

> Religious and other beliefs and convictions are part of the humanity of every individual. They are an integral part of his personality and individuality.

English law mirrors this understanding of religion by providing free-standing legal rights for believers, epitomised by the 'conscience clause' which exempts the individual from a generally applicable law on grounds of their conscientious objection (See, for example, section 4 of the Abortion Act 1967). Other legal rights are bestowed upon the individual on grounds of their 'religion'. For example, section 1 of the Adoption and Children Act 2002, in common with various other statutes regarding the care of children, recognises the right of children to have 'due consideration' to be given to their 'religious persuasion'. A further example is section 139 of the Criminal Justice Act 1988, which provides that it is a defence to carry an article with a blade 'for religious reasons'. This provision provides for the exemption of the Sikh Kirpan but is drafted broadly so that the exemption is not dependent upon membership of the collective but is an individual right. Other legal rights are bestowed upon the individual on grounds of 'religion' such as those provided by the Human Rights Act 1998 and the new law on religious discrimination (see Sandberg 2007; Hill and Sandberg 2006 and 2007). Such rights are not dependent upon individuals being a member of a particular collective but are dependent on individuals being aligned with a religion. It might be suspected that those who are part of a collective will find this requirement easier to meet. Indeed, if the State's conception of religion is narrowly defined so that only known collective religions are protected, then these rights, though addressed to the individual, become collective rights.

Indeed, a number of seemingly individual rights are actually collective rights since they are only bestowed upon individuals by virtue of their membership of a collective. For example, although Sikhs working on a building site are exempt from the normal rule requiring the wearing of safety hats, this right is not an individual right since the exemption in section 11 of the Employment Act 1989 cannot be relied upon by those who are not members of the Sikh faith. Exemptions from normal slaughter rules to permit religious methods under the Welfare of Animals (Slaughter or Killing) Regulations 1995 are also rights dependent upon membership of the collective: they only apply to licensed Muslims or Jews who use Jewish or Muslim methods for the food of Jews or Muslims. However, where a right is conferred only upon those who are not members of a religious collective, such a right is clearly an individual right since those who are granted the right are not members of a collective and are defined by their lack of membership. A rare example of such a right may be found in section 1 of the Oaths Act 1978 which provides that anyone who is 'neither a Christian nor a Jew' does not have to take the oath in the prescribed form provided that they take it 'in any lawful manner'.

Conclusion

It is clear that the legal evidence represents recognition that religion is both an individual and collective phenomenon. Although human rights instruments are phrased as individual rights and are directed at individuals, they have some effect upon religious collectives. Furthermore, although international human rights guarantees colour provisions on religion in national constitutions, many such constitutions stress the collective rights of religious organisations. This is true not only in countries where there is a State Church, such as England and Denmark, but also in other jurisdictions, such as Spain and Italy. Laws in England and Wales which defend religious groups and religious believers indicate that religion is protected both as a collective activity and as a key element of personal identity. Legal provisions seemingly protecting religious groups often have the purpose of protecting the individuals who make up such groups. Provisions which seem to protect the individual are often dependent on that individual being a member of a collective or designated as religious in some other way. This lack of a clear distinction between individual and collective rights may be interpreted as showing that Durkheim was correct. Collectivity remains a definitional attribute of religion: legal instruments show that States have not fully embraced the idea that religion is an individual and private affair (although international authorities seem closer to embracing this notion).

Moreover, the legal evidence supports the Durkheimian premise that individual cults do not constitute a different type of religion: the legal evidence suggests an understanding of religion as a phenomenon which has both a collective and an individual dimension. More broadly, this exploratory examination serves as a case study to illustrate how the study of law and legal mechanisms may enrich a sociological understanding of religion by means of a 'sociology of law and religion' (Doe 2004; Sandberg forthcoming).

Bibliography

Ahdar, R. and Leigh, I. 2005. *Religious Freedom in the Liberal State*. Oxford: Oxford University Press.

Colton, P. 2006. 'Religion and Law in Dialogue: Covenantal and Non-Covenantal Cooperation of State and Religions in Ireland.' In Puza, R. and Doe, N. (eds), *Religion and Law in Dialogue: Covenantal and Non-Covenantal Cooperation between State and Religion in Europe*, Leuven: Peeters. 93–114.

Cumper, P. 2000a. 'The Protection of Religious Rights under Section 13 of the Human Rights Act 1998,' *Public Law*. 254–265.

——. 2000b. 'Religious Organisations and the Human Rights Act 1998.' In Edge, P.W. and Harvey, G. (eds), *Law and Religion in Contemporary Society*, Aldershot: Ashgate. 69–92.

Doe, N. 1996. *The Legal Framework of the Church of England*. Oxford: Clarendon.

——. 2004. 'A Sociology of Law on Religion – Towards a New Discipline: Legal Responses to Religious Pluralism in Europe', *Law and Justice* 152. 68–92.

Durkheim, E. 2001. *The Elementary Forms of Religious Life*. Trans C. Cosman. Oxford: Oxford University Press.

Edge, P.W. 2002. *Legal Responses to Religious Difference*. The Hague: Knuwler Law.

Evans, C. 2001. *Freedom of Religion under the European Convention on Human Rights*. Oxford: Oxford University Press.

Evans, M.D. 1997. *Religious Liberty and International Law in Europe*. Cambridge: Cambridge University Press.

——. 2000. 'The UN and Freedom of Religion.' In Ahdar, R.J. (ed), *Law and Religion*, Aldershot: Ashgate. 35–61.

Hare, I. 2006. 'Crosses, Crescents and Sacred Cows: Criminalising Incitement to Religious Hatred', *Public Law*. 521–538.

Hill, M. 1973. *A Sociology of Religion*. London: Heinemann.

——. 2001 'Judicial Approaches to Religious Disputes.' In O'Dair, R. and Lewis, A. (eds), *Law and Religion*, Current Legal Issues IV, Oxford: Oxford University Press. 409–420.

——. 2007. *Ecclesiastical Law*. 3rd edition. Oxford: Oxford University Press.

—— and Sandberg, R. 2006. 'Muslim Dress in English Law: Lifting the Veil on Human Rights', *Religión y Derecho* [*Law and Religion*] 1. 302–328.

——. 2007, 'Is Nothing Sacred? Clashing Symbols in a Secular World', *Public Law*. 488–505.

Idinopulos, T.A. and Wilson, B.C. (eds). 1998, *What is Religion?: Origins, Definitions and Explanations*. Leiden: Brill.

James, W. 1982. *The Varieties of Religious Experience*. New York: Penguin.

Little, D. 2002. 'Religious Minorities and Religious Freedom.' In Danchin, P.G. and Cole, E.A. (eds), *Protecting the Human Rights of Religious Minorities in Eastern Europe*, Columbia: Columbia University Press. 33–57

Martínez-Torrón, J. 2002. 'Religious Liberty in European Jurisprudence.' In Hill, M. (ed.) *Religious Liberty and Human Rights*, Cardiff: University of Wales Press. 99–127

Platvoet, J.G. and Molendijk, A.L. (eds), 1999. *The Pragmatics of Defining Religion: Contexts, Concepts and Contests*. Leiden: Brill.

Rivers, J. 2000. 'From Toleration to Pluralism: Religious Liberty and Religious Establishment under the United Kingdom's Human Rights Act.' In Ahdar, R. (ed.), *Law and Religion*, Aldershot: Ashgate. 133–162.

——. 2001. 'Religious Liberty as a Collective Right.' In O'Dair, R. and Lewis, A. (eds), *Law and Religion*, Current Legal Issues IV, Oxford: Oxford University Press. 227–246.

Sandberg, R. 2006a. 'The Legal Status of Religious Denominations and State–Church Relations in the UK.' In *Droit des Religions en France et en Europe: recueil de Textes*. Bruxelles: Bruylant

——. 2006b. 'A Whitehall Farce? Defining and Conceptualising the British Civil Service', *Public Law*. 653–661.

——. 2007. 'Flags, Beards and Pilgrimages: A Review of the Early Case Law on Religious Discrimination', *Ecclesiastical Law Journal* 9 (1). 87–90.

——. [forthcoming]. 'Religion, Society and Law: An Analysis of the Interface Between Law on Religion and the Sociology of Religion.' Doctoral thesis, Cardiff University.

Say. D. 1991. 'Towards 2000: Church–State Relations', *Ecclesiastical Law Journal* 2. 152–162.

Taylor, P.M. 2005. *Freedom of Religion: UN and European Human Rights Law and Practice*. Cambridge: Cambridge University Press.

Weber. M. 1978. *Economy and Society*. Ed. G. Roth and C Wittich. London: University of California Press.

Chapter Twelve

Freedom in Chains:
Religion as Enabler and Constraint in the
Lives of Gay Male Anglican Clergy[1]

Michael Keenan

Constrained in 'Crisis'

The 'gay issue' is currently central to debates in the Anglican Communion. Such debates exist at local, national and international levels. Since 2003 and the nominations of Jeffrey John and Gene Robinson to the bishopric[2] this 'issue' has been framed as a 'crisis', with the debate surrounding gay issues – specifically blessing same-sex unions and ordaining gay clergy – being seen as threatening the very fabric of the Communion. However, although the 'crisis' may be recent, the 'issue' has been circulating for much longer. For example, the previous three reports from Lambeth Conferences have called for times of study, reflection, or listening.[3] This call, however, has been limited due to the continued unwillingness to allow the stories of gay clergy to be told publicly. Such unwillingness has been institutionalised in a number of different Church documents, and can be illustrated by reference to the 1991 report from the House of Bishops *Issues in Human Sexuality*, which reads:

> There is at any given time such a thing as the mind of the Church on matters of faith and life. Those who disagree with that mind are free to argue for change. What they are not free to do is go against that mind in their own practice. (House of Bishops 1991, 45)

---

1   This paper emerged from an ESRC-funded PhD study (award number PTA-030-2003-01724). I would like to thank Dr Andrew Yip and Dr Brian Heaphy for their support and encouragement throughout the undertaking of this study. An earlier version of this paper was presented at the 2007 British Sociological Association Annual Conference, 'Social Connections: Identities, Technologies, Relationships' at the University of East London.
2   Jeffrey John, an openly gay celibate man, was nominated in 2003 as Bishop of Reading in the Church of England. John withdrew from this nomination following a time of intense and vocal opposition. In the same year, Gene Robinson, an openly gay man living in a open and active same-sex partnership, was nominated and confirmed as Bishop of New Hampshire in the US Episcopal Church; again the appointment met with vocal opposition.
3   The Lambeth conference is decennial conference of bishops of the Anglican Communion. The most recent (1998) conference report committed to 'listen to the experience of homosexual persons' (Anglican Communion 1999, 33).

Therefore, although the Church calls for a time of listening and discussion, this must occur without reference to the stories of sexually active gay clergy, as these continue to be viewed by the institution as unacceptable stories. In essence, the institution continues to constrain the public telling of stories of experience, and attempts to continue to constrain practice through official statement and public discourse. Such an approach distances not only gay clergy, but also gay believers from the Church, and buttresses public understanding of traditional Christian faith as constraining gay believers' life choices. As one respondent put it, the Church is seen as 'life-denying'.

Negotiating Constraint

Institutional constraint has been discussed previously in the literature. Research on gay clergy from varying denominational backgrounds has discussed how the 'mind' of religious institutions constrains gay clergy, particularly in terms of the public presentation and discussion of their gay lives. Fletcher (1990) illustrated the increased stress that gay clergy face in undertaking their role due to the interaction of their sexuality and the institution's publicly stated attitudes towards this. Similarly, Wagner's (1981) study of gay Roman Catholic priests in the USA emphasised the fear experienced by gay priests which was related to the possible consequences of the institution discovering their sexuality – again emphasising the need for constraint on the part of gay priests. Related to this, a number of studies have discussed the lack of support gay clergy feel, due to the need for silence about their sexuality (Wolf 1989; Stuart 1993). Such difficulties lead to the very obvious constraint of sexual life discussed by many with reference to 'the closet'. This personal silence is encouraged through institutional silence stemming from the refusal to engage with the stories of active gay clergy. Therefore individuals' perceptions of the need to 'closet' illustrate the power that the institutional Church has to constrain the lives of individual clergy.

Such evidence from the literature, combined with the reaction to the nominations of Jeffrey John and Gene Robinson, illustrates that, within public talk at least, connection to Christian religious institution is a constraining factor on the 'living' of sexuality. Furthermore, existence as gay and clergy is marginal, unaffirmed and – in at least some quarters – dangerous. This begs the question, why do gay individuals stay as clergy within unaffirming institutions? Indeed, how do they incorporate their connection to institution within their stories of self, which must also incorporate their identification as gay men? In essence, how do gay clergy negotiate the coexistence of gay identity, Christian identity and clerical identity?

Although to some extent previous literature on gay clergy has discussed this issue, such discussion has been secondary to discussion of constraint. Wagner (1981), and Wolf (1989) both discuss the need for creative approaches to belief in order to find fit. Wolf for example states:

> In contrast to the 'average' priest … our respondents seem to have developed a more personally defined spirituality with regard to sexuality in the near absence of any official discussion of this issue as it relates to the clergy. (Wolf 1989, 64)

Although recognition of such negotiation exists in the literature, discussion of the process of negotiation is slight. Turning to literature on lesbian, gay and bi-sexual (LGB) Christians, such discussions have been taken further, and illustrate that non-heterosexual individuals actively negotiate with belief in order to find connection between, and meaning for, their sexual and religious selves (Yip 2000; 2002; Wilcox 2003). This research particularly highlights the importance of personal experience, and access to alternative interpretations of scripture. Within such negotiations organisational Christianity remains of importance for many individuals. Indeed O'Brien (2004, 192) suggests that finding connection between gay and Christian identity is the LGB Christian's *raison d'être*.

Wider theoretical discussions within the sociology of religion relate such negotiations with concepts of 'individualised belief' (Bellah 1985; Roof 1999), and the 'subjective turn' (Heelas and Woodhead 2005), which emphasise the central role of self in the acceptance and negotiation of belief. This situation is eloquently discussed by Geyer and Baumeister as follows:

> Historically, a central and explicit goal of religion and morality in general has been to restrain the self and to override people's tendency to act out of self-interested motives. Now people must find a way to reconcile historical conceptions of morality with the recent formulation of the self as a source of value with inherently authoritative claims. (Geyer and Baumeister 2005, 419)

To some extent such discussion may overemphasise the role of innovation in individuals' personal belief systems. The focus on the role of the individual and their self-understanding emphasises a 'tailor-made' approach to constructing personal faith stories, which links with an understanding of religion as a cultural resource (Lyon 2000). However, for many individuals traditional belief systems remain not only influential, but a significant part of their understanding of themselves and their lives (for example, evangelical gay Christians: Thumma 1991; Wolkomir 2001). Therefore negotiation of belief is required to give space to such traditional aspects of meaning. Similarly, the position of gay clergy as clergy emphasises their connection to organisational Christianity. In order to conceptualise this process it is possible to turn to Weeks, Heaphy and Donovan's (2001) discussion of non-heterosexual life experiments. Specifically, in relation to the use of the concept of 'family' among non-heterosexuals, the authors write:

> The language of 'family' used by many contemporary non-heterosexual people can be seen as both a challenge to conventional definitions, and an attempt to broaden these; as a hankering for legitimacy and an attempt to build something new; as an identification with existing patterns, and a more or less conscious effort to subvert them. (Weeks et al. 2001, 11)

This discussion views the negotiations of LGB people as connecting to the pre-existing, and simultaneously attempting to broaden existing boundaries. Taking such an understanding forward this chapter conceptualises the construction and management of belief stories among gay clergy as the negotiation of tradition and innovation.

In order to explore this negotiation, this chapter refers to three specific areas in which respondents felt enabled by a faith, which in common discussion is often viewed as constraining, these are:

- Experiencing religion as a provider of safe space.
- Viewing religion as a provider of meaning for sex and relationships.
- Accessing meaning for sexuality through religion.

Such discussion does not undermine the feeling of discrimination and constraint felt by respondents working within the Church of England. Rather, in conjunction with a sense of constraint and lack of affirmation respondents continued to feel enabled and affirmed by their identification, both professionally and personally, with the Christian faith. This was achieved through negotiation with the traditional and acceptance of the innovational.

The Study

This paper draws on interview data from eight gay male Anglican clergy; this formed part of a larger study of the negotiations undertaken by gay clergy in managing the coexistence of gay, Christian and clerical identities. At the time of interview all eight respondents were actively involved in church ministry in the Church of England. The respondents were aged between 30 and 65. Of the eight clergy quoted in this paper three self-defined as 'out'. All eight respondents were recruited through advertisement (within newsletters and support group mailings). Interviews took place between 2003 and 2005. The interviews were semi-structured in nature, undertaken in a place of the respondents' choosing (generally vicarages or church offices), and lasted between 90 and 120 minutes.

All names and identifiable information have been changed.

Finding Meaning Through Continued Religious Affiliation

Turning to the narratives of the respondents it is possible to see continuing identification with the traditional. Also illustrated is how this identification with the traditional, and simultaneous innovation upon it, enabled the respondents to manage the coexistence of what were publicly perceived to be incompatible aspects of self.

Religion as Provider of Safe Space

The first way in which identification with traditional religiosity enabled the respondents can be seen in terms of Church providing a safe space for individuals who felt distanced from 'mainstream' heterosexual secular communities and shared experiences. In discussing their life histories the respondents emphasised the importance of their faith in terms of gaining acceptance, and finding space to accept themselves. There were two specific ways in which this was discussed in the respondents' narratives. Church offered both physical space, and space for individuals to make personal connection between faith and sexuality. The following quotations illustrate these issues:

> I think in that sense I found my own youth club, because the Church, the Church building and what went on in the building became the bit that I became fascinated with. In that sense I can see why mother and father used to get really quite perturbed because I was never away from the place, but it is fascinating, absolutely fascinating. It wasn't my closet by any means, because it was a Church that was always busy doing things, and in that sense they made a wide base of contacts and views I would never have otherwise touched. (Luke)

> I was sent away to public school so I suppose it was school religion. Looking back on it, I wonder whether chapel and Church offered an alternative because, I mean I didn't accept my sexuality, and didn't understand it in my teen years or even much into my twenties. I wonder whether that was an alternative group in which I could find friendship and meaning to the macho sports-playing heterosexual with which I didn't identify. I'm a child of the 60s and it was still illegal in the 60s, and the opportunities of groups reaching out to individuals who were exploring who they were was just non-existent. (Harold)

> I think it was a positive factor because on a sort of, what today probably sounds even to myself a sort of trite sort of basis, I felt that what my faith was telling me was that God made me and made me what I was. Therefore I wasn't wanted to deny it, in the way in which I probably had been. And yes I mean cultural and social things mean that you are still very careful and very wary. But I didn't feel that I was right trying to sort of repress what I was, so I would say it was a positive influence in coming to terms with my sexuality which is unusual for some people. (Adam)

Within these quotations Church provided space in which respondents could make connections and gain affirmation. Firstly, as a social space Church was a place where respondents found acceptance at a time when among their peer group they experienced a distinct feeling of difference. Luke's narrative emphasises how he found belonging within the confines of the Church building. Being within the building, and involved in Church activities Luke found space to express his creativity. He also found a space in which he gained acceptance in terms of his evolving sense of self. Church was his 'youth club', a place where he could express himself more fully than he could in other places. Harold similarly emphasised the community aspect of Church. In particular he discussed the safety of the Church community and the very specific role he can see retrospectively that the Church played in his ability to accept himself. He discussed the Church as being separate from the secular realm of male youth, within which he felt he did not fit. Though Church was not specifically affirming Harold as a gay man, it was a space in which he could access affirmation for the 'type' of person he felt he was. Traditional Church religion was therefore important for these men because it was significant in what was their emerging sense of self. The building, the activities, the views of what an individual should be, all connected with both Luke's and Harold's understanding of themselves.

Religious belief provided a personal safe space that was related to central Christian teachings of love and acceptance. This gave some respondents the ability to connect emerging sexuality with emerging belief systems. For Adam, this emerging belief system encouraged him to be more open with himself about his sexuality than he had previously been. Though Adam's discussion of the importance of traditional belief in terms of this acceptance of himself does not refer specifically to the institution, his discussion of feeling accepted emerged from an understanding of God and Christianity, which he accessed through institutional experience. For Adam, the god he was being told about, and the god he connected with was a god that accepted him as he was, and indeed expected Adam to accept himself. In other words, if God and his Church are loving and accepting of the individual, it follows that the individual should be accepting of themself.

The respondents' discussions of Church providing safe space (whether social or personal) emphasise how the institutional, or the traditional, enabled the respondents to accept themselves. By accessing institution the respondents found space wherein they could connect with their understandings of themselves in a way that they had been unable to in secular youth culture. Finding Church enabled finding self. Therefore, although Church was by no means openly accepting of these individuals' sexualities, it provided a space wherein these respondents felt able to relate more closely to their emerging sense of self than they had been able to outside of Church. Despite the constraint of sexuality, feelings of acceptance enabled the respondents to make connections for themselves, and to gain affirmation – to innovate on the experienced tradition.

Religion as Source of Meaning for Sex and Relationships

The second area in which continued identification with the traditional was evident was specifically in relation to respondents' understandings of their experiences of sex and relationships. Traditional religious concepts and discussions provided a way of relating to and accepting experience, which had not been found through purely secular understandings. The following quotations illustrate:

> I do enjoy sex very much, I don't understand quite what it is about the two becoming one flesh, but it does seem to me that sexual activity with another person, and sometimes it's even true of one night stands, does unite and bond you with another person in a mysterious way. ... I can't imagine what it would be like not having that as a possibility at least, even if you are not having it at the time. (Stephen)

> I suppose if I'm really honest, the sense of peace I get with somebody I truly love in a sexual encounter feels like a good experience of God, I would have to say that, so in that sense there is something of holiness about it in a way, although in perceived wisdom there can't be. (Matthew)

> If there is a real love between me and somebody else, then that's God allowing me a privileged sharing in his love for that person, and because I'm a human being and I don't have a vow of celibacy then God has given me a body and a mind and a heart to express that love, the total expression of it. You know, so I think that's the 'me' that God has created, the me that seeks to love. (Anthony)

Stephen, Matthew and Anthony all related how their understandings of sex were intrinsically related to their faith. The sexual experience is imbued with meaning that goes deeper than either physicality or emotional connection. For all three of these respondents being sexually active was to some extent a spiritual experience. It was both experiencing an aspect of God's plan for them as individuals, and also being able to experience first-hand what an all-encompassing godly love feels like. It is this view of erotic love which is emphasised in certain aspects of traditional Christianity with reference to the relationship between two committed individuals of different sexes. For the respondents, the core of this belief (the spiritual aspect of erotic love) remained. However, this traditional understanding is innovated upon. For some, as Anthony illustrates, this belief is innovated to allow the inclusion of a same-sex partner. For others, as Stephen illustrates, the tradition is innovated to include multiple partners. Within both of these approaches, however, the core tradition gives meaning to sexual experience, despite the dominant institutional discourse of sin.

The coexistence of multiple interpretations, however, can mean that such negotiations are required to be continuous. Alan's narrative illustrates this:

> Two ways of looking at it in my head. There is either the sort of liberal way where it's all ok. Whatever you do – that's absolutely fine. The Harry Williams[4] thing about, you know, sex with a stranger is the closest you can be to god, and all that. That's one way you can think about it. The other way you think about it is that it's all sinful but you do it anyway. So, a bit like sort of getting angry, or being smart or, whatever, you know? And I shift my emphasis from one to the other as I would sort of change my socks really! I think probably because I'd like to think that I could do the Harry Williams thing and just say 'Oh it's all wonderful' and that's fine. But there's something in the back of my mind that I can't quite get rid of, that he might not be quite right. (Alan)

Alan's reflections illustrate the difficulty of dealing with alternative interpretations. The ability to innovate is indeed enabling, however it is held in check, or constrained by the awareness that other possible interpretations exist.

The examples illustrate the connection between religious belief and respondents' conceptions of their relationships. They also emphasise the meaning such belief can provide for these relationships. Among the respondents, the claim to Christian meanings within relationships illustrates the ability to connect 'holiness' to gay relationships. Christian belief imbues sex and relationships with a meaning that otherwise would not be attached. Therefore, being active physically within a relationship is not just acceptable in the eyes of God, but is in fact a celebration of God's creation. Again, these examples emphasise the interaction of tradition and innovation. Traditional teachings are innovated through personal experience, and alternative interpretations (for example, Harry Williams), enabling individuals to find fit.

Religion as Provider of Meaning for Sexuality

Finally, in discussing understandings of sexuality itself, the respondents again illustrated the importance of accessing and accepting traditional understandings of

---

4   Harry Williams was a gay Anglican theologian. In his autobiography *Some Day I'll Find You* (1982) Williams discussed how he praised God during sex for the joy he was giving and receiving

faith, God and Christianity. Coming to discussions of sexuality with reference to traditional Christianity the respondents found ways of accepting gay identity through traditional theology and belief. The following quotations illustrate:

> Basically it's the way God created me. I can't see that he is going to sort of perpetrate some sort of joke. You know? Y'know, the rulebook saying one thing, and then make somebody something else. (Adam)

> If I am made in the image of God, if all things come from God how can this not be? And I would encourage other people to say who they are, so I can't not say it myself. I can't believe that God likes straight people and not gay people. (Stephen)

> People have been given their sexuality as part of their God given-ness. (Keith)

> I have to sort of say to God, well you know, you made me this way, this is who I am. If I have to answer for it one day that's what I'm happy to do. (Matthew)

The above quotations highlight the use of traditional theological beliefs – God created everything and human beings are created in the image of God. The respondents accessed these traditional aspects of theology in order to find an understanding of their sexuality. Such theological beliefs were understood with reference to traditional interpretation. However, they were also used more innovatively in terms of applying such traditional understandings to personal experiences of being gay. As Wilcox suggests, religious teachings are 'seeds that sprout plants never anticipated by many religious authorities' (Wilcox 2003, 77). For the respondents, as God is creator of everything, gay sexuality is an aspect of God's creation, it is given by God, and a part of the diversity God intended in the sexual realm. Also, Stephen's narrative suggests that, because human beings are made in the image of God, his sexuality is in some sense a reflection of the image of God. In essence, gayness is an aspect of the entirety of the divine. One important aspect of such reflections is that they illustrate an understanding of sexuality as something existing beyond the choice of the individual – it is essential, an aspect of who they are, no matter what choices they make. But, perhaps even more importantly, this understanding is also something more than essential. It is what Thumma (1991) refers to as 'creationist'. Sexuality, being understood as being created by God, becomes something which the individual has a duty to embrace, an aspect of their God given-ness, indeed a gift from God. Refusal to accept being gay within such an understanding goes beyond refusing to accept the self the individual desires to be. It is refusing to accept the self that has been given by God through his creation of the individual. Therefore, as Matthew's reflections quoted above emphasise, if anyone is to blame, surely it is God, for gay sexuality is God's doing.

Such understandings on the part of the respondents again illustrate the importance of traditional religiosity in the construction of stories of self. Access of traditional theological understandings provides meaning to the individual's experience of their sexuality through their innovations upon it. Understanding is imbued with meaning through its connection to traditional theology. Here again the negotiation of tradition and innovation within individuals' belief stories gives meaning to their experiences as gay men.

The Enabling Power of Traditional Belief

The above examples from the narratives of the respondents can, as previous literature has suggested, be seen as illustrating the powerful and liberating influence of individualised belief. The innovations undertaken by the respondents in constructing their personal belief stories give them the ability to make connections and to accept gay identity. Therefore it is possible to see the distinction between freedom and constraint as simply a result of the difference between institutional religion and personal belief. However, the innovations discussed on the part of the respondents remain firmly connected to the traditional, with tradition remaining as important an aspect of their belief system as their personal innovation. This importance of the traditional can be clarified by returning to the discussion of the respondents' narratives.

Comfort Through Tradition

The initial discussion concerning traditional belief providing safe space is related specifically to the importance of institution, organisation, or indeed community. Hibbs discusses the importance of 'long-term relationship to the organisational culture' (Hibbs 2006, 157). For Hibbs, institutional Church is a place where individuals have grown and felt a sense of belonging through long-term affiliation. Indeed, he refers to Church as a 'comfort zone' (Hibbs 2006, 157). The quotations from the respondents, given above, reflect this understanding of the importance of institution. However, the discussions of Luke and Harold go beyond seeing institutional Church as the basis of faith, it is also shown to some extent as the basis of self-acceptance. As Thumma (1991), and Wolkomir (2001) suggest, affiliation to denomination can be as important an aspect of identity as sexuality. Although the Church organisations Harold and Luke refer to did not make pronouncement about the men's emerging sexualities, they did show acceptance of these men as people. In essence, Church accepted the respondents at a time when the secular communities they were a part of did not. For this reason, breaking connection to the traditional (institutional Church) could, for many, threaten connections made within personal stories of self. The traditional Church is a place where individuals find acceptance, welcome and community. Whilst sexuality may remain unspoken in such situations, it gains silent affirmation through the individual connecting the acceptance they gain from Church, to all aspects of their personal identity. That is, the traditional Church institution's welcome is innovated to refer to the individual's sexual identity. The constraining silence of institutional Church therefore also enables personal acceptance of emerging sexuality. Despite the distance perceived in public talk between Church institution and gay sexuality, in personal stories of meaning connection can be made, and the institution plays an important role in this.

Meaning Through Tradition

The continuing importance of tradition is also illustrated in the respondents' discussions of sex and relationships. Although access to alternative interpretation and self-experience was important for respondents in connecting gay life and Christian belief, these innovational understandings were also intrinsically related to traditional teachings. Further, as Alan's reflections illustrated, the possibility of sin was not fully removed. Rather, space was found for innovation through understanding the traditional as one of many possible interpretations. Through accepting the traditional as interpretation, the respondents gained space to innovate, to access the stories and experiences of others, and to connect interpretations to their own experiences. However, although alternative interpretations of Christianity allow freedom, they remain interpretations in a world of many possibilities (Giddens 1991; Plummer 2003). As such, these understandings remain, fallible, flexible and fluid. Acceptance of these ideas is transient and must be worked on, hence the central importance of negotiation, indeed constant negotiation. Such negotiations cannot be fully removed from the traditional. Excessive innovation removes the meaning from individuals' identifications with Christianity. In other words, innovation separated from tradition does not connect Christianity to gay sexuality; it simply declines to attempt connection. Therefore continued connection to the traditional (sex as spiritual) is important and can be seen to anchor the innovational. It is the constraint of the innovational which enables the individual to combine sexuality and religious affiliation.

Acceptance Through Tradition

In discussing understanding of sexuality the paper illustrated that religion gave respondents the ability to limit the need for constant negotiation. This was done through direct appeal to experience, understanding and concept of God. Within this an understanding of God as creator of everything placed the existence of individuals' sexuality in the hands of God. Therefore acceptance of religious belief and acceptance of sexuality go hand in hand. This creationist approach has a similar base point to the essentialist understanding of sexuality (Warner 1995; Wilcox 2003; Yip 2005). One's sexuality is given by God and therefore completely beyond the control, or importantly the 'choice' of the individual. Such an essentialist/creationist understanding of sexuality can be questioned as to whether it is indeed an acceptance at all. To some extent it is more accurate to refer to such an approach as a refusal to accept, a way to 'go on' by removing the need to self-accept. Sexuality is beyond the control of the individual, being something occurring naturally, or created by a divine force. Therefore acceptance of being gay is not owning one's sexuality, rather it is accepting something which one can do nothing about (Whisman 1996). Thus one is not accepting and celebrating the 'goodness' of sexuality, but similarly one is freed from blame about the 'sinfulness' of sexuality. Of course such issues are important in academic discussions of sexual identity and sexuality. However, what is important within the lives of the individuals discussed here is that a creationist understanding of sexuality gives the individuals the ability to go on. The access to and connection with the traditional theological understandings at the base of such arguments gave the respondents access to a way of understanding sexuality which not only imbued it with meaning, but also placed responsibility outside the boundaries of the individual, and into the hands of an infallible god. Connection to such a creationist/essentialist understanding is an immensely important aspect of personal stories of self. Although, here again, the connection to the traditional constrains, constraining the individual's ability to 'own' their sexuality. This constraint also enables. It enables the individual to access a way of understanding sexuality, which is both a powerful defence to institutional opposition, because of its use of traditional theological understandings, and also an important aspect of personal meaning systems. If God created gay sexuality then surely gay sexuality must be good, indeed it is an aspect of the self that God created. Therefore not to embrace this God-given gift is an insult to the divine creator.

The Dialectic of Tradition and Innovation

Central to the respondents' reflections is a negotiation of tradition and innovation that reflects the dual ability of traditional religious identification to constrain and enable. Such negotiation is reminiscent of Baxter's (1990) discussion of the dialectics at play in personal relationships. In undertaking such negotiations the individual must not move too far from either side of the dialectic. Moving too far away from tradition endangers the individual's connection to Christianity; moving too far away from innovation threatens the individual's connection to gay identity. The need for negotiation is therefore constant, as the constraining nature of traditional belief also allows access to meaning. Connection is enabled by constraint.

Concluding Thoughts

The data illustrates the continuing importance of religious beliefs in the lives of a number of late modern individuals. Although the findings presented here are directly related to the experiences of a small number of gay clergy, the issues discussed talk directly to the problems of late modern belief discussed by Geyer and Baumeister (2005). The stories of the respondents illustrate that faith stories are negotiated with reference to self-experience, institutional experience and the experiences of others. These negotiations are not limited to a specific time, place, or event. Rather they are, and indeed must be, ongoing. Being Christian is not a fixed category, its meaning must be constantly negotiated, and this negotiation must be contextualised within an understanding of the experiences of the individual. For this reason, such negotiations connect life sectors, such as sexual and professional identities, and provide a meaning framework for individuals.

The lives of many gay clergy are experienced as life circumstances which are dangerous and forcibly constrained through being situated within the institutional Church. However, these are balanced by a connection to faith which, through negotiation of tradition and innovation, gives meaning and affirms the individual. This thereby gives individuals the 'freedom' to be both gay and clergy.

Bibliography

Anglican Communion. 1999. *Section 1 Called to Full Humanity*. Harrisburg, PA: Morehouse Publishing.

Baxter, Leslie A. 1990. 'Dialectical contradictions in relationship development.' *Journal of Social and Personal Relationships* 7: 69–88.

Bellah, Robert N. 1985. *Habits of the Heart: Individualism and Commitment in American Life*. London: University of California Press.

Fletcher, Ben. 1990. *Clergy Under Stress: A Study of Homosexual and Heterosexual Clergy*. London: Mowbray.

Geyer, Anne L. and Baumeister, Roy F. 2005. 'Religion, Morality, and Self-Control: Values, Virtues, and Vices.' In Raymond F. Paloutzian, and Crystal L. Park, eds, *Handbook of the Psychology of Religion and Spirituality,* New York: Guilford Press. 412–432.

Giddens, Anthony. 1991. *Modernity and Self-Identity: Self and Society in the Late Modern Age*. Cambridge: Polity.

Heelas, Paul and Woodhead, Linda (eds). 2005. *The Spiritual Revolution: Why Religion is Giving Way to Spirituality*. Oxford: Blackwell.

Hibbs, G. Shane. 2006. *Journey of the Sacred Leader: A Qualitative Inquiry Examining the Coming Out Process in the Organizational Culture of a Religious Setting for Gay, Male, Protestant Clergy*. Lincoln, NE: iUniverse.

House of Bishops. 1991. *Issues in Human Sexuality: A Statement by the House of Bishops of the General Synod of the Church of England*. London: Church House Publishing.

Lyon, David. 2000. *Jesus in Disneyland: Religion in Postmodern Times*. Cambridge: Polity.

O'Brien, Jodi. 2004. 'Wrestling the Angel of Contradiction: Queer Christian Identities.' *Culture and Religion* 5: 179–202.

Plummer, Ken. 2003. *Intimate Citizenship: Private Decisions and Public Dialogues*. Seattle: University of Washington Press.

Roof, Wade C. 1999. *Spiritual Marketplace: Baby Boomers and the Remaking of American Religion*. Princeton: Princeton University Press.

Stuart, Elizabeth. 1993. *Chosen: Gay Catholic Priests Tell Their Stories*. London: G. Chapman.

Thumma, Scott. 1991. 'Negotiating a Religious Identity: The Case of the Gay Evangelical.' *Sociological Analysis* 52: 333–347.

Wagner, Richard. 1981. *Gay Catholic Priests: A Study of Cognitive and Affective Dissonance*. San Francisco: Specific Press.

Warner, R. Stephen. 1995. 'The Metropolitan Community Churches and the Gay Agenda: The Power of Pentecostalism and Essentialism.' In Mary J. Neitz and Marion S. Goldman, eds, *Sex, Lies, and Sanctity: Religion and Deviance in Contemporary North America* Greenwich, CT: JAI. 81–108.

Weeks, Jeffrey, Heaphy, Brian and Donovan, Catherine. 2001. *Same Sex Intimacies: Families of Choice and Other Life Experiments*. London: Routledge.

Whisman, Vera. 1996. *Queer By Choice: Lesbians, Gay Men and the Politics of Identity*. London: Routledge.

Wilcox, Melissa M. 2003. *Coming Out in Christianity: Religion, Identity and Community*. Bloomington: Indiana University Press.

Williams, Harry A. 1982. *Some Day I'll Find You: An Autobiography*. London: Mitchell Beazley.

Wolf, James G. 1989. *Gay Priests*. San Francisco: Harper and Row.

Wolkomir, Michelle. 2001. 'Wrestling with the Angels of Meaning: The Revisionist Ideological Work of Gay and Ex-Gay Christian Men., *Symbolic Interaction* 24: 407–424.

Yip, Andrew K.T. 2000. 'Leaving the Church to Keep My Faith: The Lived Experiences of Non-Heterosexual Christians.' In Leslie J. Francis, and Yaacov J. Katz, eds, *Joining and Leaving Religion: Research Perspectives,* Leominster: Gracewing. 129–145.

——. 2002. 'The Persistence of Faith among Nonheterosexual Christians: Evidence for the Neosecularization Thesis of Religious Transformation.' *Journal for the Scientific Study of Religion* 41: 199–212.

——. 2005. 'Religion and the Politics of Spirituality/Sexuality: Reflections on Researching British Lesbian, Gay and Bi-sexual Christians and Muslims.' *Fieldwork in Religion* 1: 271–289.

Chapter Thirteen

Religious Identity and Millenarian Belief in Santo Daime

Andrew Dawson

Introduction

This chapter reflects upon fieldwork undertaken in recent years with alternative and non-mainstream religions in Brazil (Dawson 2007) when I had the opportunity to spend time with members of the Brazilian new religion of Santo Daime. In the course of my research it became clear through conversations in which talk of the 'end times' cropped up that Santo Daime members (referred to as *daimistas*) were constructing their religious identities by, among other things, drawing upon a range of millenarian themes and images most closely associated with more traditional forms of Brazilian religiosity (see, for example, Levine 1992; Myscofski 1988; Queiroz 1965; Pessar 2004). Regarding millenarianism as a 'particular type of salvationism', Cohn argues that the millenarian paradigm can be identified through its characterization of salvation as

> (a) collective, in the sense that it is to be enjoyed by the faithful as a collectivity; (b) terrestrial, in the sense that it is to be realized on this earth and not in some other-worldly heaven; (c) imminent, in the sense that it is to come both soon and suddenly; (d) total, in the sense that it is utterly to transform life on earth, so that the new dispensation will be no mere improvement on the present but perfection itself; (e) miraculous, in the sense that it is to be accomplished by, or with the help of, supernatural agencies. (1970, 13)

On each of these counts, the relevant scenarios, themes and images articulated by members of the Santo Daime religion qualify as characteristically millenarian. Whilst variations exist from one *daimista* community to another, espousal of the millenarian paradigm usually reflects the ecological preoccupations of the movement as a whole. According to informants, the 'time of trial' about to begin or already upon us involves some kind of impending environmental 'catastrophe' brought on by an assortment of 'rampant materialism', 'global warming', 'pollution', 'over-reliance upon technology', and 'alienation from nature'. Although details of post-catastrophic times often remain sketchy, the new earth scenario envisaged by *daimistas* involves the re-establishment of humankind's relationship with nature, which is to be most clearly expressed through the use of environmentally friendly means of economic and social reproduction. One *daimista* referred to this process as akin to being 'thrown back to the stone age'. Given the end of technology as we know it, *daimistas* believe that those versed in the processes of natural production will be best placed both to survive the global catastrophe and to exploit the opportunities afforded by the new dispensation. Consequently, *daimista* communities are keen for members to develop a knowledge and skills base conducive to what one informant describes as 'working with nature'. To this end, *daimista* communities are often located in rural settings or at the semi-rural peripheries of major conurbations. Referred to as 'our refuge' or 'our Noah's ark', these non-urban communities are viewed simultaneously as shelters from the impending catastrophe, training grounds for the righteous remnant and anticipations of the forthcoming earthly Jerusalem.

Although the origins of the Santo Daime religion lie among the poorer sectors of the population living in the semi-rural context of north-western Brazil, the *daimistas* with whom I was working are actually members of Brazil's urban middle classes inhabiting the expanding conurbations of the central-southern states of Minas Gerais, Rio de Janeiro and São Paulo. The issue I wish to explore here concerns the fabrication of religious identity by urban middle-class *daimistas* through their appropriation of millenarian motifs traditionally associated with Brazil's rural poor. To do this, two lines of enquiry may be followed. The first explores the continuity between the traditional millenarianism most closely associated with Brazil's rural peasantry and the new era millenarianism articulated by urban middle-class *daimistas*. Comparisons are drawn between the practical-symbolic crises suffered by rural adherents of traditional millenarian forms and the existential crises endured by urban professionals espousing new era millenarianism. Like traditional millenarianism before it, new era millenarianism is held to express subjective experiences of alienation from and disenchantment with prevailing societal structures.

Unlike the first, the second line of enquiry is one of discontinuity. Instead of drawing parallels, the second line regards the use of millenarian imagery by contemporary *daimistas* as indicative of a range of dynamics typical of the late modern context within which these urban professionals are situated. Whilst notions of alienation and disenchantment are not ignored, this second line of enquiry regards new era millenarianism as primarily expressive of a number of reflexive preoccupations typical of late modern existence. Before exploring these two lines of enquiry, it may prove beneficial to say something of the organizational repertoire within which individual appropriations of millenarian motifs occur.

The *Daimista* Repertoire

Santo Daime was founded among the mixed-race, semi-rural peasantry of the Amazonian state of Acre by Raimundo Irineu Serra (1892–1971). Known commonly as 'Master Irineu', Irineu Serra is held by many to be the reincarnation of the spirit of Jesus. Based at the community of Alto Santo, Santo Daime emerged as a recognizably distinct religious movement in the mid-twentieth century (Cemin 2004, 347–82). Subsequent to Irineu Serra's death a breakaway organization known as CEFLURIS (Eclectic Centre of the Universal Flowing Light Raimundo Irineu Serra) was founded by Sebastião Mota de Melo (1920–1990). Known as 'Padrinho Sebastião', Mota de Melo is believed to be the reincarnation of the spirit of John the Baptist. CEFLURIS is today headquartered at Céu do Mapiá in the state of Amazonas

(Couto 2004, 385–411). As with Alto Santo before it, Céu do Mapiá is held to be the location at which the post-cataclysmic New Jerusalem will be founded. On the back of the organizational expansion of CEFLURIS, Santo Daime reached Brazil's major conurbations (for example, Rio de Janeiro and São Paulo) in the early 1980s before spreading to Europe, North America and Australasia.

Santo Daime is the oldest of Brazil's ayahuasca religions and is also the most internationally widespread. The word 'ayahuasca' derives from the Quechua language and means 'soul vine' or 'vine of the dead' (Labate et al. 2004, 21). When applied to the ayahuasca religions of Brazil (Barquinha, Santo Daime and the Vegetable Union), the generic term ayahuasca denotes the combination of the vine *Banisteriopsis caapi* and the leaves of the shrub *Psychotria viridis* (Dawson 2007, 67–98). Ayahuasca is a psychotropic substance traditionally consumed by indigenous inhabitants of the Amazon which passed to non-indigenous communities through its use among *mestiço* (mixed-race) communities and rubber-tappers in the late nineteenth and early twentieth centuries. Ayahuasca is regarded by *daimistas* as an 'entheogen', that is, an agent whose properties facilitate the interaction of humankind with supernatural agents or forces. The ritual consumption of Daime also symbolizes the union of base matter and supernatural force in which the latter makes itself felt through the transformation of the former.

The discursive and ritual repertoires of Santo Daime are an amalgam of popular Catholic, esoteric, indigenous, Spiritist, Afro-Brazilian, and new age beliefs and practices. The four most important rituals are the *feitio* (at which Daime is made), *bailado* (dance), *concentração* (concentration), and *missa* (mass). Both *bailado* and *concentração* usually commence after sunset, with the former lasting anything up to twelve hours and the latter not normally exceeding three or four. During these rituals participants face inward towards a central table which is usually laid with a wooden Cruzeiro draped by a rosary, statuettes of Mary and Jesus, photographs of Master Irineu and Padrinho Sebastião, candles, flowers, water, and incense sticks. Some groups may include statuettes of some of the saints and a Bible, whilst others might also have crystals, representations of Afro-Brazilian spirits and deities, and oriental icons. Once tied to the lunar cycle, the *feitio*, which can last anything up to three days, is increasingly conducted whenever fresh supplies of 'Daime' (the emic term for ayahuasca) are needed. The 'mass' is celebrated relative to the anniversaries of the death of prominent members. The demanding, if not arduous, nature of *daimista* rituals is reflected in their designation as 'trials' through which the spiritual worth of participants is tested relative to their physical perseverance. At the same time, ritual regimes prepare members for the trials and tribulations soon to be unleashed by forthcoming catastrophes.

Whereas the consumption of ayahuasca is held by *daimistas* to help generate the 'power' that is essential to their rituals, the singing of hymns is the means by which this 'astral force' is engaged, channelled, and manipulated to form a 'spiritual current' which binds participants vertically with the spiritual plane and horizontally with each other. Consequently, the ritual repertoire of Santo Daime is organized around collections of hymns known as *hinários*. The first and most important of these *hinários* is that of Irineu Serra and is known as the *Cruzeiro*. As with all *daimista* hymns, those of the *Cruzeiro* are set to the rhythms of the march, mazurka, and waltz, and in form reflect Amazonian mixed-race, popular Catholic and Afro-Brazilian influences (Luna 1986, 174–80; Labate and Pacheco 2004, 317, 330). In addition to the *Cruzeiro* and assorted hymnals of organizational and local community leaders, the discourse and practice of CEFLURIS is orientated by Mota de Melo's two *hinários*, *O Justiçeiro* (The Just One) and *Nova Jerusalém* (New Jerusalem). The figures of the popular Catholic trinity ('Father', 'Jesus', and 'the Virgin Mother/ Mary') appear throughout these *hinários*, as do the 'Divine Beings' who populate the 'celestial court'. Astral phenomena are likewise well represented, as are natural elements and the flora and fauna of the forest. Irineu Serra and Mota de Melo appear in the guise of 'Teacher' entrusted by the Virgin Mother (also referred to as 'Queen of the Forest') with 'sacred doctrines' to be conveyed by way of the 'hymns' being sung. Ayahuasca is likewise referred to as a 'Teacher' and 'Holy Light' whose consumption engenders 'truth', 'love', 'wisdom', 'understanding', 'force', 'power', 'cure', and 'cleansing'. Members of Santo Daime are constituted as a community of 'brothers and sisters' whose consumption of Daime sets them apart from the world of 'sin' and 'illusion'. Because of their allegiance to 'Daime', *daimistas* are to be much 'misunderstood' by the world at large. They are, however, assuredly on the 'way' towards 'salvation' and 'another incarnation'.

Through discursive and practical means, the ritual repertoire of Santo Daime situates the *daimista* community and its members within a millenarian worldview framed by the cosmic battle between good and evil. Irineu Serra is the 'Imperial Chief' of the army of 'Juramidam' and Mota de Melo his 'General'. Reflected in the use of ritual space, the 'soldiers' of 'Juramidam' are led by 'commandants' and organized into 'battalions' regimented according to sex, age, and marital status. As if to further underline the martial paradigm, members of Santo Daime who have consumed ayahuasca a set number of times receive a uniform to wear at official rituals.   The origins of Santo Daime among the semi-rural Amazonian poor go some way to explaining the presence of millenarian motifs within established discursive and liturgical repertoires. The millenarian paradigm has long been 'a fundamental part' of the symbolic reservoir drawn upon by Brazil's rural poor (Da Matta 1996, 5). Acknowledgement of humble beginnings does not, though, readily account for the continued articulation of millenarian preoccupations by contemporary *daimistas* whose urban middle-class status puts them poles apart from those first responsible for Santo Daime's appropriation of millenarian themes. Why, then, do middle-class *daimistas* adhere to a millenarian worldview whose origins are historically, geographically and demographically remote from their everyday existence in the urban-industrial heartlands of Brazil? As indicated above, two possible lines of enquiry might be followed in response to this question. The first line of enquiry is one of continuity in that both traditional and *daimista* millenarian narratives are said to reflect similar structural conditions and equivalent subjective states. It is to this line of enquiry that we now turn.

Line of Continuity

In a chapter of this length it is impossible to do justice to every factor responsible for the historical emergence of millenarian narratives in Brazil. Three contributory factors are, though, worthy of note. First, millenarian repertoires have tended to emerge on the back of an intense longing after change for the better. Usually provoked by rapid and far-reaching disruptions of established patterns of social-cultural and political-economic reproduction, the articulation of millenarian motifs reflects a range of practical and symbolic crises, the answer to which is held to lie in a thoroughgoing corrective transformation of existing societal structures. Consequently, the millenarian paradigm makes change for the better conditional upon widespread social transformation. Second, millenarian outbreaks in Brazil have traditionally embodied an inability or refusal to envisage change for the better arising internally through the reform of prevailing social systems. Indicative of an entrenched marginalization from overarching social-economic and political-legal structures the millenarian paradigm encapsulates the belief that any longed-for improvement can only come from means external to the system. Third, millenarian aspirations have historically reflected an inability or refusal to employ transformative strategies by which the prevailing system might be changed for the better. Undoubtedly fed by the aforementioned systemic marginalization experienced by groups peripheral to prevailing structures, the lack of transformational strategizing has traditionally reflected both the paucity of formal channels of collective representation and a deep-seated lack of confidence in any one group's abilities to bring about change through its own agency. Grounded in the daily experience of strategic impotence, the millenarian paradigm looks for change by means other than collective agitation or political representation.

Driven by practical-symbolic crisis and the resulting longing for change, systemic marginalization and strategic impotence combine to produce a worldview which holds that prevailing structures must end before things can change for the better and that this end will come by means both external to the system and other than collective agitation. Although not the only possible response, the *deus ex machina* model furnished by the rich tradition of Brazilian millenarianism has proven to be a valuable mode of signification for successive groups, communities and movements. In effect, the millenarian paradigm squares the significatory circle in that it provides a much-desired social transformation when both systemic marginalization and strategic impotence would normally dictate such a state of affairs to be an otherwise practical and symbolic impossibility.

In contrast to those groups in which millenarian perspectives have traditionally emerged, *daimista* urban professionals espousing millenarian views cannot be said to be suffering under the same conditions of systemic marginalization and strategic impotence. Whence, then, their attachment to millenarian motifs? Again allowing for complexities beyond the scope of this chapter, and pursuing the investigative line of continuity noted above, a number of comparisons might be drawn between the context of rural poverty which has historically given rise to traditional millenarianism in Brazil and the middle-class, urban-industrial context within which *daimista* articulations of millenarian motifs occur.

Systemic Insecurity

First, whereas it cannot be said that the majority of *daimistas* suffer under the same conditions of systemic marginalization as those among whom millenarianism has traditionally thrived, it might be argued that their status as urban professionals in contemporary Brazil nevertheless engenders a kind of systemic insecurity engendered by, among other things, a decreasing standard of living and a steady decline in both physical and occupational security. Much has been written upon the manner in and extent to which contemporary urban-industrial society generates both material and psychological insecurity for its members. Giddens, for example, identifies 'anxiety', 'disorientation' and 'insecurity' as integral components of subjective experience in late-modern society (1990, 153; 1991, 181; 1994, 89); just as Bourdieu highlights the 'generalized subjective insecurity' experienced by those subject to 'neo-liberal policies' of 'casualization' and 'flexploitation' (1998, 82–6). In the same vein, Beck identifies 'endemic insecurity' and 'biographical uncertainties' as now perennial features of contemporary existence (Beck and Gernsheim 2002, 3–4); whilst Bauman talks of the 'awesome' and 'distressing' 'insecurity' and *'précarité'* engendered by late-modern capitalism (2001, 41–8, 113–48; 2005, 31–3). Of course, the average life of the average urban professional is by no means as difficult or precarious as those of the poor majority in Brazil. Subjective experience, though, is very rarely a relative state of affairs. Nevertheless, consecutive decades of stagflation (1980s), neo-liberal reform (1990s) and fiscal redistribution (2000s) have eroded once secure professional comfort-zones at a time when enhanced global awareness and late-capitalist ideologies have actually increased urban middle-class expectations (O'Dougherty 2002; Quadros 2003, 109–35; Pochmann et al. 2007). Combined with the erosion of social-economic conditions, the shortfall between expectation and reality serves only to exacerbate the conditions of uncertainty, disorientation, anxiety, and distress identified by the likes of Bauman, Beck, Bourdieu, and Giddens. As with the systemic marginalization suffered by the rural poor, the systemic insecurity experienced by growing sections of Brazil's urban middle classes discourages change for the better being expected of current social structures. As such, change for the better will come from beyond the prevailing system.

Strategic Indifference

Second, whilst it cannot be said that the majority of *daimistas* experience the same strategic impotence as those for whom millenarianism has traditionally been a response, it may be argued that, for some at least, there exists a kind of strategic indifference to established representative structures and processes of collective agitation. The cause (or admixture of causes) of such indifference will clearly differ from person to person. Beck and Beck-Gernsheim, for example, maintain that urban-industrial processes of individualization are responsible for the progressive 'subpoliticization' of civil society and a subjectivity of 'political privatism' which manifest themselves in a growing disregard for political processes of representation and collective mechanisms of agitation (2002, 27, 38). Along the same lines, Castells blames the contemporary indifference to collective processes of representation and action upon modernity's 'dissolution of shared identities' and the resultant loss 'of society as a meaningful social system' (Castells 1997, 355). Arguing that 'ours are times of disengagement', Bauman holds the 'indeterminacy' of late-modern life to have engendered a kind of 'indifference' resulting in 'an incapacity to make plans and act on them' (2001, 127). In less general terms, strategic indifference may also be rooted for some Brazilians in a lack of habit born of the paucity of proper mechanisms for political representation and civil agitation which lasted from the military coup of 1964 until re-democratization in the early 1980s. Whatever the particular cocktail of causation, however, the contemporary context of urban-industrial Brazil is seen to be characterized by 'democratic deficit' and 'associative alienation' embodying both a 'distrust of' and 'disenchantment with' existing structures of representation and mechanisms of collective expression (Baquero 2001, 98–104, and 2003, 83–108; Ferreira 1999). Reflecting a lack of subjective investment in prevailing societal institutions, the implications of strategic indifference are that those desirous of social change must look for it through means other than established processes of political representation and civil agitation.

Practical-Symbolic Crisis

Although expressed in a variety of ways and to a greater or lesser extent, both systemic insecurity and strategic indifference were evidenced in conversation with members of the *daimista* community. Alongside received descriptions of the world as 'sinful' and 'illusory', society at large is dismissed as, among other things, 'corrupt', 'materialistic', 'degraded', and 'immoral'. In the same vein, *daimistas* are clearly distrustful of established mechanisms of political and civil representation. Whilst the historical persecution of groups such as Santo Daime has undoubtedly contributed to a well-developed (but not extreme) sectarian ethos, the low levels of *daimista* expectation of what contemporary Brazilian society can do for them goes beyond that of expressing a simple religious dualism. Together, systemic insecurity and strategic indifference have engendered among *daimistas* a practical-symbolic crisis which, at one and the same time, longs for resolution through a change for the better whilst accepting that such positive transformation will come from neither internal reform of the system nor strategic engagement with it. Of course, by no stretch of the imagination are the significatory resources made available by the millenarian paradigm the only means of anxious and disaffected urban-professionals such as these resolving this practical-symbolic crisis. Nevertheless, the eschatological scenario articulated by millenarian motifs does offer resolution in that it furnishes the much-desired change for the better whilst leaving systemic insecurity and strategic indifference untouched. Albeit in paradoxical fashion, it is because the millenarian paradigm resolves the practical-symbolic crisis whilst leaving its causes untouched that it continues to be drawn upon by middle-class *daimistas* living in the urban-industrial heartlands of Brazil.

Line of Discontinuity

As indicated above, there is a second line of enquiry in respect of the attachment of urban middle-class *daimistas* to the millenarian paradigm. Although the implications of systemic insecurity and strategic indifference are not rejected by this second line of enquiry, it does place much more emphasis upon dynamics which reflect a greater degree of discontinuity between traditional and *daimista* millenarian discourses. The second line of enquiry commences by regarding *daimista* espousals of millenarian themes as embodying a self-conscious strategic articulation indicative of the heightened degree of reflexivity enjoyed by the urban middle-classes of late-modern industrial society. In effect, the 'reflexivity thesis' argues that the historically recent transmutation of typically 'modern' dynamics constitutive of urban-industrial society (for example, individualization, detraditionalization, globalization, and pluralization) have resulted in an unprecedented degree of self-awareness being enjoyed by increasing numbers in contemporary, late-modern society. Using the term 'reflexivity' to designate this new-found degree of self-conscious appreciation, theorists of late-modernity argue that contemporary urban-industrial existence is, for many, marked by a strategically driven and instrumentally orientated subjectivity (for example, Beck 1992; Giddens 1991; Lash 1990). Perhaps exemplified by the professional classes of urban-industrial society, the reflexivity afforded by late-modernity permits individuals a degree of self-critical awareness, positional understanding and strategic savvy hitherto unavailable to human consciousness (for example, Beck et al. 1994). As *bona fide* members of Brazil's urban-industrial middle classes, it should be of no surprise, then, to find the dynamics of late modern reflexivity at play among contemporary *daimistas* and the organizational repertoires articulated by them.

Reflexive Strategies

Following this line of enquiry, the appearance of traditional millenarian motifs within *daimista* narratives might, for example, be regarded as a reflexive strategy employed to underwrite the utility value of organizational repertoires. By employing millenarian discourse to situate the world in the midst of a truly momentous transitional phase, it could be argued, *daimista* discourse reinforces its pragmatic worth by offering itself as a form of practical knowledge well-placed to aid individuals in meeting the very particular demands provoked by the calamitous times through which we are passing. The knowledge furnished by Santo Daime, it is claimed, allows individuals to understand the significance of current calamities and disasters by placing them in their appropriate cosmological context. At the same time, the practical repertoire afforded by Santo Daime is said to equip practitioners with a range of techniques which will enable members to endure successfully the trials and tribulations associated with the birth of the new era.

In the same vein, the reflexive character of *daimista* appropriations of traditional millenarian themes might further be underlined by regarding the espousal of millenarian motifs as part of a broader strategy to differentiate the Santo Daime religion from other occupants of the increasingly crowded religious landscape of urban-industrial Brazil. In view of the fierce competition for what remains a relatively small constituency of sympathetic urban professionals, religious production undergoes a degree of 'standardization' as organizational repertoires are progressively tailored to the same, narrow band of potential members (Berger 1967, 147). In order to stand out from the crowd, and thereby mitigate the effects of repertorial standardization, religions such as Santo Daime must find ways of differentiating themselves from others in their field. Berger calls this process 'marginal differentiation' as any group employing it must be careful not to differentiate themselves so much as to place themselves outside of the most profitable (and thereby standardized) band of organizational repertoires (1967, 147). Certainly, the *daimista* community is no stranger to the dynamics of standardization and marginal differentiation and has self-consciously employed its environmental and indigenous credentials to best exploit these dynamics. Along the same lines, then, the appearance of traditional millenarian themes within the narrative repertoires of urban middle-class *daimista* communities might be viewed as another strategic attempt to marginally differentiate the Santo Daime religion from its nearest competitors.

Self-Valorization

In keeping with late-modernity's facilitation of the 'reflexive project' (Giddens 1991, 186), the attraction of the millenarian paradigm to urban professional *daimistas* might also involve the strategic exploitation of its eschatological scenario in the cause of self-valorization. In one sense, the new earth scenario portrayed by the millenarian paradigm provides *daimistas* with both a vindication of and reward for their perseverance and faithfulness in the face of scepticism and persecution. The arrival of a new dispensation will involve not only the transformation of the world but also the transposition of group values and those who espouse them from their currently marginal status to a central position in keeping with the character of the new world order. In another sense, the appropriation of millenarian motifs is even more self-affirming because it reminds practising *daimistas* that the values and beliefs they adhere to are the very same values and beliefs by which the world will be transformed and upon which the new era will be founded. Furthermore, because *daimistas* live by these values and beliefs they will be among the righteous remnant which is to form the vanguard of the renewed world and its new civilization. The strategic linkage of contemporary *daimista* practice with impending global renewal endows both the Santo Daime repertoire and its individual practitioners with a significance of truly cosmic proportions.

The *daimista* preoccupation with what I have elsewhere called 'cosmic self-aggrandizement' is further reinforced through use of the millenarian paradigm's decimation of the prevailing structures and dominant institutions of contemporary society (Dawson 2007, 162). As with other occupants of Brazil's new era religious landscape, the *raison d'être* of Santo Daime ritual repertoires is held to be their nurture of the 'higher self' (known also as the 'inner', 'cosmic', 'true' or 'Christic' self). The 'higher self' is the interior aspect of the individual most attuned to the universal whole of which we are all a part. Only when the higher self is developed are the latent powers residing deep within each of us able to be tapped, harnessed and manipulated to the end of obtaining absolute self-realization. Evidenced through spiritual enlightenment, universal understanding and physical well-being, the self's absolute realization is, however, conditional upon the eradication of the 'ego' (known also as the 'lower self'). Originating through embodied interaction with the world at large, the ego is the part of the individual most affected by and attached to the external, material world. In so being, the ego suppresses the higher self and thereby restricts the individual pursuit of absolute self-realization.

Functioning, in effect, as the social self, the ego serves as a cipher for the plethora of forces and dynamics which stand over and against the individual. That is, the ego signifies society at large, just as its dissolution signifies the liberation of the individual from external forces and dynamics otherwise beyond its control. By annihilating the ego, the *daimista* repertoire eradicates societal determination. In so doing, *daimista* discourse and practice frees the individual from unwarranted external interference and thereby allows the unfettered pursuit of absolute self-realization. In narrative terms, then, the annihilation of the ego and the emergence of the higher self correlates directly with the dissolution of societal determination and the achievement of absolute self-realization. This is where millenarianism comes in. For, in the hands of urban middle-class *daimistas* preoccupied with the reflexive project of the self, millenarianism's decimation of the world at large reinforces this correlation. By completely reconfiguring the societal dynamics responsible for the birth of the ego, millenarianism's new earth scenario removes all forms of external determination which might otherwise hinder the absolute realization of the higher self. The renewed earth of the millenarian paradigm thereby furnishes the individual with a blank canvas upon which she is unqualifiedly free to express herself and pursue her destiny. In effect, the millenarian paradigm's removal of unwarranted societal determination underwrites the absolute sovereignty of the late modern self.

Instrumental Religiosity

The reflexive character of *daimista* appropriations of millenarian themes might further be underlined with reference to the typically instrumental and expressionistic nature of new era religiosity in Brazil. Collectively, late modern transformations of established urban-industrial dynamics have radically modified received relationships between religious communities and their respective participants. With emphasis shifting from collective to individual expectation, growing numbers of individuals increasingly interact with religious movements and organizations relative to subjective criteria guided by immediate experience and orientated to personal fulfilment. Evaluated relative to subjective needs and aspirations, religious participation is thereby instrumentalized as it comes to be viewed as a means to self-realization rather than an end in itself or the meeting of pre-existing social obligations. Perhaps two of the clearest expressions of the instrumentalization of religious belonging in Brazil are the dynamics of religious transit and bricolage. Religious transit is characterized by the concurrent participation in and consecutive switching between different religious groups, whilst religious bricolage embodies an eclectic, pick-and-mix approach in which otherwise disparate beliefs, rituals and values are individually appropriated relative to subjective tastes and preoccupations. Evidence of the instrumentalization of religious belonging, along with the dynamics of transit and bricolage, are commonplace across the *daimista* community. One informant, for example, was open enough to admit that a key reason he likes the *daimista* community of which he is currently a member is that the absence of sermons and talks gives him space to 'get on and think what I want'. In the same vein, and typical of many conversations, a community leader told me that prior to 'finding' Daime he had participated in Catholic, Umbanda, Spiritist, Theosophical, Rosicrucian, new age, and assorted neo-esoteric groups. Like so many of his contemporaries, whilst he regards himself as having moved beyond these beliefs and practices, it was clear that he continues, however unwittingly, to use them to inform his current engagement with (and modification of) the contemporary *daimista* repertoire.

Practised by urban middle-class *daimistas*, transit and bricolage express an experimental and expressionistic religiosity which at times borders on the playful. Facilitated by increasingly pluralized urban environments, transit and bricolage combine to produce a 'subjective polysemy of religious experience' in which an assortment of beliefs and rituals are picked up and played with before being discarded or appropriated along idiosyncratic lines (Brandão 1994, 30). Set against the backdrop of instrumentalized religiosity *daimista* espousals of millenarian themes might best be understood, then, not as embodying deep-seated insecurity and ambivalence but rather as reflecting expressionistic and experimental dynamics which are intrinsically playful in nature. This is not to question the seriousness and commitment with which millenarian views are expressed by Santo Daime members. It is, though, to recognize the espousal of millenarianism as part of a transient and hybrid religious identity the provisionality of which is reflexively orchestrated. In so being, the millenarian views expressed by urban middle-class *daimistas* can only properly be understood when viewed as representing just one component of an otherwise variegated biographical trajectory comprising a highly diverse and constantly changing set of beliefs.

Conclusion

Inevitably, the espousal of millenarian themes by urban middle-class *daimistas* is a far more nuanced process than a chapter such as this can suggest. Nevertheless, each of the lines of enquiry pursued above provides valuable insight into a range of dynamics which combine to set the conditions of possibility within which *daimista* appropriations of the millenarian paradigm occur. The argument from continuity has some merit in that Santo Daime adepts frequently express themselves as disaffected with prevailing societal institutions whilst, at the same time, remaining disinterested in utilizing existing means of social engagement. The appropriation of millenarianism as a way of resolving the crisis generated by the confluence of systemic insecurity and strategic indifference certainly has parallels with the traditional context which has contributed to the espousal of millenarianism by Brazil's hard-pressed rural poor. There is, then, something to be said in favour of the argument from continuity. At the same time, the late modern context within which the Santo Daime religion exists plays a massive part in influencing both the organizational repertoires by which *daimista* millenarianism is framed and the subjective dynamics of individual agency by which millenarian motifs are brought to life. Both the heightened reflexivity enjoyed by the urban middle classes and the implications of religious instrumentalization afford *daimista* appropriations of the millenarian paradigm an ineluctably strategic quality. So, whilst not ruling out the dynamics of practical-symbolic crisis explored by the first line of enquiry, the argument from discontinuity underlines the intentional, self-aware qualities of *daimista* espousals of millenarian themes. Strangely familiar by virtue of its recapitulation of established themes, yet strikingly novel on account of its late modern characteristics, the *daimista* appropriation of traditional millenarianism underscores the Janus-faced nature of new era religiosity exemplified here by the Santo Daime religion of Brazil.

Bibliography

Baquero, Marcello. 2001. 'Cultura Política Participativa e Desconsolidação Democrática: Reflexões sobre o Brasil Contemporâneo.' *São Paulo em Perspectiva* 15.4: 98–104.

——. 2003. 'Construindo uma outra Sociedade: O Capital Social na Estruturação de uma Cultura Política Participativa no Brasil.' *Revista de Sociologia e Política* 21: 83–108.

Bauman, Zygmunt. 2001. *Community: Seeking Safety in an Insecure World.* Cambridge: Polity.

——. 2005. *Liquid Life.* Cambridge: Polity.

Beck, Ulrich. 1992. *Risk Society: Towards a New Modernity.* London: Newbury Park.

—— and Beck-Gernsheim, Elisabeth. 2002. *Individualization: Institutionalized Individualism and its Social and Political Consequences.* London: Sage.

——, Giddens, Anthony and Lash, Scott. 1994. *Reflexive Modernization: Politics, Tradition and Aesthetics in the Modern Social Order.* Cambridge: Polity.

Berger, Peter. 1967. *The Sacred Canopy: Elements of a Sociological Theory of Religion.* New York: Anchor Books.

Bourdieu, Pierre. 1998. *Acts of Resistance: Against the New Myths of Our Time.* Cambridge: Polity.

Brandão, Carlos R. 1994. 'A Crise das Institutuições Tradicionais Produtoras de Sentido.' In A. Moreira and R. Zicman, eds, *Misticismo e Novas Religiões.* Petrópolis: Editora Vozes. 23–41.

Castells, Manuel. 1997. *The Power of Identity.* Malden: Blackwell.

Cemin, Arneide B. 2004. 'Os Rituais do Santo Daime: "Sistemas de Montagens Simbólicas".' In B.C. Labate and W.S. Araújo, eds, *O Uso Ritual da Ayahuasca.* 2nd edition. Campinas: Mercado de Letras, 347–82.

Cohn, Norman R.C. 1970. *The Pursuit of the Millennium: Revolutionary Millenarians and Mystical Anarchists of the Middle Ages.* London: Paladin.

Couto, Fernando de La R. 2004. 'Santo Daime: Rito da Ordem.' In B.C. Labate and W.S. Araújo, eds, *O Uso Ritual da Ayahuasca,* 385–411.

Da Matta, Roberto. 1996. 'Understanding Messianism in Brazil: Notes from a Social Anthropologist.' *Encuentros* 17: 1–13.

Dawson, Andrew. 2007. *New Era – New Religions: Religious Transformation in Contemporary Brazil*. Aldershot: Ashgate.

Ferreira, Marcelo C. 1999. 'Associativismo e Contato Político nas Regiões Metropolitanas do Brasil: 1988–1996. Revisitando o Problema da Participação.' *Revista Brasileira da Ciências Sociais* 14. http://www.scielo.br/.

Giddens, Anthony. 1990. *The Consequences of Modernity*. Stanford: Stanford University Press.

——.1991. *Modernity and Self-Identity: Self and Society in the Late Modern Age*. Cambridge: Polity Press.

——. 1994. 'Living in a Post-Traditional Society.' In U. Beck, A. Giddens and S. Lash, eds, *Reflexive Modernization*, 56–109.

Labate, Beatriz C. and Pacheco, Gustavo. 2004. 'Matrizes Maranhenses do Santo Daime.' In B.C. Labate and W.S. Araújo eds *O Uso Ritual da Ayahuasca*, 303–44.

——, Goulart, Sandra L., and Araújo, Wladimyr S. 2004. 'Introdução.' In B.C. Labate and W.S. Araújo, eds, *O Uso Ritual da Ayahuasca*, 21–33.

Lash, Scott. 1990. *The Sociology of Postmodernism*. London: Routledge.

Levine, Robert M. 1992. *Vale of Tears: Revisiting the Canudos Massacre in Northeastern Brazil, 1893–1897*. Berkeley: University of California Press.

Luna, Luis E. 1986. *Vegetalismo: Shamanism Among the Mestizo Population of the Peruvian Amazon*. Stockholm: Almqvist and Wiksell International.

Myscofski, Carole A. 1988. *When Men Walk Dry: Portuguese Messianism in Brazil*. Atlanta: Scholars Press.

O'Dougherty, Maureen. 2002. *Consumption Intensified: The Politics of Middle-Class Daily Life in Brazil*. Durham, NC: Duke University.

Pessar, Patricia R. 2004. *From Fanatics to Folk: Brazilian Millenarianism and Popular Culture*. Durham, NC: Duke University Press.

Pochmann, Marcio, Pereira, Marelo, Barbosa, Alexandre, Silva Ronnie and Amorin, Ricardo. 2007. *Classe Média: Desenvolvimento e Crise*. São Paulo: Cortez Editora.

Quadros, Waldir. 2003. 'Classes Sociais e Desemprego no Brasil dos Anos 1990.' *Economia e Sociedade* 12.1: 109–135.

Queiroz, Maria I.P. de. 1965. *O Messianismo no Brasil e no Mundo*. São Paulo: Dominus Editôra & Editôra da Universidade de São Paulo.

Index